MW01124274

SHAPING THE ARCHIVE IN LATE MEDIEVAL ENGLAND

Sarah Elliott Novacich explores how medieval thinkers pondered the ethics and pleasures of the archive. She traces three episodes of sacred history – the loss of Eden, the loading of Noah's ark, and the Harrowing of Hell – across works of poetry, performance records, and iconography in order to demonstrate how medieval artists turned to sacred history to think through aspects of cultural transmission. Performances of the loss of Eden blur the relationship between original and record; stories of Noah's ark foreground the difficulty of compiling inventories; and engagements with the Harrowing of Hell suggest the impossibility of separating the past from the present. Reading Middle English plays alongside chronicles, poetry, and works of visual art, *Shaping the Archive in Late Medieval England* considers how poetic form, staging logistics, and the status of performance all contribute to our understanding of the ways in which medieval thinkers imagined the archive.

SARAH ELLIOTT NOVACICH is an assistant professor at Rutgers University, where she specializes in medieval literature. Her research interests include poetry, drama, gender studies, and visual culture.

CAMBRIDGE STUDIES IN MEDIEVAL LITERATURE

General Editor
Alastair Minnis, *Yale University*

Editorial Board
Zygmunt G. Barański, *University of Cambridge*
Christopher C. Baswell, *Barnard College and Columbia University*
John Burrow, *University of Bristol*
Mary Carruthers, *New York University*
Rita Copeland, *University of Pennsylvania*
Roberta Frank, *Yale University*
Simon Gaunt, *King's College, London*
Steven Kruger, *City University of New York*
Nigel Palmer, *University of Oxford*
Winthrop Wetherbee, *Cornell University*
Jocelyn Wogan-Browne, *Fordham University*

This series of critical books seeks to cover the whole area of literature written in the major medieval languages – the main European vernaculars, and medieval Latin and Greek – during the period c.1100–1500. Its chief aim is to publish and stimulate fresh scholarship and criticism on medieval literature, special emphasis being placed on understanding major works of poetry, prose, and drama in relation to the contemporary culture and learning which fostered them.

Recent titles in the series
Martin Eisner *Boccaccio and the Invention of Italian Literature: Dante, Petrarch, Cavalcanti, and the Authority of the Vernacular*
Emily V. Thornbury *Becoming a Poet in Anglo-Saxon England*
Lawrence Warner *The Myth of "Piers Plowman"*
Lee Manion *Narrating the Crusades: Loss and Recovery in Medieval and Early Modern English Literature*
Daniel Wakelin *Scribal Correction and Literary Craft: English Manuscripts 1375–1510*
Jon Whitman (ed.) *Romance and History: Imagining Time from the Medieval to the Early Modern Period*
Virginie Greene *Logical Fictions in Medieval Literature and Philosophy*
Michael Johnston and Michael Van Dussen (eds.) *The Medieval Manuscript Book: Cultural Approaches*
Tim William Machan (ed.) *Imagining Medieval English: Language Structures and Theories, 500–1500*

A complete list of titles in the series can be found at the end of the volume.

SHAPING THE ARCHIVE IN LATE MEDIEVAL ENGLAND

History, Poetry, and Performance

SARAH ELLIOTT NOVACICH

Rutgers University, New Jersey

CAMBRIDGE
UNIVERSITY PRESS

CAMBRIDGE
UNIVERSITY PRESS

University Printing House, Cambridge CB2 8BS, United Kingdom

One Liberty Plaza, 20th Floor, New York, NY 10006, USA

477 Williamstown Road, Port Melbourne, VIC 3207, Australia

4843/24, 2nd Floor, Ansari Road, Daryaganj, Delhi – 110002, India

79 Anson Road, #06–04/06, Singapore 079906

Cambridge University Press is part of the University of Cambridge.

It furthers the University's mission by disseminating knowledge in the pursuit of
education, learning, and research at the highest international levels of excellence.

www.cambridge.org
Information on this title: www.cambridge.org/9781107177055
10.1017/9781316819265

First published 2017

Printed in the United States of America by Sheridan Books, Inc.

A catalogue record for this publication is available from the British Library.

Library of Congress Cataloging-in-Publication Data
NAMES: Novacich, Sarah Elliott, author.
TITLE: Shaping the archive in late medieval England : history, poetry, and performance / Sarah
Elliott Novacich.
DESCRIPTION: Cambridge : Cambridge University Press, 2017. | Series: Cambridge studies in
Medieval literature ; 97
IDENTIFIERS: LCCN 2016045372 | ISBN 9781107177055 (hardback)
SUBJECTS: LCSH: English literature – Middle English, 1100–1500 – History and criticism. | Religion
in literature. | Holy, The, in literature. | Christianity and literature – England – History – To 1500.
| Civilization, Medieval, in literature.
CLASSIFICATION: LCC PR275.R4 N68 2017 | DDC 820.9/3823–dc23
LC record available at https://lccn.loc.gov/2016045372

ISBN 978-1-107-17705-5 Hardback

This book is for my dad, Stephen, who knows how to ask a good question, and my mom, Elizabeth, who recognizes art everywhere.

Contents

Figures

Acknowledgments

I would like to thank Alastair Minnis and Roberta Frank, who first helped me to get started on this project, and who made me love the Middle Ages. Thanks also to Jessica Brantley, Nicole Rice, Denys Turner, and Matthew Giancarlo, whose far-ranging interests luckily include medieval drama, iconography, Dante, and Isidore of Seville.

The following friends and colleagues have been generous with their time, reading drafts, making key suggestions at key moments, and just generally helping the writing process to be a good one: Arthur Bahr, Seeta Chaganti, Ann Coiro, Susan Crane, Rebecca Davis, Elin Diamond, Lynn Festa, Shannon Gayk, Andy Heisel, Ben Yousey-Hindes, Eleanor Johnson, John Kucich, David Kurnick, Marisa Libbon, Lauren Mancia, Mukti Lakhi Mangharam, Jacqueline Miller, Laura Saetveit Miles, Liz Appel Mixter (and her wonderful thoughts on the ark), Ingrid Nelson, Jonah Siegel, Jennifer Sisk, Michelle Stephens, Henry Turner, Rebecca Walkowitz, Carolyn Williams, Diana Witt, and Abigail Zitin. I am grateful for the thoughtful suggestions and guidance offered by my department, the anonymous readers at Cambridge University Press, and Linda Bree. Brepols Publishers (Turnhout, Belgium) has kindly granted permission to reproduce part of "Uxor Noe and the Animal Inventory," from *New Medieval Literatures* 12 (2010), in Chapter 3.

Special thanks are reserved for Marcus Elder, master of languages, Julia Fawcett, a wonderful scholar and friend, and my extended family, for their indulgence and support. I also am especially indebted to the generous support of Larry Scanlon and Stacy Klein, whose multiple read throughs have helped me to produce this final product.

Most of all, I could not have written this book without Josh.

A Note on Citation Style

For Middle English quotations, I retain the thorn (þ) and yogh (ȝ), as well as v/u and j/i spellings. The endnotes offer author and title, as well as translator and editor when required; full citations are in the bibliography. All Middle English translations are my own, unless otherwise noted.

Abbreviations

CCCM   *Corpus Christianorum continuatio mediaevalis*
CCSL   *Corpus Christianorum, series latina*
EETS   Early English Text Society (o.s., Original Series, e.s., Extra
       Series, s.s. Supplementary Series)
PL   *Patrologia Latina.* Ed. J.-P. Migne. Paris, 1844–1865

Introduction

This book begins with a famous ending. In the York Mercers' play of the Last Judgment, performed for nearly two centuries in the northern English city as part of a larger, community production of sacred history, now preserved in a fifteenth-century manuscript known as the "Register," God orders the assemblage of a formidable inventory. His angels must gather together "Ilke a leede þat euere hadde liffe" [each person that ever had life]; and take care, he warns, "Bese none forgetyn, grete ne small" [let there be none forgotten, neither great nor small].[1] That is not all: besides the "ilke a leede," assembled in fleshly or spectral form, the many thoughts and deeds by which they are to be judged also somehow become apparent at the angels' call, each record taking form as a kind of uncontrollable autobiography, marked upon the body or perhaps, as contemporary iconography suggests, in their suddenly legible hearts.[2] These inscriptions or sometimes vocalizations of "rekenyng" [reckoning], as the York angels call them, provide a sorting mechanism: each soul will, ready or not, bear his or her complete history to the "grette assise" that God instates (ll.94–5), and there, according to the "Anima Mala" [bad souls], all the "wikkid werkes . . . / þat we did ofte full pryuely, / Appertely may we se þem wreten" [the wicked works . . . that we often did in secret, we may see them openly written] (ll.129; 131–2).

The amount of narrative God's angels summon to the playing space is thus conceptually enormous: nothing less than a detailed personal history for every creature that ever lived. Of course, only a limited number of bodies would fit onstage for this momentous judgment, but these would be understood as representative, evoking the late medieval audience gathered physically before them, and suggestive also of "euery-ilke a gaste," every single soul who came before: the entire population of history, now risen to be counted (l.85). It is a complete cast, and it both forms and witnesses a complete account of human history as that history veers toward its close.[3] The players playing the assembled dead, at last reunited with their fleshly

I

forms (sounding, presumably, like the rustle of costumes), and the crowds assembling to watch them play all gather around God and his deputized angels, who "sounderes þame" [divide them up], some to heaven and some to hell (l.73):

I ANGELUS: Goode and ill, euery-ilke a gaste,
              Rise, and fecche youre flessh þat was youre feere,
              For all þis worlde is broght to waste.
              Drawes to youre dome, it neghes nere.
2 ANGELUS: Ilke a creature, bothe olde and yhing,
              Belyue I bidde ʒou þat ʒe ryse;
              Body and sawle with ʒou ʒe bring,
              And comes before þe high justise;
              For I am sente fro heuene kyng
              To calle ʒou to þis grette assise,
              þerfore rise vppe, and geue rekenyng,
              How ʒe hym serued vppon sere wise.   (ll.85–96)

ANGEL 1:   Good and ill, each and every soul, rise and fetch the flesh that was your body, for this whole world is brought to waste. Come to your judgment, it draws near.
ANGEL 2:   Each creature, both old and young, I bid that you now rise; bring with you body and soul, and come before the high justice; for I am sent from the king of heaven to call you to this great assize. Therefore, rise up and give reckoning of how you have served him in various ways.

The play describes an annotated, cosmic roll call, one that God will read with absolute comprehension, for, as he assures the "Anima Bona" [good souls] at York, he has seen them feed the hungry and clothe the cold, and he understands those actions as signifying love toward himself (ll.309–12). Complete knowledge and unerring interpretation are performed as entirely recoverable in the play. Even the devils admit as much: "For nowe," says one, "schall all þe soth be sought" [for now shall all the truth be sought] (l.226).

This book is about late medieval representations of extraordinary inventories, such as the sort assembled in the York Doomsday play. It investigates what such representations might reveal about medieval perceptions of history, narrative, and the accumulation of knowledge. I examine how various late medieval texts and performances represent the desire to amass collections that fully account for the world: how they attempt to compress time and space onto page or stage to offer, at times, a record that rivals the completeness of original creation. I refer to this desire to accumulate as much knowledge as possible, in both material and narrative form, as an *archival* one, and I use the term for a number of reasons. First of all, "archive" suggests a flexibility of inventory, encompassing the sense of "library," "treasure trove," and even codicological compilation, since a codex might be an archive unto itself, as in the massive Book of Life consulted by the angels at the end of time, or the famous Domesday book, sharing with its namesake cosmic roll call a similar sense of exhaustiveness and dread.[4] And though in modern usage, "archive" sometimes denotes collections more narrowly defined – "the organic relationship of record to the generator of that record"[5] – twentieth- and twenty-first-century theorists have expanded its conceptual range to describe the collection and transmission of knowledge more generally.

But even more importantly, the idea of the archive, in its Latin and Middle English manifestations, synonyms, and near-synonyms, and through its perceived etymologies and constellation of associations, generated extensive descriptive and allusive power during late antique and medieval centuries. In his seventh-century *Etymologies*, Isidore of Seville links the Latin "arc(h)ivum" (archive) to the word "arca" (ark), which, as we will see in later chapters, also can refer to ships ("arca noe," Noah's ark of the flood), and hearts ("arca cordis," the ark of the heart). Isidore writes:

> A strongbox (*arca*) is so called because it prevents (*arcere*) and prohibits seeing inside. From this term also derives "archives" (*arcivum*, i.e. *archivum*) and mystery (*arcanum*), that is, a secret from which other people are "fended off" (*arcere*).[6]

Medieval etymological work consistently echoes portions of Isidore. Hugutio of Pisa's twelfth-century *Derivationes* emphasizes the idea of the "arca" as a protected space that wards off intrusion, circuitously connecting the term to "arcanus" (arcane) or "secretus" (secret), that from which others are held off ("a quo ceteri arcentur"), and further linking the "archivum" to the "librarium" (a place for books, often a bookcase) and "armarium" (a bookcase or cupboard).[7] The thirteenth-century *Summa Britonis* suggests that the "archarius est qui custodit vel facit archam vel custos thesaurorum": he is the one who protects or makes the "archam," the guardian of the treasure houses.[8] In the eleventh century, Ælfric uses "archivum" to translate the Old English "boochord" (book horde),[9] and the Latin word continues to be used to refer to collections – of parchments, tally sticks, treasures, and more – throughout the medieval period.

The details in this etymological work suggest an emphasis on enclosure, secrecy, and protection, as well as the need for a figurehead to guarantee these things: a God, for instance, to acknowledge a list of names, thoughts,

and deeds whose compilation proves beyond reproach. These aspects
associated with the words "arca" and "archivum" can be discerned in the
representations of archival projects that this book explores. But my examination also moves beyond explicit statements of archival etymology and
definition to consider how both the form and content of late medieval
engagements with sacred history, including works of poetry, prose, iconography, and performance, reveal a vested interest in cultural transmission
and the archival labor that underpins it: how, for instance, a play like the
York Doomsday, which does not use the word "archive" even once, seems
nonetheless continually to investigate the idea of one. It is in such texts,
images, and records of performance that I propose to reveal elements of
medieval archival imagining, or ways of thinking about the compilation
and appraisal of inventories and the methods by which they are organized,
preserved, and ushered through time.

   In addition to engaging with suggestive, premodern etymologies, my use
of the word "archive" also responds to the rich and varied critical histories
and more speculative theories of the archive that have been produced in
recent decades, some of which involve the Middle Ages, but many of which
skip over those centuries all together. Postmodern theoretical interest in
the archive, lead most notably by Foucault and later by Derrida, has
increased the critical uses to which the word might be put. I want to
superimpose this conceptual flexibility onto the allusive reach of the
medieval "arca"/"archivum" in order to see what sort of resonances and
disjunctions might be found. Such a diachronic approach risks a certain
amount of self-reflexivity, a tendency to coil inward as it pursues ideas
central to the archive itself: continuity and its ruptures. But it also permits
the Middle Ages, situated at the beginning of English literary history, to
take up its rightful place in discussions about how that literature appre-
hends time, transmission, tradition, and loss.

   This introduction thus offers a summary of the ways in which comparatively modern discussions of the archive have conditioned our approach to
the past as well our efforts to define our work as literary critics, work that,
in recent decades, has taken something of its own archival turn, even
inspiring what some might term a "fever." It then moves into medieval
considerations of the archive – bureaucratic, poetic, and especially
moments when these categories overlap – to consider the elements shared
between medieval and modern approaches to the collection, organization,
and transmission of knowledge in its various forms. My intention is to
demonstrate how medieval works take up questions central to current
conversations about archival theory and practice, though, of course, in

different forms and at times with different stakes. Finally, by returning to the sacred history culminated by Judgment Day, I present three other famous episodes that investigate archival processes: the creation and loss of Eden, that garden of exemplars; the loading of Noah's ark ("arca noe"), the ship that attempts to forge continuity between ante- and postdiluvian worlds; and the Harrowing of Hell, in which Christ liberates the repository of an embodied past. Like the Mercers' play, medieval engagements with these earlier episodes of sacred history permit the interrogation of aspects of archival labor, putting pressure on and delighting in processes such as compiling inventories, protecting records, making copies, and turning backward toward the past. Implicit in this turn to sacred history is the idea that a culture's conceptions of the value of archival work might be explored through its narrative traditions, particularly when a narrative tradition so crucially structures that culture; to put it another way, poetry about and performances of sacred history can be seen both to produce and examine English medieval intellectual history, particularly as it relates to questions regarding the transmission of knowledge.

1   The Archive (and the Archives)

Archivists, historians, and literary and cultural critics, medievalist or otherwise, frequently imply a division between the "archive" and the "archives."[10] The singular refers to an abstract conceptualization of the storage, preservation, and transmission of knowledge, and the plural more specifically indicates the buildings, rooms, or institutions in which collections take form: all the places scholars go to find things, especially the past. Carolyn Steedman has examined this divide between theory and practice in a tongue-in-cheek meditation on Derrida's influential essay, "Archive Fever." At first passing lightly over the fraught longings for origin that characterize his description of conceptual maladies, she describes the health effects of the literal dust inhaled by readers toiling in actual archives: the headaches, for instance, about which the prolific French historian Jules Michelet used to complain after visits to the reading rooms. Steedman acknowledges how Derrida's approach has helped to sharpen the way scholars think about power, knowledge, and interpretive license, or "the hermeneutic right," as he puts it, the one exclusive to the archivist, and which God wields with such authority at Doomsday.[11] But one of the interpretive risks of such an approach, she suggests, is that the archive then can be "inflated to mean – if not quite Everything – then at least, all the ways and means of state power,"

eventually producing a suspiciously "capacious metaphor" that nonetheless leaves aside the dust of real reading rooms.[12]

Derrida is not the first to expand the term "archive" beyond its designation of a specific place, collection, or practice. In the *Archaeology of
Knowledge*, written three decades before "Archive Fever," Foucault
defines the archive as "the law of what can be said."[13] Not, then, one of
the more traditional definitions he specifically rejects – "that which
collects the dust of statements that have become inert once more, and
which may make possible the miracle of their resurrection" (as with
Michelet, for instance, inhaling the dead in the reading rooms, giving
them life in a strange inverse of God's original exhalation[14]) – and not
"the library of all libraries."[15] For Foucault, the archive is that which can
"reveal the rules of a practice that enables statements both to survive and
to undergo regular modification. It is *the general system of the formation
and transformation of statements*."[16] Rather than a site of documents and
dust, it is a system by and within which we live and think and speak.
Conversely, in her book on the interplay between medieval documents
and poetry, Emily Steiner turns away from the singular archive of postmodern theory, regarding it as too "abstracted from the materialities and
genres of preservation."[17] In fact, she explicitly salvages some of the
definitional work discarded by Foucault, including the description of
"the institutions, which, in a given society, make it possible to record and
preserve those discourses that one wishes to remember and keep in
circulation."[18]

Though it might appear as something of a critical standoff, those
theorizing the dustless archive and those thinking about and from within
actually dusty archives frequently cross paths, producing not so much
a détente as a critical canon, a way of making the overlap between these
categories into its own kind of poetics. Arlette Farge's *The Allure of the
Archives*, recently translated into English, combines a deep familiarity with
the everyday experiences and materialities of institutional reading rooms –
heaps of paper, the kind of string that ties them, the handwriting, the
"everything and nothing" – with a sharp warning about the forms of
authority shaping those traces of lives once lived.[19] "The archive," she
writes, "is a vantage point from which the symbolic and intellectual
constructions of the past can be rearranged," but it is also a place of
surprising encounters with both ineffable and material presences: a note
scrawled on smuggled laundry, a handful of miraculous seeds, the not-
quite real memory of the bodies from which they issued.[20] Farge writes
about lives whose records exist by virtue of a collision with authority, but

also lives whose suggestiveness exceeds the documentary formulas imposed upon them. Archivists, themselves, frequently write about the shaping mechanisms of authority: both the forms of authority associated with those in the past who have bequeathed us their records, and the authority of those who today receive, appraise, organize, and permit access to them. They emphasize the crucial need to resist perceiving their procedures as neutral, acknowledging the interpretive frameworks through which their work is carried out and demonstrating how the need to recognize and articulate such frameworks matters, in a postcolonial world, for example, or in one bewilderingly inundated by new, digital forms of record.[21]

Literary critics as well as historians and archivists have taken up these questions concerning the records and silences of the past. How to find things obfuscated through organizational strategy or by the accidents of history has become increasingly significant to literary studies in the long wake of new historicism, one of whose central injunctions is expansion of the archive: expansion of what counts as a text, what gets deemed worthy of scholarly interest, and who gets to be remembered.[22] Reassessments of the archive and the attendant conversations about theory and practice also resemble a number of the questions and opportunities surrounding the more recently revitalized field of book history,[23] in which scholars approach the material book, encoded with dynamic histories, as an anchor to a world otherwise reduced to memory, and as irreducible proof that the past is not something that we inevitably create in our efforts to reveal.[24] But critics of this growing field suggest that the attention paid to material remains and the admittedly obsessive, sustained study that such difficult, recalcitrant objects require can end up substituting the material object for the past itself.[25] Such critiques cast the archive and its contents as fetishes, mistaken by painstaking scholars for the world that they purport to record.[26]

The study of medieval literature has a unique stake and perspective in such conversations, both as a field of study with a rich history in the dusty archives and as one continually confronted with the problem of the distant past and the tenuous connection between its often obscure objects of study and the present. Medievalists study a past not only particularly remote in time, but also one whose records frequently were expunged or recreated.[27] The dissolution of the monasteries during the Reformation left only a portion of those institutional inventories, and the early modern centuries that followed, as Jennifer Summit, Theresa Coletti, and Gail McMurray Gibson have shown, remade the Middle Ages through their own strategies of collection and revision.[28] The texts that survive in material form thus frequently are elevated to the status of quasi-relics, partially out of reverence for the tenacity and fragility their transmission across centuries suggests, and partially, perhaps, because of the estrangement such a passage across time produces. These objects offer information discernable only through skills closely associated with traditional archival research, such as paleography and codicology, but they also carry traces of their own inscrutability, hints about all the information obscured by the silencing effects of time. Medievalist scholarship continually must confront such indications of continuity and rupture, or profound recognition tempered by a sense of the elusive. Along with the solid weight of a book in the hands, the smell of vellum and faded inks, one also encounters – or rather notes that one *fails* to encounter – all the hands, now invisible, that once held it, the mouths and eyes that read, and the kingdoms, schools, parishes, and days that shaped such moments.

These questions of our engagement with the past, material and ineffable, accessible and vanished – including what to look at and how to see it, or in what forms "definitive and usable historical knowledge" might be found[29] – pervade critical conversations about texts such as the York Doomsday play, with which this introduction began. But such questions also are useful to medieval drama writ large, whose performances are more surely disappeared than other objects of study. For what kind of recorded past, or what kind of knowledge, might we access about a medium often thought to elude archival endeavor through its inherent ephemerality?[30]

Nevertheless, medieval drama has invited *considerable* archival research. Over the past several decades, an increasing awareness of the richness that local historical context provides for understanding popular performance has motivated one of the most committed turns to the archives in medieval studies: the Records in Early English Drama (REED). The project was initiated over forty years ago by Alexandra F. Johnston and Margaret (Dorrell) Rogerson, whose spearheading efforts to excavate, organize, and publish the civic registers and recording efforts of medieval bureaucrats have considerably enhanced our access to a large amount of information about medieval plays and other entertainments. Johnson, Rogerson, and a team of meticulous researchers locate, gather, and compile documents relating, sometimes obliquely, to medieval English drama and performance culture, including "memoranda, minutes of council meetings, accounts, letters, wills, ordinances, and legal contracts which touch upon and illumine practices of long-standing custom and ceremony."[31] The project describes its goals as the comprehensive compilation of a massive reference series, one that collects information, termed "raw material," with as little interpretive mediation as possible, into one place.[32] Over a decade into the project, Theresa Coletti published an influential essay raising some of the same kinds of objections as those critiquing aspects of archival research and book history. She suggested that REED pursued an exhaustive historical record, conducted within "a fiction of its own neutrality," without sufficiently investigating its own interpretive methods, and that its scholars sometimes errantly seemed to believe in a whole, true, or recoverable past.[33]

The REED project and the criticism it has elicited interest me in several ways. First of all, the volumes of records are tremendously *useful*.[34] REED provides an extraordinary amount of information that permits one to envision those vanished performances, such as the ones put on by the Mercers' guild, in new ways, with props, costs, arguments, and otherwise unimagined juxtapositions between performance activities and "regular" life. The published records help to evoke an assemblage of bodies in costumes with scripts, complaints, and desires, who have left behind enigmatic, textual traces of these things. But secondly, through the articulation of its methods and the volumes produced year after year, REED offers its own faith in the power of the archive and in the idea that there is efficacy in gathering as much as possible into one place, that eventually, as Coletti claims the project implies, it might lead one to see and to understand a kind of totality, whether of a particular facet of culture, a city in the fullness of its lived century, or a whole world now vanished. The REED project thus offers a version of archival desire that some critics might designate as fetishistic: a yearning to reconstitute, out of many scattered parts, whatever whole or sense of fullness might be salvaged, a record whose extensiveness potentially rivals or replaces the world (the past) that it records.[35]

The exciting developments and reasonable hesitations attending the archival turn in literary studies tend toward a few implicit questions. Which precise mixture of theory and dust might offer the sharpest resolution as we look backward toward the past? How far are we to be lulled away from theoretical lenses by the concrete facticity of material in our hands, codices attesting to so many earlier readers, writers, editors, artists, patrons, and sellers? Or, how far from these material links to the past should we stray as we become rerouted through the pressing questions of the present, lost in the words of our own arguments, blithely woven far from the doors of the archive? This book proposes that such questions, foregrounded by conversations surrounding the archival turn generally and projects such as REED specifically, *also* animated medieval conversations about the archive, that is, about how to access, shape, understand, and preserve the past and the present so that they might be comprehended and transmitted to future populations. I am interested in how medieval thinkers and scholars queried the value, risks, pleasures, and critical blind spots of archival activity; how they imagined the dangers and enticements of reaching back toward a past passed on to them; the attempts to decipher the various forms in which it arrived; and the prestige and unnerving power associated with one's own efforts to archive the always-unspooling present.

This book demonstrates how imaginative medieval works anticipate crucial elements of the intellectual debates over archival endeavor in which Coletti and the editors at REED, or those studying the "archive" and "archives" across disciplines, participate. Medieval imaginings of the archive do not break down neatly into questions of theory and practice, but they illuminate the hopes bound up in a fully recoverable past and a fully recordable world, and they frequently foreground the collateral damage of such aspirations: that which is left out of purported wholeness; the dangers wrapped up in the search for a specific past or origins; and the vise grip upon the future that the desire for exhaustive recording frequently entails. The next section turns to specific medieval texts in order to demonstrate how we might begin to uncover the desires and hesitations wrapped up in ways of imagining the archive, and it shows how both bureaucratic and poetic texts reformulate and anticipate some of the questions rehearsed above.

2   Sacred and Compendious Histories: The *Liber Albus*, the *House of Fame*, and *Paradise*

The kind of revisionist history described by scholars such as Summit, Coletti, and Gibson was not a strategy invented in the early modern period. Patrick Geary suggests that medieval writers and historians regularly reshaped their own inherited pasts, revering tradition even as they labored to mediate it through "transmission, suppression, and re-creation."[36] Rather than being a period merely organized into being by the Renaissance, the Middle Ages worked to organize itself, with its subjects continually rewriting histories of the past through the revision and new production of historical documents and archives.[37] And importantly, as Michael Clanchy argues in *From Memory to Written Record*, the production of those records began to increase dramatically in the second half of the medieval period.[38] Documentation spread through the work of royal, municipal, and ecclesiastical bureaucrats and scribes, who produced and sorted through contracts, receipts, charters, wills, and books of account, storing these more earthly reckonings in large rolls of parchment, wound up and preserved in cabinets, waiting for uncertain futures and accumulating authority like interest.[39]

Alongside the proliferation of documents emerged a number of works that commented on this bureaucratic and textual increase, even occasionally exclaiming over a newfound capacity to organize and better comprehend the world through it. Such texts were both practical and imaginative; they offered sound advice for bureaucrats as well as Borgesian visions of unending record for those differently moved by a world newly flooded with parchment. In the twelfth century, for instance, Richard fitzNigel (sometimes Fitzneale) wrote the *Dialogue of the Exchequer*, which explains the nuts and bolts of his daily labor, but which also encourages an imagined interlocutor to search for "mystic meaning" in the work of the royal office:

> For it is a worthy thing to seek flowers of mystic meaning among the thistles of worldly matters. Indeed, holy mysteries can be found hiding not only in the things you have just noticed, but in the whole account of the exchequer. For the diversity of duties, the great authority of the judiciary, the seal bearing the royal image, the sending of summonses, the writing of the rolls, the accounting for one's stewardship, the collection of debts, and the condemnation or absolution of defendants are symbols of the strict accounting that will be revealed when the books of all are opened and the door shut.[40]

Echoing the event of the Last Judgment from the book of Apocalypse – "the books were opened"[41] – fitzNigel connects the work carried out in the royal bureaucratic office to the kind of amassing of knowledge performed in the York Doomsday play, suggesting that one might be read as a symbol of the other. In the "sending of summonses," one perhaps can hear the echo of angelic trumpets, and in the winding up of rolls, envision the Book of Life.

Two centuries after fitzNigel's *Dialogue*, and after the plague had decimated a large portion of the European population, the compiler of the *Liber Albus*, or the White Book of the City of London, expresses a desire for more detail-oriented work like fitzNigel's:

> Forasmuch as the fallibility of human memory and the shortness of life do not allow us to gain an accurate knowledge of everything that deserves remembrance, even though the same may have been committed to writing, – more especially if it has been so committed without order or arrangement, – and still more so, when no such written account exists; seeing too that when, as not unfrequently happens, all the aged, most experienced, and most discreet rulers of the royal City of London have been carried off at the same instant, as it were, by pestilence ... it has been long deemed necessary ... that a volume ... should be compiled from the more noteworthy memoranda that lie scattered without order or classification throughout the books [and] rolls, as well as the Charters of the said city.[42]

Here, our compiler puts his faith in the archive as a mechanism of salvation, as disaster reminds one of the ephemerality of knowledge and the ease with which it might be lost. Even as he admits such a project to be impossible, the writer of the prologue permits himself briefly to contemplate accumulating "an accurate knowledge of everything," the kind of compendium that links one age to the next, even when it feels like everything has changed.

This would be the kind of ordinary saving that is salvific, and the desires and hesitations wrapped up in such a project can be related to the massive, global projects of preservation represented by episodes of sacred history, such as, for instance, the cosmic roll call of Judgment Day. In a way, the interpretive trajectory of this study moves in a direction *opposite* to fitzNigel's musing. Rather than discerning "mystic meaning" or possible salvation in bureaucratic practice, it considers how representations of sacred events might be understood to comment on the desires and concerns underpinning more ordinary archival labor. To put it differently: instead of unearthing poetry in the labors of a bureaucratic office that stocks, accesses, and shapes archives, I look at the kinds of archival desire that mystery plays stage and that poetry considers. This is not to insist upon a division between bureaucratic and more "literary" kinds of writing, since to separate bureaucratic from spiritual or aesthetic endeavors would be to deny the richness of meaning certain bureaucrats clearly discerned in their labor and, in some cases, the influence of such labor upon their poetry.[43] This study, however, places attention more squarely on the poetry and performances of sacred history produced alongside the sharp increase in bureaucratic documentation, investigating how such engagements with that central, religious narrative spanning from Creation to Judgment Day might be seen to interrogate the desires and anxieties bound up in more quotidian forms of textual proliferation and collection. It examines how ideas of the archive and the assembled accumulation of the past influenced the form and content of works that seem less connected to bureaucratic procedure (less than the *Dialogue of the Exchequer*, for example), while keeping in mind the material realities of the archive in the later Middle Ages, about which scribes among their rolls and reckonings might wax poetic.

For the era during which textual saturation was both relatively new and newly central to state and ecclesiastical institutions produced a variety of kinds of writing. Mountains of text were written, used, and preserved by anonymous copyists and royal appointees, but also by the poet Hoccleve, who compiled the *Formulary*, an extensive collection of both template and specific letters, contracts, and forms,[44] and by Geoffrey Chaucer, who worked as a bureaucrat while writing several important works, including the *House of Fame*.[45] In that poem, the eagle-guide marvels at the fictional Chaucer's textually dense life: "For when," he says "thy labour doon al ys, / And hast mad alle thy rekenynges … Thou sittest at another book."[46] Here, Chaucer as insatiable reader shuttles between his bureaucratic "rekenynges" – the term recalling the personal testimonies of "ilke a creature" at Doomsday – and books read for pleasure, before moving on to the word-filled realm of Fame, where "ryght thus every word, ywys, / That lowd or pryvee spoken ys" moves through the air, multiplying like ripples after a stone is cast into a pool (ll.809–10). The archives – those specific rooms of specific documents authorizing a present in relation to its past – sometimes enclosed writers who wrote about such spaces, whether in loving description of their bureaucratic labor or in the poetry of dream visions.

Similarities between descriptions of mundane and cosmic records frequently hinge on the contemplation of the possibility of wholeness. For instance, the preface of the *Liber Albus* seems to set out modest goals of collection:

> not only those laudable observances which, though not written, have been usually followed and approved in the said city, to the end that they may not be lost in oblivion hereafter, but also those noteworthy memoranda which have been committed to writing, but lie scattered in disorder in manner before-mentioned.[47]

But it also suggests, in its opening lines, that these scattered memoranda, strewn "without order or classification throughout the books [and] rolls," might, if reassembled, *build* toward the envisioned but always unreachable goal of "an accurate knowledge of everything." This description of ideal bureaucratic labor that eventually might accomplish a complete collection recalls the famous three tercets at the end of Dante's *Paradiso*, a poem gently parodied in Chaucer's *House of Fame*. Dante's verse describes the moment after the pilgrim-poet has passed the last of the circling spheres, though, of course, temporal designations already are under pressure:

> O grace abounding, through which I presumed
> to set my eyes on the Eternal Light
> so long that I spent all my sight on it!
>   In its profundity I saw – ingathered
> and bound by love into one single volume –
> what, in the universe, seems separate, scattered:

> substances, accidents, and dispositions
> as if conjoined – in such a way that what
> I tell is only rudimentary.[48]

Both the preface of the *Liber Albus* and the *Paradiso* tercets suggest a number of key relationships that hover around understandings of the archive: that between the divine and human, or impossible and possible orders of creation, and, when "all knowledge" fails to be "ingathered," that which takes form instead.[49] In his description of the cosmic codex, Dante plays between what can and cannot be represented: there *is* a book, "one single volume" ("un volume") capable of showing everything at once, but it is not one that humans themselves can write, read, or even remember beyond a rapturous state, the state in which ("O grace abounding") Dante perceives it. On the other hand, the description of the single volume is itself bound up beautifully in the poet's own tercet; his poem both includes and in a manner equates itself with this cosmic text shot through with light. Dante receives his textual vision from the height of the Empyrean, God's privileged vantage point, after a journey consisting of thousands of lines. When the envisioned compendium of universal knowledge and history ("substances, accidents, and the interplay between them") takes the form of a text, it thus recalls the medium of the masterpiece the poet himself is just about to wrap up, as well as the *logos* that is or gives rise to creation. We are reminded that the scattered pages of heaven, hell, and earth, although seen here as bound within a rapturous state, also might be reassembled through much patient human work and care, and through careful poetic form. This also is the kind of care for which the preface of the *Liber Albus* advocates, so that information, written in disorganized fashion and scattered to the four winds ("sparsim et inordinate scripta") might be compiled into a "volumen."

The *Paradiso* tercets intimate the possibility of gathering in everything at once even as they point out the impossibility of doing so. Dante cannot transcribe the "single volume" for us, the readers of his *Comedy*, but he can integrate its apprehension into his own verse. Even as the volume logically includes Dante himself and his *Comedy*, the *Comedy* in turn includes the description of the single volume. There is play, in these stanzas, between divine creation and human art, and, importantly, the suggestion that wholeness can be intimated in different ways.[50] There need not be a one-to-one concordance between reality and record, as long as there is a representational strategy that, even as it creates a sparer account, gestures toward its own kind of fullness.

A number of medieval genres favor length and capaciousness in what would seem to be a different kind of strategy for the representation of available knowledge: encyclopedias "on the nature of things" (*de natura rerum*), a textual form frequently modeled on Isidore's *Etymologies*; theological *summae* and endlessly proliferating commentaries; *mappae mundi* filled with scriptural text and imagery; chronicles numbering tens of thousands of lines, beginning with creation and then tapering off, at long last, into national histories or a spare list of kings. These "compendious genres," as Steiner has called them,[51] suggest a desire to gather all that can be gathered, to see it, to contemplate it, to learn from it, and to be awed by the representational power of one's own making, even when one only can falter toward a goal as lamentably unreachable as that of the *Liber Albus*. In fact, complete knowledge seems often to be admitted freely as merely a dreamed of ideal, rather than a reasonable writing strategy.[52]

Still, the attempt to create an inventory of universal knowledge often can seem to rival the idea of divine creation itself: a cosmic volume enclosed within a poetic masterpiece, for instance, or texts composed according to hexaemeral schemes, overtly acknowledging that they take the six days of divine creation as their model.[53] Of course, works whose subject matter is history in its (scripturally informed) entirety ostensibly seek to gather and abbreviate knowledge that already is distilled, if scattered. Likewise, the information required by the *Liber Albus* already is written, but apportioned across too many books and rolls to be useful. In this sense, compilers attempt to synthesize human knowledge rather than rival the divine "labor" of creation itself. But acts of homage and contestation can be hard to disentangle, and celebrations of divine creation, in the hands of certain artists, can seem to exceed the status of "mere" report or record, as with the cosmic volume within the final canto of a masterpiece.

In the case of the *Paradiso*, the simplicity of Dante's single volume prevents its transcription; any attempt to delineate its pages would, in a way, scatter them again, disintegrate the integrity of the volume and fracture its totality. Chaucer plays with just this chaotic potential in the *House of Fame*, humorously evoking Dante's vision of a comprehensive, crucially textual creation.[54] Chaucer's poem describes a site in which all the words ever spoken cohere, corporeally manifest, and mix together, each one finding its allotted berth up in the air, in "his propre mansyon" (l.754). These are the scattered leaves, or the scattered words, gathered together like shavings to a magnet. The eagle that carries him skyward explains to Chaucer:

Now hennesforth y wol the teche
How every speche, or noyse, or soun,
Thurgh hys multiplicacioun,
Thogh hyt were piped of a mous,
Mot nede come to Fames Hous.   (ll.782–6)

Every noise ever created – articulate or otherwise, human speech or
mouse squeak – is gathered in by the House of Fame to form a clamorous
record, one in stark contrast to Dante's volume whose simplicity is shot
through with light. This vision of words in the air, hovering and con-
current, comically cacophonous in comparison to Dante's sublime
volume, brings to the fore the question of the difference between single,
simple, eternal wholeness and the kind of collecting that endeavors
toward it. The *House of Fame* presents the never finished process of
record making, as opposed to Dante's rapturous vision that fleetingly
comprehends the kind of completion that exists past the point of history,
taking form at the final moment of the Last Judgment or beyond the
circling spheres.

As in the *House of Fame* or the *Liber Albus*, the episodes of sacred
history whose archival endeavors this book examines also eventually
are complicated by all of the things the eternity beyond the spheres is
free of: time, desire, regret, doubt, confusion, differing perspectives,
and a plasticity of memory. Like the initial example of Judgment Day,
these episodes – the creation and loss of the Garden of Eden; the biblical
flood and Noah's building of the ark; and the Harrowing of Hell, in
which Christ descends to the underworld to encounter a collection of
history – consistently and creatively were reimagined by late medieval
thinkers and artists. The events provided a general framework for the
world as medieval Christians variously apprehended it, and they helped
to suggest how sacred history might give "ordinary" history meaning, or
how everyday archival labor might share in the importance of a more
cosmic assemblage of knowledge. Representations of these sacred events
reveal medieval ways of thinking about the archive and its limits,
dangers, and irresistible allures. It is out of various representations of
these episodes that this study assembles or reassembles components of
a late medieval archival imagination, pursuing how artists and thinkers
approached the ordering of collections; the desire and uneasiness of
accumulation; the study of stasis and change; of original and record; and
the ingathering of what is widely dispersed across the past, the present,
and even the future.

3　Garden, Ark, and Underworld

The book is organized around the three episodes concerning Eden, the flood, and the Harrowing of Hell, not because they are the only ones whose medieval representations reveal aspects of archival desire, but because, as in any collection, some things must be selected and some left out. (This, as we will see, is the uneasy truth that begins to dawn upon the medieval Noah as he surveys the drowned world from the safety of his ark.) But these particular episodes also invite consideration of major components of archival process: respectively, the relationship between original and record, the compilation of inventory, and the question of how archival access forges unruly relationships between the past and present. In fact, all of the episodes involve questions of temporality; though I began this introduction with a consideration of Judgment Day, an episode in some ways bumping up against the limit of eternity, each of the three episodes treated in the chapters concerns the archival impulse to stall or transcend time, to turn it back upon itself, or to usher it along more quickly.

Like the Judgment Day example, the episodes involving Eden, the flood, and the Harrowing of Hell were refracted across a wide variety of media, manifested in imagery, interrogated by exegesis, adapted to poetry, inserted into chronicles, embedded in *mappae mundi*, and intensely familiar to wide swathes of western, medieval Christendom. All three episodes also took form as mystery plays, linked together with numerous other sacred events to form, at times, marathon performances of sacred history, now often referred to as English Corpus Christi or cycle drama, though the terms are disputed.[55] This dramatic tradition is associated, to varying degrees, with the medieval towns of York, Chester, and Wakefield (with which the Towneley manuscript has an uncertain relationship[56]), and the region of East Anglia, where it is believed the N-Town cycle manuscript was made. Much of what we know about the potential for large-scale productions comes from York; the plays in the N-Town and Towneley manuscripts might have been performed only in part, or in a much more private way, if at all.[57] The sacred content the plays include, the forms and historical circumstances of the performances, and the compilation of the play texts are all of interest to our conceptualization of the archive. I offer a brief overview of the dramatic tradition to demonstrate how the plays, through their mundane, practical concerns, as well as their theological sticking points, worked as a resource for imagining the archive.

Vernacular, religious plays were performed from the fourteenth through the sixteenth centuries, mostly in the north of England, their content spanning from the story of creation, through Christian redemption, and toward a projected apocalypse. At York, most certainly, amateur actors, sometimes organized through guild membership, participated in these connected series of discrete plays tied to major scriptural and extrabiblical events, including the fall of the rebel angels, the creation of the world, the fall of Adam and Eve, Moses's reception of the law, the sacrifice of Isaac, the nativity, the trials and passion of Christ, the Harrowing of Hell, various heavenly ascensions, and, as we have seen, the culminating Judgment Day. The duration of the performances, running possibly from sunrise to sunset, and sometimes across as many as three days, and the dispersal of its stages throughout civic spaces, gesture toward the cosmic proportions of its content. The plays of an almost impossibly full day, or perhaps two or three, enact the unfolding of a world understood as the monumental work of six, as well as its subsequent history and prophesied future. Such performances could occur on a large scale that involved a considerable number of actors, participants, and the city itself, within which stages, or pageant wagons, processed through different stations for performances of the individual mysteries ("mystery" in its now archaic, possibly obsolete sense, meaning "craft" or "trade"). Spectators could follow the wagons through the city, or wait in one spot to see them arrive, perform, and pack up, one after another, witnessing sacred history taking form beneath the city gates, in front of the mayor's house, or before the Minster.

The idea of collection mattered to this dramatic form. The "cycles" had their own investment in the scattered leaves of the book that Dante's poem describes, or the relationship between potentially reconstituted parts and whole, an investment evident both in the textual records that remain and in the kinds of performances to which those records gesture or attest.[58] The feast of Corpus Christi originally celebrated by at least some of the productions intimates the dizzying possibilities between whole and parts, the body or corpus of Christ, dispersed in Eucharistic pieces (in which a *whole* presence yet inheres, in each single crumb[59]) and the congregational body that eats of it and becomes embodied as a unity through those consumed pieces. As multiple Gods perform upon disparate stages, intimating beginning, end, and the expanse of sacred history across which those points are plotted, they enact and play with the work of gathering parts into whole, and of seeing the whole at once. The performances suggest the desires and difficulties that attend this work of seeing, hearing, and tasting everything, everything miraculously contained within something both finite and comprehensive. Especially in the large-scale productions at York, voices from multiple plays might blend together within the civic space, some caught and others lost, producing, perhaps, a sensation that the whole world might be apprehended for no more than a split second before it inevitably dissipates into something else, before the ark docks, the stage comes apart, and the pageant wagon rolls on. The crowds disperse in order to reassemble elsewhere, perhaps with the lingering sense that an attempt at fullness or completion fleetingly has been glimpsed within a temporarily charged space.

The complex temporalities of performance and the tendency for medieval sacred history to be perceived typologically are mutually reinforcing in these moments, and together they offer rich resources for representing the archive. The stage on which sacred history is performed offers a generous, flexible repository for time and space, a timeframe bookended by the "nought" out of which the world is made and the eternity toward which it veers, a frame almost endlessly expandable and thus in some sense ideal for archival activity and increasable inventories. The duration of the still ongoing sacred history is intimated through the lengthy performances, and their episodic, reiterative nature – the capacity to be told and witnessed in various orders, in chronological reverse, or in echoing loops – is emphasized through the multiple, repeatable plays. To break down this dynamic: a finite episode (e.g. the flood, the nativity, the passion) is staged before an audience, but this play also participates in an ongoing cycle of performances, a cycle spiraling through the days of festival, through the years, and eventually through centuries. Perhaps some participants imagined their annual or semiannual performances of sacred history as circling within a slower spiral of real time, extending, according to the logic of sacred history itself, toward Judgment Day.

Both the length of the performances and the centuries over which the tradition variously endured suggest a certain weight or momentum of time: the continual replaying of a long and familiar story that spirals, like the liturgical calendar, both forward and in circles, toward an always anticipated culmination or an ideal audience – God before the lists at Judgment Day, say – who might witness the completion of the story and so effect its being finally, satisfactorily "performyd": finished, accomplished, a thing done.[60] But the dynamism of performance, its liveness and liveliness, and its propensity to invite new possibilities and transformations, also disrupts the stasis that the accumulative encapsulation of a complete world would seem to require, making the site of performance less of an ideal archive, and more an ideal space from which to investigate the attempts – wildly successful, seemingly incomplete, or utterly doomed – at archival endeavor.

Roughly half the book considers the mystery plays that enact the episodes involving Eden, the flood, and the Harrowing. The rest examines works of poetry, prose, biblical paraphrase, devotional writing, and iconography contemporary to them. I am interested, for instance, in the "compendious" genres, in images of hell, and in poems of infernal descent, in which verse itself becomes a means for tempering or turning back the onslaught of time.[61] These other works can provide a richer context for English religious drama even as they themselves at times include traces of a performance sensibility within their non-embodied forms. The mystery plays, in turn, widely familiar and performed for centuries, help to contextualize such imagery and non-dramatic texts. This is not to insist on a strict divide between texts that are associated with performance and those that are not; Carol Symes has demonstrated the practical difficulties of doing just that, and she argues compellingly for a more generous understanding of the ways in which performance permeated various facets of medieval culture, and how it might be seen in places where we are not accustomed to look.[62] Symes' work contributes, alongside studies by Jody Enders and Jessica Brantley, to ways of thinking about performance when it is not relegated, conceptually or architecturally, to designated theatrical genres and spaces, and how it might be used as a methodological tool for interpreting works not immediately grouped under those rubrics.[63] This book, too, considers texts that for various reasons complicate a divide between the dramatic and non-dramatic, or performance and non-performance: textual records of lost performances, for example, or the genre of the lai, balanced between written poetry and the memory of song. Examination of such texts, and the move to consider mystery plays alongside other kinds of works in general, can contribute to the work of bringing medieval drama and performance into the larger fold of medieval literary studies, where it historically has struggled to find critical space.

But while we can find formal similarities between the mystery plays and the metrical chronicles – a marathon production that first calls for silence with a sonorous "sum alpha and omega" and a thirty-thousand line history that commences with the direct address of "Lordynges þat be now here / if ȝe wille listene & lere"[64] – I still do not want to diminish the singular identity of the mystery plays to which I turn in Chapters 1, 3, and 5. They are but one medieval performance genre out of many, and I am interested in them *for* their idiosyncrasies, including their incredible historical duration and popularity. They are, as V.A. Kolve bluntly puts it, the "the most truly popular drama England has ever known."[65] As public theater, the plays and the records that they have left can reveal how large portions of late medieval communities were engaged in thinking about the organization of space and time, and how audiences participated in performances of archival endeavor, even as they experienced, outside of the suspended reality of the plays, the acts of cultural transmission promised and effected by the performances themselves. And, of course, I am interested in *this* particular kind of drama because it specifically stages the creation and loss of Eden, the construction of Noah's ark and the flood, and the Harrowing of Hell, the three episodes that structure the rest of the book.

The first chapter of the book, "Model Worlds," starts with the beginning of sacred history, examining the creation and loss of Eden, as well as later gardens that take the earthly paradise as their model. The chapter argues that Eden, a site of creation and collection, works as a model world, but in two, sometimes contradictory, senses. For subsequent phases of history (all medieval Christian history is subsequent to this beginning), the garden functions as a collection of exemplars, a lost vision of perfection that has been imperfectly emulated in fallen form. But it also – and simultaneously – works as an archive of ideals, a record of the ways in which perfection historically has been imagined. Understood from the first perspective, Eden offers a pre-historical vision of perfection to be copied; in the second, Eden becomes a copy of earthly imaginings. I look closely at the mystery plays that perform the creation and loss of the garden – and, in the York plays specifically, a few moments of static perfection in between – to argue that such performances make it difficult to discern which world, the earth or the earthly paradise, is the copy or record and which is the original.

The chapter also investigates how one goes about charting the boundary between such ontological and geographic categories. To that end, I consider how the plays perform the nebulous edges of both the earthly paradise and the medieval stage itself: how an unenclosed performance space stages a garden whose most necessary postlapsarian feature is its fortification. Such performances invite us to think more about the relationship between the archive and the world, or copy and original, and about how these categorical distinctions dissolve within performance space. It returns us also to the various desires and frustrations associated with the archive: the fever for origins, and the movement backward in time toward a beginning that is always already its own kind of afterward.

Moving on from the difficulty of distinguishing between the archive and the world, or between record and original, I then turn more specifically to the problem of compiling an inventory and to the story of Noah's flood. Chapters 2 and 3 focus on the story of the flood in order to think about the exclusions and inclusions upon which the creation of an inventory is predicated, as well as the desire for exhaustiveness and the interpretive authority invested in the archivist who presides over those decisions and communicates that desire. I argue that Noah's ark ("arca noe") functions as an archive ("archivum") in performances of the flood, and that the patriarch's project of loading a vessel with remnants of a vanishing past conceptually reinforces what Isidore understood as an etymological link. Noah collects elements of the antediluvian world – his own family and the animals, embarking two by two – and arranges them to ride out the vicissitudes of history, or the crisis of weather God sends to cleanse the earth whose creation he has begun to regret. Here, as in the compilation of the *Liber Albus*, an archive of knowledge is assembled in response to disaster.

The first of the flood chapters, "Ark and Archive," looks at various medieval engagements with the Genesis story, including work by the twelfth-century theologian Hugh of Saint Victor, who employs the ark as a mnemonic device, figuring it as an "arca cordis," or "ark of the heart." Examining the "arca noe" alongside the "arca cordis," the chapter looks at possible relationships between history and memory, and the ethical consequences of confusing one for the other. It further considers a number of medieval chronicles and romances, investigating how the intertwined yet oppositional desires for an exhaustive account and more controllable, genealogical and political narratives are underwritten by the story of the flood-time archivist. Chapter 3, "Uxor Noe and the Drowned," returns to the mystery plays to pay particular attention to the plight of Noah's Wife, who, in her enhanced medieval role, derides her husband's monumental project. In the plays, Noah refuses his wife's cooperation as co-leader of the ark, though still insists that she board his floating archive. She is not permitted to record history, but becomes recorded, as another item of inventory, or another beast, herded into his archive. The chapter considers the implementation of categories under duress, and explores the catastrophic consequences the project has for future gender identities and politics.

Chapters 4 and 5 take on the issue of archival temporalities by turning to the episode of the Harrowing of Hell and other medieval narratives of infernal descent. In these chapters, I read hell simultaneously as a site of dead letter records and as irrepressible past, a storehouse that struggles to contain its overwhelming quantity of history, spectrally embodied as the ever-accumulating centuries of the dead. I consider the propensity for time to run backward when one descends into the underworld, and the ways in which the past overtakes the present when the dead are raised. Chapter 4, "Infernal Archive," explores the dynamics of hell as an archive and these unruly temporalities by looking at medieval accounts of voyages to the underworld and back, in works such as Middle English versions of the Harrowing of Hell and the *Gospel of Nicodemus*, Dante's *Inferno*, the Middle English lai *Sir Orfeo*, and accounts of Saint Patrick's Purgatory, the legendary Irish portal to the otherworld. Chapter 5, "The Harrowing of Hell: Closure and Rehearsal," examines Christ's journey to hell and back – his descent into the underworld and his liberation of the patriarchs and prophets of the Old Testament understood as confined there – as it was performed on mystery play stages. Medieval iconography and some stage designs featured a hell mouth through which Adam and Eve, Abraham, Moses, Isaiah, and others departed from their infernal confines. I read these always-open jaws as indicating the thwarted suppression of history; they are the rupture through which the past leaks, and from which stories pour out of the underground to complicate the new narratives being forged on the surface (the stage) of the earth above.

These moments in sacred history concern thinking about the world *in toto*: for instance, an *entire* world lost and the seeds for a new one preserved aboard an ark. The conceptual archival projects that such episodes represent occur on a massive scale: the creation of a completely representative inventory, ringed by Eden's walls; the preservation of two of everything, salvaged aboard Noah's ship; and access to a record of all that has ever been, encountered by Christ as he descends into infernal history. The tremendous scope of these archives frequently corresponds to the medieval textual and visual genres that transmit them, including the lengthy chronicles and the performances of sacred history that stretch on for hours or sometimes even days, beginning with the fall of the angels and culminating in the cosmic roll call of the Last Judgment, as in the Mercers' play.

These medieval archival models, playfully constructed through poetry, riotously staged by mystery plays, and variously conjured by other creative projects, illuminate both the desires and dangers associated with efforts to gather as much as possible into one place. Through these models, we can discern medieval perceptions of how categories of record structure social organization and narrative form, and how methods of accumulation condition one to anticipate the way stories begin and end. As with the extensive Judgment Day narratives, housed in nearly infinite penitential hearts, or Dante's single book, or Chaucer's deafening "hous," these episodes suggest both grave concerns and utopian giddiness about the ways components of a whole world might be brought together: about the difficulties of recording; the parts inevitably left out; the interpretive postures that cannot be escaped; the future that is altered by gathering in and shaping the past; the past that gets revised as the future looms ever nearer to receive it; and the present that is overwhelmed by such archival frenzy.

The chapters that follow thus explore a number of relationships wrapped up in imagining the archive, including that between stasis and dynamism, disappearance and accumulation, preservation and salvation, and patriarchal control and the kind of meaning produced by a witnessing, free-roaming crowd. These explorations are tethered to sites, sacred and otherwise (garden, ark, and hell, and also sometimes hearts, codices, boxes, and bodies) and to episodes that provide insight into the way medieval thinkers approached time and collection, and how they expressed both a delight in and anxiety about archival projects. The archive suggests the intersection of one time with another, the transmission of transformational knowledge that can effect change and be changed through centuries. It also involves labor that attempts to mediate that intersection among past, present, and future, though often, as we will see, it is the collision among them that draws the artist.

CHAPTER I

Model Worlds

This chapter begins with a scene that has become, in many ways, emblematic of beginnings: Adam and Eve stepping from the earthly paradise into the earth, leaving behind a garden characterized by its stasis, perfection, beauty, and abundance, and into a world that eventually becomes the one we know. I argue that the relationship between these grounds, the paradise planted "from the beginning" and the larger, extensive, fallen earth that spreads out from it, offers one way of approaching the distinction between originals and records.[1] Just as it can be difficult to delimit the site of origins from the archive that accumulates around and after it, it can be difficult to tell where Eden ends and the rest of the earth begins. Medieval representations of the creation and loss of the garden frequently illuminate the unclear, inconsistent distinction between categories of original and record, or original and copy, and even between designations of before and after. By considering medieval efforts to define that supposedly initial, sacred ground against the larger world into which Adam and Eve fall, we also can question the ontology of the archive and how it might be defined against that which it archives.

In an important sense, Eden (or the earthly paradise, I use the terms interchangeably[2]) functions as a site of origins in the Middle Ages, a garden of exemplars from which the more expansive earth might take its cues, copying species and the rules for relationships among them in fallen form. According to this schema, despite the errant nature of human history, those on earth should attempt to hew as closely as possible to the model garden God initially creates with such divine care. This is a relationship of original and copy: first comes Eden, a place of perfect sufficiency and abundance, and then, after the fall, comes the earth, the great expanse into which Adam and Eve reluctantly and fearfully step, with zoological procession presumably trailing morosely behind them. In this larger earth, with its more generous horizon, life continues but with a difference, and with ideals remembered only well enough for subsequent regret, duplicated in faint echo, or through a glass darkly.

But scriptural uncertainties and medieval representational strategies also put pressure upon this version of a radically initial, pristine Eden, held off as separate from a lesser and secondary earth. Through exegetical questioning, poetic wordplay, and especially the unclear borders of representation effected in zones of performance, different works contest both the primary status and physical edges of the garden. Earthly records of Eden also can prove so earnest, exacting, or otherwise extraordinary that they sometimes appear to supersede the primacy attributed to that place planted "from the beginning," making it seem as if a record might challenge or trump an original. This makes it hard to locate and to articulate with authority the exact perfection from which we have fallen, but that lack of certainty also permits the kind of speculating capable of producing various versions of Eden. As Alastair Minnis points out, different descriptions of Eden have been used to sanction "both egalitarianism and slavery, equality and inequality, and the dignity and inferiority of womankind," just for starters.[3] According to *this* schema, then, the garden gets recreated as a circle of privileged ground containing ordered perfection as different historical moments imagine it. The search for origins, rather than uncovering a pre-historical starting point, instead creates its own exemplars, so that representations of Eden record fallen histories of imagined perfection. The earthly paradise thus can function *both* as the original creation that human history endeavors fruitlessly to replicate, copying its rules and patterns in fallen form, *and* as a record of the fallen world: a site of origins reconstituted through layers of suspect historical desire, remade through visions of perfection we must historicize.

Clifford Geertz has pointed out the multivalence that the word "model" carries in English, how it has "both an 'of' sense and a 'for' sense."[4] It can be descriptive, "a model *of*" something that aids in the "apprehension" of that thing (of what Geertz calls a "pre-established nonsymbolic system"), or it can be a model *for* reality, as when something in the physical world is built in accordance with a model, with "model" taking on the sense of a blueprint.[5] The ambivalence of the term helps us to understand how Eden, too, can function either as an initial design, a divine blueprint for the earth, or how the conjured memory of it can contain traces of the historical moments in which one struggles to imagine that initial design: either a divine model for the larger world, or a model that those in the world themselves create in the struggle to imagine their mythic origins.[6] One of the points I want to make in this chapter is that both senses of the word can inhere in the same medieval representation of Eden.

The nature of the model matters to how we perceive the nature of the inventory that Eden purportedly contains and organizes. Inventory might be comprised of ideals or exemplars, terms that suggest an originating standard, even as they harbor traces of retrospective desire. Or it might be made up of copies or records, categories fully imbued with a sense of belatedness or secondariness. But "copy" and "record" also differ slightly from each other. Though they are related in their loose opposition to the sense of an "original," they are not interchangeable, as "copy" would seem to participate in a more exacting mimesis, and "record" to leave more room for invention. This, then, is a second point: it is the entangling of these qualities – an exacting mimesis that endeavors to trump reality itself, and the kind of creative latitude that permits newness – that interestingly complicates projects to recuperate and represent mythic origins.

With the figure of Adam stepping out of the garden in mind, then, this chapter first interrogates the difference between the earth and Eden in geographical and conceptual terms, demonstrating how thinkers, working exegetically, poetically, and from within the genre of the travelogue, both clarified and muddled the difference between these grounds. In the second section, I turn to performances of the creation and loss of Eden, demonstrating how the pageant wagon stages – theaters without walls – foregrounded the difficulty of geographically curtailing and ontologically defining the garden through its simultaneous production of performance and sacred space. From there, I consider the contested relationship between original and record, or between the world and a record of the world, through the involuting, dazzlingly disorienting representational strategies of late medieval poetry and theology. The final section examines the relationship between the archive and narrative through a study of Adamic language, the words first uttered, with such power, in the soon-to-be-lost garden.

1   Forms of Erthe

Tradition teaches that the postlapsarian grounds of the earth and the earthly paradise differ significantly: one is a rarified realm of seeming eternity, from which an entirely sufficient array of fruits and flowers spring, and the other is a humbler vastness encircling this privileged center, conditioned by time, change, and the need for labor. In this section, I consider how that iconic image of Adam's outward stride – that one suspended moment of crossing over – might help us to query the difference between them. Perhaps, after all, the sensation of earthiness on either side of the threshold feels rather similar during departure: beneath the *front* feet of Adam and Eve, the clayey surface of the more extensive earth into which they fall, and, beneath the back, the paradisiacal ground, momentarily indistinguishable in color and consistency. In many images, the fall appears as no fall at all, but rather as a level step across indeterminate ground.

It is after the human pair crosses this momentous threshold that the difference between earth and Eden is supposed to become clearer. Many medieval depictions insist upon it; images of postlapsarian fortifications proliferate, intimating enclosure and protection through stonewalls, gates, armed angels, fire, water, and, in one play, curtains.[7] An image from an early fifteenth-century French manuscript surrounds the forfeited garden with a rising body of water, hinting at the flood to come even before Adam and Eve fall.[8] Other images, such as one found in the Hours of Catherine of Cleves, feature small, barred conduits in the garden wall, a reminder both of the once-permitted passage between the worlds and the current impossibility of such movement.[9] In the fourteenth century, Mandeville's *Travels* includes a description of the earthly paradise so set apart from the world that even the mechanisms for enclosing it are hidden. The text insists on the garden as being beyond image-making, beyond imagining. Mandeville writes that "[o]ff Paradyse cann I noȝt speke properly for I hafe noȝt bene þare,"[10] but he continues anyway, relying on the testimony of others, which seems only to contribute to the invisibility of the garden, for they, too, have only encountered an obscured edge. According to Mandeville, "wyse" and well-traveled men say it is not only the interior of the garden that cannot be apprehended; the walls themselves are covered with moss and branches, so that it is impossible to know of what kind of stone they are made: "Paradys es closed alle aboute wiþ a walle, bot whareoff þe walle es made cann na man telle."[11] One cannot see the protected interior, and one cannot even see the form of protection that surrounds it; Eden has become entirely invisible to those outside of it.

But neither the spare details of scripture nor many of the descriptions of elaborate fortifications indicate whether there would have been a visible partition between these realms before or during the moment of expulsion, something to mark out the place where the walls or a ring of fire soon would appear. The confusing double narrative in the opening chapters of Genesis contributes to the difficulty of determining how different earth and Eden are at the time of their creation. After God makes heaven and earth ("caelum" and "terrum" in the Vulgate) and all the things within them, he rests on the seventh day. But then the story of creation recommences with its own disconcerting "but":

> But a spring rose out of the earth, watering all the surface of the earth. And the Lord God formed man of the slime of the earth: and breathed into his face the breath of life, and man became a living soul. And the Lord God had planted a paradise of pleasure from the beginning: wherein he placed man whom he had formed (2.6–8).[12]

Man and woman already have been created according to the first chapter of Genesis – they are the handiwork of day six – but their formation is repeated in this second chapter, along with the first specific designation of a separate "paradise" in which they are "placed" to dwell. The double narrative results from the conflation of two traditions, but theologians disentangled the chapters in different ways, trying out various suppositions to explain what otherwise reads as not-quite-exact repetition.

My interest here is not in the attempts to synthesize Genesis for the sake of narrative coherence, but in the room this temporal confusion makes for thinking about whether Eden and the rest of the earth are created sequentially or simultaneously, and how chronology conditions understandings of their relationship to one another. Is the earthly paradise ground that gets cordoned off sometime after a more general moment of creation, set apart for Adam and Eve, who are made from the earth outside of it, or is the garden a still more sacred center where the generative powers of creation initially and exclusively churn? Is there a difference – geographical, chemical, ontological, in *some* way visibly or otherwise sensibly apparent – between one part of the ground and the other that results from the sequence of their creation? Augustine's writings on Genesis formed an influential part of the exegetical effort to address these uncertainties,[13] and medieval poetic attempts also delighted in the confusion of possibility, adding a playful linguistic layer of same-but-different to the geographical ambiguity. The tantalizing question of consistency and difference across the two realms persisted across centuries, reinvoked every time Adam was represented as stepping outward, leaving one parcel of ground for another, abdicating eternity for the onslaught of time.

For instance, switching from the substance of land to water, the fifth-century Syrian bishop Severian writes that when the four rivers of paradise pass that essential threshold between Eden and earth, they become polluted.[14] By the fourteenth century, the chemical nature of the elements still are under question, as the prophet Isaiah comments more vaguely upon possible distinctions in the *Cursor Mundi*, suggesting that the materiality of the greater world, even if not polluted, still lacks the vague, *je ne sais quoi* of Eden:

> Of all thinges þat we here se,
> On hei, on lau, on land, on see,
> War o gretter strengh and pith,
> Ar adam had fordon þe grith.[15]

> Of all the things that we see here, on high, on low, on land, on sea, they were of
> greater strength and pith before Adam destroyed the peace / refuge.

Then again, Isaiah perhaps is cited to mark a difference less noticeable across the geographic boundaries of Eden and earth at the moment of Adam's departure, and more apparent over time, in the long wake of his fall. After the expulsion, the *Cursor Mundi* possibly suggests, all of the greater earth also becomes suddenly less Edenic.

Middle English itself contributes to this ambiguity between places, since "earth" or "erthe" can refer both to the loam of the ground and to the global cosmos: different elements, registers, and portions of creation. The circular Middle English lyric "Erthe toc of erthe" exploits this semantic flexibility, mingling specific places and layers of dirt, all of which the word "erthe" designates:

> Erthe toc of erthe erthe wyth woh,
> Erthe other erthe to the erthe droh,
> Erthe leyde erthe in erthene throh,
> Tho heuede erthe of erthe erthe ynoh.

> Earth took earth from the earth with sadness.
> Earth drew the other earth to the earth.
> Earth laid the earth in an earthen tomb.
> Then had earth of earth earth enough.[16]

In her reading of the enigmatic lyric, Gillian Rudd suggests that the word "Adam" also participates in the web of allusive meaning, as the name recalls "the possible derivation of *adamah*, earth."[17] Rudd demonstrates how one might read Adam as molded from the ground in these incantatory lines, and also recognize him as delving into the earth himself, spade in hand and sweat upon the brow. The way that earth gets syntactically and physically shifted around in the poem suggests, according to Rudd, a "précis of the fall" itself.[18] Earth is drawn, piled, and shaped in the lyric, but each instance of the word continues to evoke the meaning of the others: these are the many possible forms of "erthe," or of that *something* that God creates after the light. The earth of the earthly paradise, the earth of the world outside paradise, and the earth of Adam himself share a conceptual and physical connection, making it hard to determine at which poetic or geographical instance one form of "erthe" lapses into another, or, to recall the Syrian bishop, when and where one drop of water suddenly loses its pristine quality.

These considerations of not-quite disparate "erthes" intersect with the subject of the archive because they reveal difficulties associated with the longing for origins. Derrida writes that a component of archive fever is the fever for beginnings, the "desire to return to the origin, a home-sickness, a nostalgia for the return to the most archaic place of absolute commencement,"[19] a description that conjures, for me, Mandeville's somewhat mournful lingering over the invisible walls of paradise, related to him by other men who likewise could not see them. Derrida's fever is a desire to know which original moment of inception shapes subsequent history, whose archival accumulation proceeds from, overwhelms, and effaces it: the "arkhē," as he calls this beginning (countering Isidore's Latin etymology with Greek), "*there* where things *commence*," and "*in this place* from which *order* is given."[20] The ability to articulate details of that origin, to know its qualities or essence after one has cleared away the history that seems only to be intervening, finally to know "the most archaic place of absolute commencement," assigns the seeker tremendous authority over the future. This is particularly true when that beginning or origin is understood as sacred,[21] for then its disclosure permits one to articulate, admonishingly and with great plans for recuperation, the perfection from which we have fallen.[22] But what if one struggles to locate this place of beginning, or to demarcate its edges? What is the limit of the beginning? In the next section, a consideration of the mystery plays that take up the creation and loss of Eden, traditional site of origins in medieval Christian sacred history, reveals how those performances stage the desire for recovering a place of absolute beginning even as they dispute the possibility of such a project.

2   Performing the Beginning

York had the greatest number of plays associated with Eden and the acts of creation that preceded it. The records include (after the Fall of the Angels) the Creation, the Creation of Adam and Eve, Adam and Eve in Eden, the Fall of Man, and finally the Expulsion, thus separating out into separate performances a number of events – and more or less non-events, such as the static portrait of the human pair in Eden – that the N-Town, Towneley, and Chester plays variously combine. In all of these versions, Adam seems to take form outside of the garden, followed by Eve; the two, naked and unashamed, then are brought into paradise. In York, the Creation of Adam and Eve intimates this shift from the earth, where God makes Adam out of "þe symplest part of erthe þat is here" – the "here" seeming to designate ground not part of Eden proper – and into the garden, where the newly formed humans are brought in the manner of a homecoming (l.25). The play then ends with God asking Adam and Eve to "comys forth" with him (l.94), and the next play, Adam and Eve in Eden, begins with *Deus* introducing the humans to their new garden home: "this is the place," he says, in the very first line (l.1). In N-Town, they are welcomed by the ringing out of the divine voice, and "the place" gets a name: "Now come forth, Adam, to paradys."[23]

But the "here" of their first formation also seems to hold considerable charms for the newly awakened humans, some apparently quite similar to those they will encounter in "paradys." When Adam first opens his eyes, in the "here" where he has been made, he instantly delights in his surroundings, praising a "world" that he notes is both "long and wide" and exclaiming, at York:

> A, lorde, full mekyll is þi mighte
> And þat is sene in ilke a syde,
> For now his here a ioyfull syght
> To se þis worlde so lange and wyde.   (ll.45–8)

O Lord, full great is your might, and that is seen on each side. For now a joyful sight is here, to see this world so long and wide.

Eve echoes his sentiment about the breathtaking dimensions in language that begins to sound like the traditional description of the inventory housed in Eden, with its cornucopia of birds and beasts:

> And selcouth thyngis may we se here
> Of þis ilke warld so lange and brade,
> With bestis and fowlis so many and sere;
> Blessid be he þat [hase] us made.   (ll.57–60)

And various, marvelous things may we see here, of this same world so long and broad, with so many various beasts and fowls; blessed be he who has made us.

God goes on to tell Adam and Eve that, "In paradyse sall ȝe same wone, / Of erthely thyng get ȝe no nede" [In paradise you shall dwell together and of earthly thing have no need] (ll.73–4). The second line might be read to suggest that they will need no earthly thing, as in, they will not experience need at all, but it also sets up a certain opposition between "erthe" and "paradise"; the human pair, if they play their cards right, will not need anything associated with the earth outside of the earthly paradise: they will not need anything linked to the "here" with whose beauty they are, at first, so taken.

This initial, tentative, distinction between the earth and the earthly paradise becomes, as we have seen in other works, enhanced after the fall; what begins as a shift from one wondrous portion of the world to another, from the "here" to a perhaps slightly more glorious "there," gets reaffirmed and reinforced, according to scripture, with a flaming sword. The first set of stage directions of the *Jeu d'Adam* calls for this reinforcement of boundaries through elevation and the use of a curtain, even before the moment of the fall:

> Constituatur paradisus loco eminenciori; circumponantur cortine et panni serici, ea altitudine ut persone, que in paradiso fuerint, possint videri sursum ad humeris.

> Let paradise be constructed on a raised place; let curtains and silk hangings be arranged around it at such a height that the persons who are in Paradise may be visible from the shoulders up.[24]

The directions imply that Eden must be walled before the expulsion. It makes the question of how the actors are clothed before and after the fall less pressing than in the English plays, but presumably allows the audience, from its fallen vantage point on earth, still to see the face and arms of Eve as she bites into the fruit.

But unlike in the *Jeu d'Adam*, it is not entirely clear how the difference between earth and the earthly paradise would have been staged by the English plays. Most likely a raised area, such as a pageant wagon, indicating Eden would have been involved, possibly with the suggestion of a low wall,[25] but it is difficult to know how, at York, for instance, Eden could be staged in such a way so as to make it seem *less* "lange and wyde" or "lange and brade" than the greater world around it, those qualities by which Adam and Eve are most dazzled when they first awake outside of the garden, presumably upon the ground of the city. It would be hard to shut out the magnificent breadth of this newly created world in an age before enclosed theaters, or to imagine the sightlines of the actors playing Adam and Eve running up against some unmarked limit or truncated horizon: that invisible border upon which fortifications later were to be built. If Adam and Eve were created on the street and then brought to an elevated pageant wagon stage for the audience to witness, then that designated playing space would have been set apart from civic ground, but incapable of visually excluding it.

Much work has been done on the staging resources used to designate and demarcate representational space in this era before enclosed theaters. Most critics employ the terminology of *locus* and *platea*, wherein the *locus* tends to be associated with the pageant wagon stage, or a space representing a specific place and time, and the *platea* with the ground around it, onto which actors and props spill to accommodate the practical logistics of potentially crowded staging. Jerome Bush, in a study of the Digby *Mary Magdalene*, describes it this way:

> A *locus* is localized space. Usually, a *locus* is representational, if not illu-
> sionary, in nature. It is a man-made object or structure fashioned within
> a clearly defined stage space . . . On the other hand, the *platea* is unlocalized,
> nonarchitectural, and nonrepresentational space. In most cases the *platea* or
> "the place" is constituted by, rather than constructed on, a natural setting or
> a permanent structure: the village green or a city square. It is part of both the
> audience's everyday life and the play's staging.[26]

The division is a helpful starting point, a fruitful opposition with which the performances can begin to play. For it is difficult to stop the spread of representational potential, or to point to a place that does not represent.[27] Medievalists have been quick to point out this difficulty of containing the theatrical zone for which the *locus* at times might serve as epicenter. In these plays of far-flung locations, staging Jerusalem, Egypt, or heaven, the city itself is made to collude through its performance of geography, and frequently gets cast as a biblical site. In *Signifying God*, a study of the York plays, Sarah Beckwith describes the effect that performance and the city have upon one another; she reminds us of the difficulty of separating York from Jerusalem, *platea* from *locus*, reality from representation: "No physical markers separate a specific 'theatrical' space from everyday life: there is no inherent, independent stage for acting."[28] In these civic performances, played in the street by local tradesmen, it can be difficult to pinpoint the line where performance ends and everyday life begins, or fully to extricate scriptural from medieval time.

Natalie Crohn Schmitt has written about her efforts to direct Adam and Eve in Eden as part of the 1998 production of the York plays in Toronto:

> [I]n blocking our production of the Fullers' play, we chose to have God first
> appear on the decorated pageant wagon which served to represent a low-
> walled Eden, the like of which appears in numerous late medieval

illustrations, the wall setting sacred space off from ordinary space . . . Adam and Eve, representing human kind before the Fall, wended their way to the wagon at audience level.[29]

The episodes associated with the creation and fall include at least two crossings between earth and Eden: Adam and Eve's homecoming into Eden after their creation, and then their expulsion from it. Schmitt's careful discussion of staging choices, however, reminds us that, because there are so many individual mystery plays, guilds, and wagons participating in the extensive productions, at any one time there will be a number of stages, choreographed crossings, and Edens, walled or otherwise, taking form. As Beckwith puts it, there might be "up to twenty Christs, twelve Maries, several different 'Gods,' and a few Satans wandering the city giving multiple performances at several sites."[30] Such a dynamic destabilizes the relationship between the earth and the supposedly singular paradise, even threatening to overwhelm iconic crossings with the heavy foot traffic of a festive city.

In Schmitt's Toronto production of Adam and Eve in Eden, the new human pair moves through the *platea* toward the *locus* of the raised stage, through the audience toward Eden. Following the map of scripture, they wend from the outer regions of that human-generating clay into the prepared garden. But at the same time, they appear to move backward into history, or *through* history, by weaving their way through a postlapsarian crowd. The crowd is staged as postlapsarian because they stand outside the theatrical Eden, but also, within this medieval Christian context, they wait on the "real" postlapsarian ground of York, a fallen earth that needs neither costuming nor suspended belief to play its part. The ground plays itself; it is the "here."[31] To then step back (or down) from the stage of Eden to the earth, or to look out from the perspective of Eden to earth, is also to move from the *locus* ("the place," in God's words in the York play) into the *platea* of the city, from the suspension of time into time itself, into history.[32] At the point of departure, Adam and Eve lean toward their future in the last of their indivisible moments, poised to fall into that "here" they once briefly knew, the place with the wider horizon, and perhaps down onto the plains of what would become Damascus. They move forward into what is both history and future: the conditions for history, and time unrolling out like the land before them.

In some ways, this surely must be staged as a mournful moment. As the actors ready to join the audience on the fallen *platea* in the York Expulsion

play, there is a sense of irreparable loss that comes both with the end of
their privileged existence and the end of the performance. Adam
laments:

> In worlde vnwisely wrought haue wee,
> This erthe it trembelys for this tree
> And dyns ilke dele!
> Alle þis worlde is wrothe with mee,
> þis wote I wele.
>
> Full wele Y wote my welthe is gane,
> Erthe, elementis, euerilkane
> For my synne has sorowe tane,
> þis wele I see.   (ll.112–20)

In the world we have wrought unwisely. This earth, it trembles because of this
tree, and each dell makes a din! All of the world is wroth with me, this I know
well. Full well I know my wealth is gone, earth, elements, everything, for
my sin, taken up by sorrow. This I well see.

After eating the fruit, Adam perceives changes in what he refers to as both
"this worlde" and "this erthe"; he would seem to be referring to Eden, but
perhaps the designation shifts from one line to the next. Either way, the
"erthe" trembles ("trembelys") and, anthropomorphized, expresses rage
("alle this worlde is wrothe with mee"). Alongside the trembling comes
a great noise: "dins ilke dele," which I read as "each dell or dale made
a din," or "each portion [of the garden or the world] made a din." Middle
English "dele," however, also can refer to sawed boards, the lumber,
perhaps, out of which a pageant wagon might have been constructed.
It is not only the ground that begins to tremble and sound when the
humans eat, but also the stage upon which that transgression gets reenacted
that thunders as its actors prepare to take their leave. The fact that Eden is
on wheels in these performances, or the stage placed upon the street,
emphasizes further the sense of *departure* with which Adam and Eve are
cursed. In fallen York, even Eden wanders; it achieves stasis for the space of
a moment, when actors and audience pause and view the inventory
lavished upon the stage, and then, according to the processional quality
of the performances, either wagon or crowd (or both) pack up again,
following the expelled players on their not so solitary way.

But the departure is not only mournful, for this momentous footfall
also produces new sacred space. Beckwith's reading of the York plays
describes performance space not as an ontological given, but as an effect
produced between the congregant actors and audience as they reenact and

reexperience sacred history. The stage is not a single address, but differentiated and "articulated into being," incrementally and variously made out of the city itself, whose every stone has the potential to be dramatically co-opted.[33] In her discussion of the Resurrection play, Beckwith relates this production of performance space to sacramental practice or Eucharistic process:

> It is a presencing of Christ in the community of the faithful. And since theater . . . is radically incomplete without its witnessing participants, the audience, York's Resurrection theater manifests the possibilities and resources of the insight that "nothing can be present to us to which we are not present."[34]

Beckwith employs sacramental contract – the efficacy of sacrament as contingent upon active and faithful witnessing – as a way of thinking about performance, which is "radically incomplete without its witnessing participants."[35]

Such a formulation seems especially apt for the play of the Resurrection, but the approach runs into interesting confusion in performances endeavoring to represent the loss of paradise. Performances of the departure from Eden's gates produce and unleash a theatrical zone that conceptually extends beyond the limits of any witnessing community. Theatrical spaces, when they logically include the entire world – the world into which Adam and Eve fall, the world, so long and broad and wide, into which the players descend from the stage – may be articulated into being, but perhaps not afterward easily curtailed. Performances of the Expulsion, commemorating an event that long ago made the earth into a fallen ground, purport to remake this whole earth into an expansive stage and then to *cast it as* that fallen ground. In this way, the plays reconfirm the whole world, long and broad, as the site where performance must continue for the next great act of Adam and Eve: the performance of human history. It becomes a site theatrically "set apart," staged and perfectly cast as fallen ground. The world is at once theatricalized and fallen, or, we might say, "set apart" and fallen, and so "sacred" and fallen.[36] The relationship between the stage as its own privileged theatrical zone, one set apart with difficulty from the civic space it borders, can be understood as commenting on the relationship between the sacred zone of Eden and the rest of the earth that spreads out from it.

Such a paradoxical dynamic suggests a way of thinking about the world as redeemed through the performance of the fall. The play of the Expulsion pulls the familiar ground out from beneath the feet of the fallen audience.

At first, Eden is that strange new land at which they get to peer, enabled by performance to discern that from which postlapsarian humans – the regretful Mandeville, his wise men – are cordoned off. But when Adam steps off the stage, his outward stride remakes whatever medieval city upon which it lands into foreign ground, or dramatically recalls that it always has been that. Even as the flaming sword reinforces the impassible divide between staged earth and staged Eden, the departure of the players, playing at falling, permits the sense of the sacred zone of performance to spread, and the whole world becomes different: playing itself even as it plays "as if."[37]

There is a tremendous potential for authority in articulating the details of a shared site of origins, and in the promise that it might one day be recovered as pristine, untouched by the confusion of history, and clear in its order and injunctions. When Adam and Eve step across realms soon to be divided by formidable walls, the crushing finality of the scene suggests that such defenses are built not only to keep the pair out should they try to return, but constructed to establish and insist upon the difference between "here" and "there." The sprouted-up walls insist that there is, from our fallen perspective, a more circumscribed paradise of absolute beginning, and that it might someday be recovered as an absolutely clear corrective to the errant ways of history. But in the medieval plays of the Expulsion, that difference is muddled, as footfall makes fallen ground into a zone of performance, in which each new moment might offer a new instant of inception, absolute beginning again, origins reoriginated through performance. Rather than simply revealing a site of beginning by drawing aside the proverbial or theatrical curtain, the plays stage this moment of beginning, again and again allowing an unclear, ordinary, and expansive "here" – where God finds the "simple earth" with which to make a body – to achieve the status of Derrida's "*there* where things commence."

3   Reality and Record (Some Garden Varieties)

In the previous section, I argued that the English mystery plays destabilize Eden as a site of origin, through dramaturgical maneuvers (multiple, unenclosed stages serving as the *loci* of the purportedly singular garden) and through an understanding of the way performance and sacred spaces are created. I want now to take this understanding of the unstable relationship between the earth and the earthly paradise and return to the issue of original and record. It would seem that many earthly, imperfect searches for the perfection of the earthly paradise trouble the trajectory of sacred history, in that the search itself, instead of revealing a radical beginning, ends up producing more record, more archive, making Derrida's arkhē, the place of commencement, further recede. One might say, following Allen Frantzen's argument in *Desire for Origins*, that the search produces not only more archive, but its own version of origins, creating a closed circuit in which seekers attempt to discover that which they themselves have articulated into being.[38] This loop, in which one searches for an ideal of one's own making, replays itself in various forms, as descriptions of an initial, perfect place and time, whose rules should structure all later attempts at perfection, have a tendency to reveal tenets close to the hearts of their narrators.

Medieval engagements with Eden reveal a tendency to produce origins characterized by historically conditioned values. Minnis, as we have seen, argues that the search for origins offered an "enabling context" for exegetes presuming to reveal the nature and rules of Eden, and who exerted influence upon property laws, dietary restrictions, and gender relations.[39] Eric Jager sees this dynamic operating beyond exegesis, calling the "myth of the Fall ... an imaginative construct or projection of medieval culture itself, which wrote its own historical reality into the mutable narrative details and symbolic values of this myth."[40] And writing of beginnings more generally – all beginnings, or any beginning – D. Vance Smith argues that its forms "are really meditations on temporality, meditations that are also rooted *in time*, in the pressing circumstances of times that make such meditations and their formal images necessary."[41] All forms of beginnings, all articulations of beginnings, can be historicized, even the designation of the sacred one understood as the most radically original of origins.

Frantzen carries out his examination of the search for origins within the context of modern scholarship, suggesting that today's scholars no longer really believe in the possibility of recovering a mythic, singular origin past that vanishing point of history, one "conceived of as a totality ... a self-contained, complete unity from which all else derives"; to believe that "such an origin could be recovered," he writes, "would be to return to a prelapsarian world, or something equally unimaginable."[42] Though his general formulation conditions my own approach in this chapter, medieval representations of the precise space Frantzen understands as "unimaginable" – the prelapsarian world – in fact *also* critique the association of Eden as a place of absolute, singular commencement, unsettling the very concept of a mythic origin sited before the advent of history. This deconstruction of a sacred totality hinges on representations of the confused relationship between the earth and Eden. The previous section considered the playful confusion between the earth and

Eden that the mysteries stage; here, I look at how that confusion animates a variety of other texts, as well as the idea of gardens generally, and how such play complicates the relationship between the search for origins and the creation of records: between the different valences of the word "model," that is, and ultimately, between the world and a mere record of it.

In the Middle Ages, the abundance of the earthly paradise was inevitably imagined through a scrim of loss, bringing ideas of plenty and absence into close quarters. Abundance, at this time (perhaps at all times), was the result of collection, however deliberate or haphazard, concentrated or gradual. But Eden then poses a puzzle, since it does not require collection, as it does not experience dispersal prior to its state of plenty. Collections gather in that which previously has been dispersed, either geographically or temporally, responding to a sense of precariousness.[43] And there *is* no precariousness in Eden before the fall; the garden remains immune to the havoc that time wreaks up until the moment that time begins. Its collection of fish and flowers are not salvaged remnants, but divinely crafted exemplars.[44]

Despite this difference, there persists a desire to think of Eden as a site of collection and the use of gardens as both an actual site and metaphorical figure for collections. Eden, famous for its loss, nonetheless emits through its iconic visuals a sense of permanence: it is set apart from everything else, filled with flora and fauna, and frequently encircled by some kind of fiery or architectural protection, an island safe even after the fall, static in the midst of unwinding history.[45] There is, perhaps, something about gardens in general that offers a similar sense of protection and stillness. The Genesis description of an entirely sufficient Eden, a world unto itself, influenced constructions of the *hortus conclusus*, in whose promises of containment and splendor medieval visual artists, landscape designers,[46] and poets reveled. (The medieval *hortus conclusus*, triangulated with the garden from the Song of Songs, also was associated with descriptions of Mary's womb, whose salvific contents promise to restore the losses of history, offering its own kind of sufficiency.[47]) In some sense, the reassuring walls of the enclosed garden keep out history, permitting a world that can be tended without the interruption of crisis,[48] but in a different sense, gardens also function as a site for the layering of history and for geographical compression. In his study of heterotopias, or spaces of accumulation and juxtaposition, Foucault writes that the garden is "the smallest parcel of the world and then it is the totality of the world."

> The traditional garden of the Persians was a sacred space that was supposed to bring together inside its rectangle four parts representing the four parts of

the world, with a space still more sacred than the others that were like an umbilicus, the navel of the world at its center (the basin and water fountain were there); and all the vegetation of the garden was supposed to come together in this space, in this sort of microcosm.[49]

The garden endeavors toward a state of all-times-at-once, microcosmic collection: the whole world in miniature.

In her work on the museum in the early modern period, Paula Findlen describes how controlled natural imagery became associated with sites of collection; Pliny, she points out, conflates the grotto with museums in his influential *Natural History*, inviting subsequent thinkers to approach "gardens and groves" as "museums without walls."[50] The garden also was employed metaphorically to refer to collections less obviously botanical, such as encyclopedias and other compendia.[51] Medieval gardens were apt figures for thinking about the art of *compilatio*, which characterized so much of manuscript culture, and even works composed more or less as organic wholes might invoke the garden to suggest the ingathering of information. An important manuscript from twelfth-century Alsace was known as the *Hortus Deliciarum* (Garden of Delights),[52] and Matthew Paris wrote the continuation of a chronicle called the *Flores Historiarum* (Flowers of History) in the thirteenth century. In the twelfth century, the theologian Honorius Augustodunensis used the fecund image of the garden as suggestive of the most important work of *compilatio* he knew: "the monastery bears the image of Paradise, and an even more secure Paradise than Eden ... The various kinds of fruit trees are the different books of the bible ... "[53] But Findlen also interestingly suggests that "Eden, and by extension, the universe, was God's museum."[54] Such an understanding would seem to correspond to ideas of the world as a manifestation of God's thinking: the material copy of that which is contained in the divine mind. Still, thinking about Eden as God's museum raises the question of whether, if God creates Eden "from the beginning," the garden can be a museum of creation *and* creation itself. That is, both a record and a world.

To press harder on this idea of original and record, I want to consider two passages that tackle it head on. One concerns a medieval garden; the other takes place in a twentieth-century cellar, though, it would seem, with that medieval garden clearly in mind. The first is the famous description of the pleasure garden that appears in *Le Roman de la Rose*, a poem begun by Guillaume de Lorris around 1225, continued by Jean de Meun roughly fifty years later, and translated (as *The Romaunt of the Rose*) by Chaucer toward the end of the fourteenth century.[55] In the poem, a dreamer discovers the fountain or well of Narcissus, the deceptive surface that reflects the world with such convincing specificity that it destroys the man who gazes for too long into it (a plot borrowed from the third book of *Metamorphoses*, where Ovid describes a clear fountain and protective grove of trees). At the bottom of the well are two crystals, which capture and exactingly reflect the world around them; these crystals, in Chaucer's words, disclose the entire garden in which they are found, "[r]yght as a myrrour openly / Shewith al thing that stondith therby" (ll.1585–6).[56] No detail is so small or obscured that the crystals fail to capture it, reflecting the entirety of the garden (or, one half per jewel) back as if it were "peyntid" on their luminous surfaces, or perhaps within them (l.1600).

It would seem that the crystals that contain and reflect the garden of delights in different versions of the *Romance of the Rose* were on the mind of Jorge Luis Borges (among other things, an accomplished medievalist) when he wrote his short story, "The Aleph," in the mid-1940s. The writer's prominence and the extensiveness of his oeuvre mean that his penchant for exhilarating spirals of the surreal have garnered the description "Borgesian," but Borges himself seems to suggest that the inspiration for much of this style is medieval.[57] "The Aleph" tells of another would-be lover who encounters an incredible device of reflection; he wanders, this time into a cellar, wherein rests an "iridescent sphere" containing either the entire world or an image of it:

> The Aleph was probably two or three centimeters in diameter, but universal space was contained inside it, with no diminution in size. Each thing (the glass surface of a mirror, let us say) was infinite things, because I could clearly see it from every point in the cosmos. I saw the populous sea, saw dawn and dusk, saw the multitudes of the Americas, saw a silvery spider-web at the center of a black pyramid, saw a broken labyrinth (it was London), saw endless eyes, all very close, studying themselves in me as though in a mirror ... saw the Aleph from everywhere at once, saw the earth in the Aleph, and the Aleph once more in the earth and the earth in the Aleph ...[58]

Borges attempts to outdo the description from *The Romance of the Rose*. Unrestrained by optical logistics, the aleph proposes a new kind of seeing: instead of needing to look at two crystals to "openly / sheweth al thing" in two parts, one look into the aleph reveals all space at once, "with no diminution in size." This point about size is especially confusing, for if there is both an aleph *and* an earth to be seen within it, and no difference in size, there would seem, in fact, to be two worlds. The narrator calls it "the inconceivable universe."[59]

Borges' aleph shares with the crystals of *The Romance of the Rose* the miraculous capacity to contain and reflect, apparently down to the smallest detail, the material worlds that in turn contain them. The aleph thus suggests a complex relationship between the containing and the uncontainable, and it is through this intimation that Borges pays most obvious homage to the description of Narcissus' gem-filled pool, in which it is not immediately clear what contains what, or which deceptive surface records or reflects which purported original.[60] In these images from *The Romance of the Rose* and in the lines from "The Aleph," vast spaces and nearly infinite inventories are described as contained within finite spaces, whether in crystals or the iridescent cellar-sphere. Both descriptions ask how the categories of larger and smaller, or the external and the internal – that is, the garden and the crystal, or the earth and the aleph – relate to one another. In each pairing, one term seems to designate an original that the other copies, reflects, or records. However, the relationship within each pair is never stable, because at times records or copies threaten to supersede originals, bursting out of their containment and attempting in turn to enclose the "real," antecedent, or original world they reflect.

Borges' teasing inversions of reality and record, and of inside and outside, do more than coyly refer to a famous source text; they play with a feature that I see as categorizing one kind of medieval approach to the relationship between reality and record writ large. Seeta Chaganti has discussed the spatial dynamics of enclosed enclosures, especially in relation to reliquaries (though also as it is intimated in poetry), in which "contained and containing are interchangeable, and the borders between them are indeterminate."[61] The dynamic of contested enclosure matters in late medieval theology as well; in her revelations, for instance, Julian of Norwich contemplates a complete cosmos collapsed into a finite space when, in a vision, Christ shows her "a little thing the quantity of an haselnot" [hazelnut]"; it is, she is told, "all that is made."[62] Later, in her tenth revelation, when Christ appears with wounded side, Julian looks into that gap to discover "a fair, delectable place, and large inow for alle mankind."[63] The side wound evokes the womb of the Virgin (so often allegorized as a garden), a space enclosed by a finite body yet holding something sufficient for the salvation of the world.[64] What seems like an optical illusion in *The Romance of the Rose* or "The Aleph" becomes, in Julian's revelation, central to her theology: a way of understanding how the advent of Christ alters the working of space and time, how that which is within also encompasses, and that which encompasses also resides within. Borges' play of inside and outside – "in the Aleph I saw the earth and in the earth the Aleph and in the Aleph the earth" – perfectly characterizes the enclosing enclosures of the anchoress's vision, in which the side of Christ, like a miraculous garden-pool crystal, holds space sufficient for the physical and temporal expanse of mankind.

Admittedly, we have strayed far from Eden proper in this discussion of crystals, bodies, hazelnut-sized somethings, and alephs, all disparate examples that demonstrate how thinkers put pressure on the unstable relationship between original and record, and between reality and representation. But like engagements with Eden, these examples can work as mechanisms that test out the potential and limits of representation, and the capacity for a record fully to encapsulate and reflect back the world that encloses it. In a way similar to the mystery play performances of creation, fall, and expulsion, moreover, these examples threaten to upend basic ontological properties: that which is supposedly the record of collection seems, through an insistently exacting mimesis, to become reality itself. This, after all, is how Narcissus becomes entranced, as well as doomed.

This ontological indeterminacy – the problem of distinguishing an original from its record, or the enclosed from its enclosure – can contribute to a way of thinking about the archive, whose exacting representative powers sometimes permit it to rival the world it records. This rivalry inevitably troubles the very definition of an archive. We have seen, in the Introduction, how ideas of the archive in some theoretical formulations risk encompassing "Everything"; this was Steedman's critique of Derrida's postmodernist engagement with the subject. And, as she points out, Derrida enhances a diffusion already attested to in Foucault's *Archaeology of Knowledge*, where the archive grows so expansive as a subject that it threatens to become unwieldy. In a bid to give the archive definitional boundaries, then, we might say that one thing the archive is *not* is that which it archives: the world, or the portion of the world, that it mediates into record. On the other hand, the line between these things, between the world and the record of the world, between the radical beginning and all that comes after, is precisely what I argue these medieval texts work to unsettle. The idea of the archive, in this chapter and in the ones that follow, is characterized by its tendency to burst out of its definitional confines as a mere site of record. It might be conservative in its efforts to preserve, to transcend or accumulate layers of temporality, but the archive also has the tendency to transform itself into reality, or into a disguised reality, becoming a record that masquerades as that which it records.

4 World of Words

In the final section of this chapter, I interrogate one more relationship through representations of the earthly paradise: that between the archive and narrative, categories variously constituted through division and accumulation, and predicated on both fragmentation and the idea of a recoverable whole. Subsequent chapters implicitly take up the relationship between the archive and narrative, but I want to broach the subject more directly here through a brief history of the concept of Adamic or Edenic language, the kind of powerful speech with which Adam first named things, and through which the human pair (briefly) communicated in the garden.

In Eden, a prelapsarian Adam was thought to have heard and understood God without grammar, *logos* without words, and then, beyond the gates, the ordering of time compelled the beginning of a more familiar kind of language. In *The Tempter's Voice*, Eric Jager turns to Augustine to explain it this way:

> The temporal and material qualities of language thus exemplify for Augustine the nature of language as a fallen medium subject to time, to bodily decay, and to death – each syllable dying away to make room for the next, like the order of history and of earthly human life itself.[65]

Human speech is, for Augustine in *De Genesi ad litteram*, predicated on syllabic division, unlike the speech of God, who is capable of communicating through an "eternal Word."[66] Thoughts and words, as much as they can be called these things, are, for God, simultaneous and instantaneous, and not subject to the division that produces narrative.[67] Even with the demands of syllabic speech, should one imagine Adam and Eve using it to communicate before the fall, certain words would seem entirely superfluous. Words such as "before" and "after," for instance, designate ideas that would not have intruded into the simultaneity belonging to the divine work of creation. Describing or responding to time would seem less necessary within such circumscribed perfection, a space of stasis where, as Eve so unpresciently promises at York, "Thys frute full styll shall hyng" [this fruit shall hang very still] (l.78).[68] It is the fall from Eden into earth that introduces a more insistent need for a vocabulary of a nostalgically apprehended "before" and an anticipated "after."

Centuries after Augustine, Dante will suggest in *De vulgari eloquentia* that Adam speaks the very first word, breathing back "El" at the creator who literally inspires him. That word might be a question, Dante writes,

but it also might be an answer, responding to God who nevertheless
need not speak "using what we call language," but who communicates in
a way beyond what we can articulate.[69] Dante's treatise charts the
splintering off of language subsequent to that question or answer "El,"
tracing the scattering of people and their vernaculars over extensive
geographies. He argues that differences between tongues occur because
"in the aftermath of great confusion" languages begin to change and veer
away from one another (I.IX; 21).[70] Umberto Eco has examined this
nostalgic look backward toward a perfect language, another place of
absolute commencement – to the place of the breathing out of "El" –
and the desire both to understand its loss and to recuperate it. For many
medieval Christian thinkers, Eco explains, words simultaneously were
invented and spoken by Adam, and they aptly corresponded to the
intrinsic nature of what they named.[71] For, although Dante needs to
speculate regarding the articulation of God's name, Genesis clearly
records man's naming of the animals: "for whatsoever Adam called
any living creature the same is its name" (Gen 2.19).[72] This perfect
correspondence begins to open up after the fall, and language fractures
further after Babel into multiple tongues, which gradually grow more
and more incomprehensible to one another.

An Adamic or universal language, the dream of a number of centuries
both medieval and postmedieval, reconstitutes original perfection by
recombining what has been dispersed, reunifying the many into one
comprehensible whole that recloses the gap between the name and the
named. Howard Bloch examines how the medieval desire to search for
origins often took this philological form, the constant looking backward
for a linguistic beginning that is only ever a smokescreen:

> Such discovery [of origins] is, of course, illusory: even the earliest objects of
> human knowledge no doubt have a prehistory and are, therefore, little more
> than a screen beyond which we cannot see. But the pleasure of grounding
> our understanding in a place, investing our desire in an original object, is, as
> the medievals knew very well, akin to finding a pleasurable place – a "locus
> amoenus" – where the mind's anxious quest comes to rest for as long as such
> rest does not itself become an object of longing.[73]

But in some sense, this place of rest (here figured as a *locus amoenus*, a lovely
place, a garden) is a return not only to perfection, but also to silence.[74]
When the work of etymology is completed, and the essence of things
rediscovered through the history of naming, the syllabic divisions recom-
pressed or reconstituted into one "eternal word," we potentially are left, in

that moment of recovered beginning, with a language only God can hear: the recovered "fruyt" again hangs "full styll," presumably in peaceful silence.

Such a search for perfection shares features with archival desire: first, according to Derrida's characterization, a looking back through all of history toward the place of commencement that such history purportedly conceals, and second, the desire to refill the garden with a complete and completely remembered inventory, and to stop up the gate through which man fell. But there also would seem to be important differences between understandings of archival process and the creation of narrative. An archive collects and accumulates, drawing in together disparate parts of the world and recombining what has been divided, whereas narrative, as we have seen, is predicated on division, or, in medieval Christian terms, in taking apart the eternal world to make many words: starting with "El" and winding up with a world full of language, or shattering the aleph in order to make a story.[75] When the narrator of Borges' short story reaches the cellar in which the iridescent sphere is held, he also reaches the "ineffable center" of his tale, for it is here, he claims, "that a writer's hopelessness begins."[76] "What my eye saw," explains the writer within the story, "was *simultaneous*; what I shall write is *successive*, because language is successive."[77] We might think of this as the kind of translation that occurs across Eden's walls, when the eternal word gets imperfectly translated into language. But in another and perhaps more obvious sense, the archive and narrative are so similar to one another that they are, at times, almost indistinguishable. Both are records capable of being transferred across time; in the Middle Ages, a codex or a scroll could be as much of an "archivum" as the chest or room in which it was stored, and a codex, or more abstractly, a text, was (and is), to begin with, a collection of words.

Of course, as we have seen, creation, not merely collection, happens in Eden, as Eden does not respond to any prior dispersal. Rather, it is subsequent acts of human creation that take divine world-making as a figure that would seem to be engaged in collection, in making copies of parts of the initial wholeness or sufficiency that characterized the prelapsarian earthly paradise. Perhaps, though, even without calling the initial abundance of Eden a "collection," it still makes sense to refer to this fallen work as re-collection, or an arduous, difficult kind of remembering. This project of re-collecting begins after the fall and so after the loss of that perfect wholeness. Narrative, from this perspective, can be understood *both* as a dividing up, as an eternal word getting endlessly fragmented and disseminated, *and* as re-collecting, reconstituting, or reaccumulating.

Such re-collecting comes with the risk of making the wrong fragment into a new centerpiece for that recovered wholeness, that is, of putting the world together askew, according to one's own priorities and historically contingent perspective.[78] We might say that the desire to gather what has been dispersed, to put the world back together again, to archive (perhaps frantically) the fragments of a lost order and pattern, characterizes the project that certain exegetes take up and that Mandeville does not presume to begin.

Eden, then, has an ambivalent relationship with narrative because it can be associated with both silence and the accumulation of text. The loss of the garden propels the beginning of narrative, and the anticipated regaining of paradise brings it to a close. The anticipation is important. One can speculate that perfect recovery of Eden through philological endeavor – the search for an initial language – eventually produces silence, but that silence always remains a far-off one. In the meantime, imperfect attempts at regaining paradise, through performance, poetry, or exegesis, leave a corpus of writings. It is not only the story of sacred history that the fall impels – this history wending through floods, covenants, and sacrifice – the fall also produces the multiple tractates, sermons, plays, and poems that attempt to reimagine or reproduce that initial garden whose loss produced such history in the first place. The mythic loss of Eden becomes the impetus for the many historical descriptions of possible perfection, articulated in the many vernaculars (one might call all languages after the breathed-out "El" vernaculars) that its loss creates.

These works of recovering Eden variously employ the trope of impossibility, or else they make it hard to distinguish recovered origin from recuperating record. That is, to return to Frantzen, they suggest a scenario in which the origin is in fact difficult to separate from the structure built around it: the earth, we might say, spreading out from Eden, or the record proliferating through the search for the beginning.[79] These two strategies – admission of impossibility and the confusion between origin and record – are mutually reinforcing. The first kind of rhetorical move occurs, for instance, in the *Cursor Mundi*, which takes pains to leave the full beauty of Eden beyond the writer's reach:

> Her es blis þat lastes ai,
> Neuer night, bot euer day;
> Es nan forsoth wit hert mai think,
> Ne writer nan mai write wit inc
> þe mikel ioy þat þam es lent.   (ll.645–9)

Here is bliss that lasts always, never night, but ever day; there is no one truly with heart who may think, nor may any writer write with ink, the great joy that is lent to them.

Despite the fact that its description includes nearly one hundred lines of poetry, one of the essential qualities of the earthly paradise in the *Cursor Mundi* is that no one *truly* ("forsoth") can imagine the joy that infuses the apprehension of its other qualities, much less commit them to ink ("ne writer nan mai write wit inc"). This true center is a blank page, like the one Mandeville conceptually leaves for it, situated within an earthly world of plenty and teeming difference, or within the world described through the tens of thousands of *other* lines of the *Cursor Mundi*. It is a kind of absent middle around which the rest of the world or text turns.

A late fifteenth-century manuscript illustration presents a helpful example of the second scenario, in which it is hard to distinguish origin from record, or to tell when the record becomes the origin.[80] The image, in a French translation of Boccaccio's *Fall of Princes*, at first seems to suggest that it is only Adam and Eve who might ever find the words to describe the ineffable beauty within the walls of paradise, and even they, after eviction, need help. In the image, the two appear as autobiographical poets, looking for a scribe (see Figure 1). They are represented at multiple moments in time on the folio page, gradually aging and moving somewhat to the right and downward, falling slowly like the hands of a clock or the spokes of fortune's wheel. They begin near God in the garden, then eat the fruit, cower beneath the flaming sword, spin, plant, nurse, witness the death of Abel and turn away from Lamech's arrow. At the bottom left of the page, they walk hunched over with canes, toward the writing desk of a figure identified as Boccaccio himself. Eve rests her hands on the desk; Adam points toward him. They seem to be telling the story they have just lived, and he is committing it to writing.

But perhaps this is to misread the trajectory, and instead the bodies might be seen as moving upward and backward through time in order to illuminate the history Boccaccio writes. In some ways, it is the same question asked earlier of God: is the image of Boccaccio creating or making a record of creation? Does the illumination suggest that his text encloses the vitae of Adam and Eve, copied as they tell it, or that the text in fact gives life to them? The potential for reading the image via multiple trajectories returns us to the idea of enclosed enclosures: the earth within the aleph and the aleph within the earth, or the beautiful garden, seemingly real, reflected

Figure 1. *Adam and Eve leaving Eden.* From the *Cas des nobles hommes et femmes malheureux.* France, probably Tours, c.1480, MS G.35 fol.1 r.

in the crystals and in Narcissus' unblinking eyes. What produces what, and where is the beginning?

The page illustrates the idea of Eden oscillating between being *all* narrative (that is, "merely" narrative) and being beyond narrative all together, its truth beyond the power of ink. In the first sense, it is a collection of the musings of theologians and poets, a paradise made of paper, or an origin made of record. In the second, it also eludes narrative as it eludes sight: one cannot see directly past the walls without mediation, and one cannot even describe the walls. And so it is longing that refills the garden with its inventory, the nostalgia of centuries, forging a "there" out of "here." Such longing creates an "even more secure paradise," in the words of Honorius, because a re-created Eden – refracted across multiple representations, all slightly more off-kilter than the dream of a magic crystal or aleph describes – produces a garden both more capacious and harder to lose.

CHAPTER 2

Ark and Archive

In her reading of Ranulf Higden's *Polychronicon*, an early fourteenth-century work recording the history of the world as he knew it, Emily Steiner proposes that the shift from the geography of book one to the history of book two accords with a difference intimated in scripture: "from Adam's fall, the chronicle can begin."[1] No longer limited to a description of the natural world, the chronicle will record the subject of fallen man, who has "his own history in time."[2] Steiner suggests that movement into the genre of the chronicle is, for Higden, "at once an affirmation of continuing life and an act of mourning."[3] The following two chapters demonstrate how medieval engagements with the biblical flood respond both to this sense of affirmation and to the call for mourning by taking Noah's ark as a figure for thinking through the work that chroniclers like Higden purport to do: collecting, organizing, preserving, transmitting, or setting aside the events of the past. The movement from the fall of man to the flood of the world is a movement into new genres, but also into different emphases in archival imagining.

As if in extended elaboration of Isidore's "arca"/"archivum" etymologies, the *Polychronicon* and other chronicles invested in British history, especially those in the sea-centered, Brut tradition, use the story of the ship that outsails the flood to authorize and critique processes of remembering and forgetting. The scriptural episode becomes a paradigm for preserving the past generally, as drowning and salvation are mapped onto erasure and recording. Of course, to relate Noah's labor to the task of chroniclers means to compare stocking and sailing a mythic ship with the writing of history, not to mention equating animals and people with words. But despite the obvious differences between these categories, I am interested in how the twinned activities of selection and exclusion draw archival processes and the work of historiography together, and how the story of the flood invites us to view both activities as participating in a bold but limited project: crafting a version of a world that was and ordering its events and populations into a coherent past.

The *Polychronicon* itself rather self-consciously describes the crucial work that historical narrative performs; John Trevisa's late fourteenth-century, Middle English translation of Higden's Latin chronicle calls "storie" ("historia" in the Latin) a "wytnesse of tyme" and suggests that it might operate as a mechanism of a certain kind of salvation: "Dedes þat wolde be lost storie ruleþ; dedes þat wolde flee out of mynde, storye clepeþ aȝen; dedes þat wolde deie, storye kepeþ hem euermore" [Deeds that would be lost story rules (or orders); deeds that would flee out of mind, story calls them up again; deeds that would die, story keeps them for evermore].[4] The *Polychronicon* will go on to read the event of the flood as a blotting out of the past and as a historical link, which subsequent historical accounts are bound to perpetuate: "And so þe flood was i-made, and occupied þe erþe wel nyh al a ȝere. . . . þis ȝere endeþ the firste age of þe world from Adam to Noe . . . " [And so the flood was made, and it occupied the earth almost a year. This year ends the first age of the world from Adam to Noah] (2:237). The rising waters end the first age, expunging the past even as the ship carries proof and memory of it into the present; subsequent histories will have to depend upon the dramatic intersection of the first two ages of the world for all knowledge of the antediluvian earth.

In this chapter, I am interested in the narrative strategies that express the collateral damage of producing and perpetuating such a coherent past, one that might be contained within finite space and arranged according to such specific instructions. Some medieval representations of the flood fore-ground the struggle to imagine the parts of the antediluvian world that are lost, or the gaps that loss has left, acknowledging the "dedes" that flee out of mind, and the ideas, people, and narratives abandoned by the ark or altered by the act of embarkation. In the York play of The Flood, the transition between these ages of the world takes the form of a domestic crisis; Noah's Wife, more or less an invention of late medieval England, directs attention away from a world that will "waxe agayne"[5] and toward the things that won't:

> My frendis þat I fra yoode
> Are ouere flowen with floode　　　　　　　　　　　(ll.151–2)

> My friends that I have gone from are overflowed with the sea.

The play stages the act of recording, an act necessary for the affirmation of life and nonetheless committed to the act of mourning.

The texts and performances I examine in this chapter and the next elaborate upon ideas of destruction and renewal bound up in the scriptural details of the flood. They consider those things that fail to be saved and, more subtly, the mediating effects that selection and salvation have upon an inventory. Chapter 2 focuses largely upon chronicles and romance, demonstrating how these works, so concerned with cultural preservation and transmission, engage with the figure of the biblical ark as well as other archival ships that shore up records in anticipation of crisis. I look at chronicles and romances together because of their occasional generic inextricability, but also because of the different, interrelated vessels that anchor them: the ship that traverses the world and the bark of the body that likewise renews it, various *arcae* variously corresponding to political and natural bodies.[6] Chapter 3 turns to biblical drama to demonstrate how performance troubles attempts at streamlining the story of the past, both by having the unruly stage symbolically and architecturally double as the ark of authority, and by introducing the compelling figure of Noah's Wife, a figure unafraid of mourning.

This first chapter on the flood thus shifts from the opening of Genesis to that book's first intimation of apocalypse, and from a garden eventually walled off from a more extensive earth to an ark coasting upon the rising waters of the flood. In Chapter 1, I argued that conjurations of Eden conflate original and record, and that the earthly paradise functions in text, visual art, and performance simultaneously as a site of origins and as one of re-collection. But the divine regret that severs ante- and postdiluvian worlds in the story of the biblical flood disentangles these categories of original and record, so that there no longer is one place in which both ontological categories inhere. The following sections consider the archiving and mourning involved in these now separate places: the drowned world and the salvaged remnants collected in the boat above it.

1   Remembering and Forgetting

The association between water and oblivion is an old one. Early on, there is Lethe, both a river and a spirit of forgetting, and across the centuries, writers continue to fit a discourse of remembering and forgetting, and collection and loss, onto images of land and water, with "land" including such disparate refuges as arks, more ordinary ships, islands, shores, and floating museums. The twelfth-century historian Orderic Vitalis, author of his own extensive chronicle, imagines the histories we fail to save, all the "admonitions of the ancients" disappearing "as hail or snow melt in the waters of a swift river, swept away by the current never to return."[7] Hundreds of years later, proving the enduring nature of the metaphor,

Nietzsche describes how portions of the past are lost, "forgotten, scorned, and washed away as if by a gray, unremitting tide," and how "only a few individual, embellished facts rise as islands above it."[8] Most spectacularly in recent memory, or at least most opulently, is Alexander Sokurov's early twenty-first-century film, *Russian Ark*, which pays specific homage to the scriptural episode of the flood. Filming an apparition of Russian history in the fabled Hermitage Museum of St. Petersburg, Sokurov pursues one long, single take through the enormous institution, chasing down history through its long halls and galleries, and memorializing it through the gestures, rustling costumes, and half-heard conversations of a teeming cast. In the closing moments of the film, the camera reveals that the museum, with its several centuries of people crowded into numerous galleries, floats; a balcony opens onto an endless expanse of water. Despite its ponderous weight, the museum plies the waves just like the legendary ark that moved over similarly un-chartable territory so long ago.

There is both obvious power and nerve-wracking fragility attending the image of the floating museum and the biblical vessel that ghosts it; both are solid refuges of authority that seemingly could sink at any moment. The watery expanse stretching outward from the Hermitage in Sokurov's film implies that much has been submerged already, and the empty vista poses a number of unsettling questions, versions of which medieval accounts of the flood also elicit: are these the *only* centuries, "dedes," and people that are to be recorded? Is there no one else out there, if only to hear the famous music streaming through the windows? What lies beneath the water, invisible to those on the balconies opening onto such unexpected ocean? The abundance the large museum holds immediately invites curiosity for all that it lacks: for those things which, following the model of the biblical ark, the museum either relinquished, decided against, or never held in the first place, the rest – all those "dedes þat wolde flee out of mynde" – lying somewhere beneath or beyond the water, lost, submerged, and unrecorded.

Water, these episodes and turns of phrase suggest, must always be withstood, whether flowing through or into the river of time, the river Lethe, or the flood of oblivion, because it threatens to erase or at least to blur whatever it purifies, poisons, or washes away. What is saved from water finds salvation or becomes "salvage": driftwood, shells, remnants that sometimes can be fit as fragments onto the mosaic of history, endeavoring always toward coherence with its fractured pieces. In the story of Noah's ark, *official* salvation takes form as a monolith: a museum, a fortress, an imperial palace, an authoritative history lording it over the water. Sokurov's unexpectedly buoyant structure evokes the biblical ark not just because it miraculously floats; what also matters is that it floats alone. There is no need for a lookout; its movement and waves disturb no one. The coasts (were there coasts) are clear: a blank slate, a *tabula rasa*, a watery surface wrinkled only by slow and solitary movement. Medieval images of the biblical flood similarly suggest the silence of a world put to sleep, but many also depict the drowned pinned beneath the hull and the sole family looking out across a recently submerged landscape, the toll of destruction still visible (see Figure 2). Noah's family travels through time, ferried by the ark over the dead into the next age and into a new postdiluvian world. To make it aboard the ark is to make it into the Book of Life, but also to make it into official history: into the history books, into scripture and adaptations of scripture, into collective memory, and into a general, sanctioned, historical consciousness. The flood narrative suggests that ship and sea correspond to saved and lost, life and death, but also to remembered and forgotten, archive and oblivion.

In medieval engagements with the flood, Noah presides over these categories, vested with the authority to supervise not only what will be kept, but also what that thing called "history" will be, now that it is needed in a new way as one epoch is cut off from another. His labor is fraught and dramatic, underpinned by the losses whose presence is never wholly eradicated, and by an interpretive authority that increases exponentially as he attempts to leave the past behind. Approaching the ark as an archive not only positions Noah as head archivist, but also as the originator of the role, the first to compile an authoritative collection, and the figure who will influence subsequent efforts. In the very beginning of their study, *The Cultures of Collecting*, John Elsner and Roger Cardinal refer to the flood-time patriarch as the first collector:

> Adam had given names to the animals, but it fell to Noah to collect them . . . Menaced by a Flood, one has to act swiftly. Anything overlooked will be lost forever: between including and excluding there can be no half-measures. The collection is the unique bastion against the deluge of time. And Noah, perhaps alone of all collectors, achieved the complete set, or so at least the Bible would have us believe.[9]

Elsner and Cardinal suggest that Noah "suffers the pathology of completeness at all costs,"[10] but Susan Stewart hints at the erasure involved in the patriarch's work and his guilty collusion with revisionist history. His collection might be complete, but only according to its own rules:

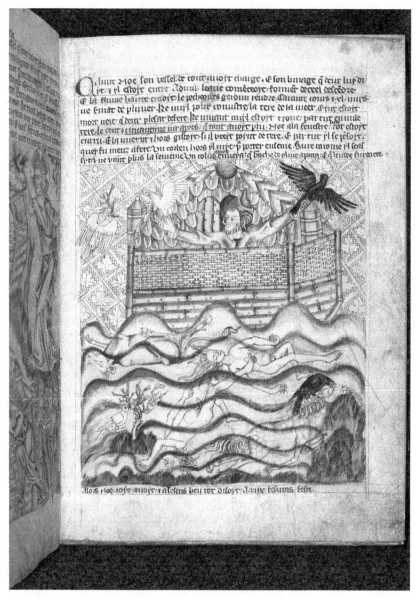

Figure 2. *The Flood and the Ark.* From *The Holkham Bible Picture Book.* England, c.1327–1335, Add MS 47682 fol. 8 r, at the British Library.

> We might therefore say, begging forgiveness, that the archetypal collection
> is Noah's Ark, a world which is representative yet which erases its context of
> origin. The world of the ark is a world not of nostalgia but of anticipation.
> While the earth and its redundancies are destroyed, the collection maintains
> its integrity and boundary. Once the object is completely severed from its
> origin, it is possible to generate a new series, to start again within a context
> that is framed by the selectivity of the collector.[11]

Both passages depict the patriarch as pulled, in his own brief and panicked
moment, between past and future, between the anticipation of a world he
sails into and stocks, and the need to record the life Adam first carefully
named. He is dependent upon this ancestor, who first helped to differ-
entiate among Eden's creatures, and dependent also upon God himself, for
whom he acts, according to Stewart, merely as a "broker."[12] Noah assists in
shaping a world that is derivative, "or so the Bible would have us believe,"
and yet frighteningly, exhilaratingly, and suspiciously new, its original
model erased, the scaffolding kicked away and submerged beneath forty
days of rain. For the collection, suggests Steward, "replaces history with
classification"; it shifts attention away from the world it collects and onto
its own rules of arrangement.[13]

When activities of remembering, commemorating, and archiving
employ the ark as a paradigmatic site of collection – through metaphors
of land and water, by emphasizing the episode in universal chronicles
similarly invested in recording, or even through scriptural name-
dropping[14] – they also employ this ambivalent archivist, a figure balanced
between chaos and control, past and future, dangerous authority and
dangerous obedience. It is this problem of further singularity – not only
one ship, but one ship captain – that ushers in the question of the
relationship between history and memory. In the Middle Ages, the
word "ark" could conjure Noah's ship ("arca noe"), as well as the ark of
the covenant ("arca testamenti"), and more ordinary containers of documents and material collections ("arca").[15] But it also could be used in the
phrase "arca cordis," or ark of the heart, a site of devotion and memory.
In the next section, I turn to the writings of the twelfth-century theologian Hugh of Saint Victor, who describes the superimposition of the ark
of the flood upon the ark of the heart. In this blurring of global and
singular, bureaucracy and interiority, history and memory, Hugh and
other medieval thinkers foreground an ethical problem that I see as
inherent in even the sparest of biblical flood stories: the right to interpret,
to preside over a momentous inventory, and to exclude in one's account
of the past as one endeavors to create a new world.

2   Hugh of Saint Victor's Ark of Memory

In the *Polychronicon*, Ranulf Higden indicates his familiarity with Hugh of Saint Victor when he discusses how to comprehend the dimensions of the ark, particularly its relation to the "instar corporis humani," which Trevisa translates as "þe liknesse of manis body" (2:234–5).[16] By demonstrating how the architectural dimensions of the ship are analogous to the human form, Higden and Trevisa suggest that the ark that records the world might bear a resemblance to a person who endeavors to remember. In her comprehensive study of the medieval *ars memoria*, Mary Carruthers describes how the ark in its various manifestations could function as a mnemonic device, its familiar form easily divisible into discrete spaces suitable for arrangement and storage. One could break information up into manageable components and place these "chunks" within the compartments of the ark or whichever site – Carruthers also lists dovecotes and money pouches – the imagination conjures.[17]

The multivalent ark was Hugh of Saint Victor's mnemonic site of choice, apt for his work on devotional memory.[18] Contemplating the ark across two interrelated works, *De archa Noe* and *Libellus de formatione arche* (both c.1125–1131),[19] Hugh literalizes and elaborates upon associations embedded in Latin phraseology to set out his mnemonic method, reimagining the "arca cordis," or devotion filled heart,[20] as a spiritual site with Noah's *nautical* ark inside of it. Noah's archiving of the antediluvian earth occurs within the ark of a heart ("cor, cordis" etymologically connects to "record") and across an interior landscape visualized as the space of ship and sea. Hugh's inward gaze reveals a chaos of flood waters, tempests, and stormy oceans, a drowned and windswept landscape battered by fixation on earthly things and lacking the kind of stability whose anchor is contemplation of the divine.

Hugh's spatial dynamics thus are shifting and relative at best. The ark, whose contemplative construction is set against such a wild background, at times approaches the magnitude of the world itself, even as it is squeezed into the no-place that is the human heart.[21] Despite this architectural flexibility, the devotional labor Hugh describes still requires numbers, dimensions, lists, categories, and compartments for the organization and storage of "chunks" of information deemed worthy of memory. Medieval thinkers who worried about the mathematical dimensions of the ark (and there were several[22]) could not have been soothed by Hugh's suggestion that one duplicate cubic measurements in the uncharted regions of the human heart. For how can a place that is, in effect, *no* place hold a ship that

holds the world? But Hugh remains untroubled by the potential incon-
sistencies of combining contemplative and architectural processes, or of
rebuilding an iconic shape in a shapeless site.[23] To structure the process of
contemplation and memory, he exhorts his readers to build an ark within
each of their own hearts, a structure whose generous biblical proportions
will "afford length, breadth, and height fully sufficient to contain enough
seed for the renewal of the entire world."[24] These many replica ships evoke
the original Genesis instructions; they are "three hundred cubits long in
faith of Holy Trinity, fifty cubits wide in charity, and thirty cubits high in
the hope that is in Christ."[25] "[L]ong in good works and wide in love," they
sail within hearts whose measurements abide scriptural specifications even
as they remain immeasurable.[26] Within the heart's stormswept and shore-
less interior his imagined ark gets rooms, decks, ladders, and a mast that is
the tree of life, the book of life, and Christ himself.

Each measurement has significance; the holy cubits count out not
only planks for flooring but also suggest through the creation of length
and width the longevity of church history and the geographic extent of
the Christian flock. And when the ark at last starts to take shape as
something that might withstand the inner tempest, Hugh begins to
write across its various surfaces, modeling the task to which his readers,
too, must turn: "Then, I begin from the bow of the Ark, below, and
write Adam's name first in the following way ... "[27] Biblical and papal
genealogies emerge; holy graffiti spreads; and thirty books of scripture
and additional commentary, both spiritual and physical directives, find
the still blank spaces. Though Hugh carefully delineates *which* words
one should write, the imagined ship also seems to hold a narrative that
attempts exhaustiveness; at the beginning of the architectural plans,
Hugh draws two squares for the *alpha* and the *omega*, intimating the
completeness of that which will arise from his preliminary sketching:
a full story with a beginning and an end. In *De archa Noe*, he
emphasizes further this notion of plenitude, likening the ark to a full
memory, an archival vessel, and another world entirely:

> This ark is like a storehouse (*apothece*) filled with all manner of delightful
> things. You will look for nothing in it that you will not find ... There all
> the works of restoration are contained in all their fullness, from the
> world's beginning to its end; and therein is represented the condition of
> the universal church. Into it is woven the story of events, in it are found
> the mysteries of the sacraments ... There the sum of things is displayed,
> and the harmony of its elements explained. There another world is
> found.[28]

Here, recalling Stewart's description of the collection, a place of bounded integrity takes form, an array of events, sacraments, and names whose harmony provides its own interpretation: that herein resides completeness, a collection of sacred history both accurate and sufficient.

In fact, though, this ark in the heart would seem to suggest a number of new worlds, some of them, if not discordant, then at least confusing. There is the new postdiluvian world meant to spring from its well-stocked store rooms, and the new world within the human interior whose secret recesses and cavernous spaces the light of contemplation illuminates. This last is the world once lost but newly found through contemplative endeavor: the world in Christ, the forgotten kingdom of heaven now concealed by "the dust of sin cast on the heart of man."[29] The field of the heart ("agro cordis") holds a lost paradise seemingly drowned in both water and soil, but through contemplation and compunction, one might recover or uncover a more perfect world.[30] Hugh's ark is a mnemonic aid in that it allows one to commit large portions of scripture, commentary, and genealogies to memory, but its construction also serves as part of a more momentous remembering, one that brushes away the earth from a buried picture of a prelapsarian world. And then there is a fourth world:

> When the ark is complete, I draw an oval around it, which touches it at its corners, and the space enclosed by the circle is the orb of the earth. In this space, I draw the map of the world in such a way that the bow of the Ark is turned toward the east, and the stern of the Ark is turned to the west. The arc of the circle that extends to the east on the bow of the Ark is Paradise, like the lap of Abraham, as it will appear afterward once the Majesty has been drawn. The other arc, which extends to the west, [holds the resurrection and final judgment of all: on the right are the chosen, on the left, the condemned. In the northern corner of this arc] is the Inferno, where the damned along with the rebellious spirits are driven downward . . . Once the machine of the universe has been constructed in this way, in its higher part the Majesty is drawn from the shoulders upward, and the feet downward, [as though sitting on a throne], but standing out from the background, with His arms extended in either direction, so that He seems to embrace all things.[31]

In this passage, Christ holds the mappable earth in its entirety. This world in turn holds the ark of the flood, which holds "enough seed for the renewal of an entire world." And finally – or rather simultaneously – this world-framed, world-containing ark is imprinted upon the human heart, the ark of the heart. The conjured image of these overlapping spaces – worlds, hearts, and ships containing and in turn being contained, embraced, or imprinted upon by one another – suggests a paradox of carefully measured spacelessness. A map of the world takes shape in an unchartable interior; a ship archives one world even as it traverses another reconstructed within the archival heart.

In advocating that one inscribe the image of Noah's ark upon the heart, Hugh does not simply play with a literalization of the "arca cordis" metaphor; he also points up the blurred categorical distinction between the physical and spiritual connotations attending the idea of the "arca." Latin and vernacular etymologies attest to this confusion: the body's torso, according to Hugutio's *Derivationes*, is an "arca" because it holds secrets ("secretum," "archanum") that others cannot reach.[32] Similarly, the fifteenth-century Middle English translator of Guy de Chauliac's surgical treatise writes, "The breste is þe arke of þe spiritual membres."[33] This torso, breast, or chest also can evoke Moses' ark of the covenant, or the "arca testamenti," the portable chest of stone-inscribed law. Such descriptions can make the "arca" seem like a physical container with visible edges, rather than the nebulous site of a more spiritual interior. And yet, in Hugh's mnemonics, the "arca," with its etymological associations of embodiment and other physical kinds of containers, emerges at the spiritual center of the body, where measurable space would seem to dissipate: the ark is both chest and heart, body and spirit. Hugh's mnemonic poetics are both serious and playful: once one has visualized the nautical ark as inscribed with text – writing on the bow, up and down columns, on stairs and in rooms – then one superimposes it upon the heart, that is, upon the "chest," "thorax," or "ark" again. The ark-that-is-ship is set upon the ark-that-is-heart, and here it contends with the interior ocean it has been conjured to withstand.

Some of the mnemonic sites Carruthers explores, spaces conjured within the imagination of the individual (or within their heart, depending on instructions), also resemble more external, shared, even institutional archives, for the archive and individual memory overlap through a number of conceptual models.[34] The ark is that kind of multivalent model: it can function as an external, collective site, shared by society, storing, say, a purportedly global history in stormy weather, but it also operates metaphorically as a comparatively private vessel of memory. That is, it can be conjured as a mnemonic device, but it also provides a conceptual model for the shared site of record outside an individual's heart or mind: the book, the cabinet, the treasure room, the chest atop the poles balanced on the shoulders of the traveling Israelites, the ship upon the water. The compact Latin verse cited in the *Summa Britonis* testifies to the broad and varied reach of the short word: "Temporibus tres esse tribus cognovimus archas: / Prima Noe, Moysi fuit altera, tertia Christi; / Lignea prima, secunda metallica, tertia neutrum" [at times we know there to have been three arks, first Noah's, then Moses' was second, the third, Christ's; the first of wood, the second of metal, and the third neither of these].[35] In Robert Mannyng's *Chronicle*, which I discuss below, the term "arke" refers both to hearts and to sites of bureaucratic collection within the same (admittedly rather long) poem.[36]

These various manifestations of "arca" complicate the division between the already intertwined categories of physical and spiritual, between the container-chest (wood, metal, or flesh) and the container-heart (flesh or spirit). The archive that exists in the world blurs into the memory-site constructed in the individual's imagination. And because descriptions of seas, ships, deserts, cathedrals, and other sites within a person's interior mimic the places shared by entire communities in the outside world, the force of metaphor challenges the division between these two categories, at times, for instance, making the world of the body indistinguishable from the world in which the body moves. The troublesome nature of the human heart – both flesh and spirit – muddles things further. Is the heart a space that stores memory in only the metaphorical sense? Or is the human chest also a more physical receptacle into which one could place text as one places it within Moses' chest of law?

A number of medieval devotional works implicitly seem to pose these questions through their description of miracles or stories of straining after intense religious experience. The fourteenth-century writer Henry Suso attempted to put "real" text into his heart, writing words upon that "arca" with the edge of a knife,[37] and the widely copied *Legenda Aurea* includes the story of Ignatius of Antioch, who, when dying, insisted that he felt the two words "Jesus Christ" already etched there.[38] When the latter was dissected it was discovered that one could, in fact, read the words, "inscribed in golden letters," that he swore had been written into his flesh.[39] In the early fourteenth century, another miraculous discovery accompanied the death of Margaret of Città di Castello, whose body yielded up a stone that had been lodged within her container-heart; in her canonization documents, her dissectors swear they found an engraving of Joseph of Arimathea's face beside a portrait of Margaret's own.[40] Margaret's heart solicited spiritual and anatomical curiosity, and the report of her miraculous body poses both technical and larger conceptual questions for medieval devotional practice. How did a stone get in there? Was her saintly flesh somehow *like* stone, despite the difference Saint Paul's crucial scriptural exchange of material implies? Can one's heart or body take form as an ark of collection, drawing together conceptions of the *arca testamenti*, a visible container filled with inscribed stone, and the *arca cordis*, a visionary place filled with visionary text? How are we to understand the different methods of inscription and record-compilation with which these are connected? How are we to read or trust them?

These various anecdotes provide extreme examples of a more central problem that chronicles, romances, and plays address: the conflation of the categories of individual memory and external archive and the blurring of the line between the body and the outer world. What *happens* when an individual's memory is permitted to suffice as an archive? What happens when a vision of the world, held within the heart, has the authority to re-create the world without? This is the problem of Noah's ark, or Noah's archive, held within the mnemonic site of the ark of the heart, or else gliding upon the waves. The flood episode describes how one man is charged with storing worthy things in the many separate quarters of a ship constructed to ride out an event whose destructive potential otherwise threatens to erase the past, as well as all visions of the past that fail to coincide with his inventory. The injunction to sort and arrange precious berths in time for the impending days of rain helps to form a crucial and lasting connection between the archive and disaster, and it stages a radical centralization of power, compacted into the panicked heart of a single man.

Threatened worlds, the flood and subsequent stories suggest, call out to be remembered, and remembered, moreover, in a specific and productive way. They become, in the perception of their retrospective narrators, a "useable past,"[41] one instrumental for the construction of an anticipated world, in a pattern that continues to bear out long after the time of mythic history.[42] Still, the biblical age probably surpasses later ones in terms of its monuments to the encyclopedic, survivalist urge. Even before the ark, rumors of approaching doom motivated the apocryphal antediluvian construction of gigantic pillars, made, unlike Babel, to withstand whatever disastrous form God's wrath should take. Trevisa writes:

> þat tyme men wiste, as Adam hadde i-seide, þat þey schulde be destroyed by fuyr, oþer by water, þerfore bookes þat þey hadde i-made by grete trauaille and studie þey closede hem in tweie greet pileres i-made of marbyl *[lapidea, marmore]* and of brend tyle *[lateritea]*. In a piler of marbyl for water, and in a pyler of tyle for fuyre; ffor hit schulde be i-saued in þat manere to helpe [of] mankynde. Me seiþ þat þe piler of stoon scaped þe flood and is ȝit in Siria (2:233).

That time, men knew, since Adam had said it, that they should be destroyed either by fire or by water; therefore they had books made through great labor and study; they closed them in two great pillars made of marble and of burnt tile: in a pillar of marble against the water, and in a pillar of tile against the fire, for it should be saved in that way to help mankind. I say that the pillar of stone escaped the flood and is still in Syria.

It is a short conceptual trip from these monuments, proto-libraries built so that they someday might "helpe" mankind, to the ark, the latter a vessel that likewise attempts to preserve an official record of the world, receiving its cargo in the form of animal-pairs rather than as sets of books. One must wonder, though, about the relationship between these two endeavors, for the earlier patriarchs' pillars go unmentioned in the Vulgate account and mystery plays of the flood that follow. Does Noah unstock any of the antediluvian library to load it into his own *arca*? Do the waters overflow and destroy the pillars despite their anticipatory marble casing? Or do these two monuments – pillars and ship – together interrupt the glassy surface of the sea somewhere near Syria, holding inevitably different records of the antediluvian past, accounts that posterity might reconstruct as visions of two different worlds? The *Polychronicon* suggests that only the marble one lasts – "me seiþ þat þe piler of stoon scaped þe flood and is ȝit in Siria"– and yet the idea of two universal archives highlights the problem of the universal archive in general, and the monolithic control it is afforded to construct an undisputed narrative of the past. A universal archive allows the archivist's memory – or mnemonic construction – to suffice as the sole record of an infinitely more complicated reality.

We might, in fact, think of Noah's ark as always floating within the private realm of the patriarch's heart; Hugh's exhortation that we let the ark navigate within us emphasizes the ontological confusion already embedded in the flood story itself. Who can tell, in an emptied world, whether Noah's archive is a ship on the water or an ark within his own heart? What is the difference between the "real" world and the imagination of the patriarch invested with the authority to redesign it? The antediluvian world seems to lose its claim on history, on existence, when Noah's archiving endeavor transforms it into the recollection of a single soul. Those who live before the deluge are either vanished or distorted by his selective account, and those who make it aboard the ark – including Noah's wife, mother of the world to come – likewise risk an ontological shift: are they alive, or are they, too, only ideas accounted for by Noah's mnemonic device? Do they exist in his ark of timber or within his ark of the heart? If the latter, is Noah's wife as "real" as he is?

The story of Noah the ark-maker – Noah the archivist – exemplifies the danger of the memory of one individual compiling the only record of a vanishing world. Noah's ark might be endlessly reshaped and rebuilt by theologians meditating on its architectural dimensions and by film directors riffing on its long-ago adventure, but despite these many incarnations its important feature remains its singularity, its isolation on the water. Noah builds only one ark. That is, only one ark gets built. One early (third- or fourth-century) text suggests a woman, "Orea" or "Norea," burns the one he is working on, making him start again.[43] Genesis excludes the disruption, of course, as well as any other protestation against the monumental responsibility with which God invests the patriarch alone. In canonical scripture, Noah constructs and completes only one ship, in time for the destructive event that will eliminate other voices that might have contributed to a more complex and nuanced version of his record of the antediluvian earth.

The medieval engagements with the flood story that I look at are concerned with teasing out the ontological, narrative, and ethical consequences of the universal archivist, variously affirming and questioning the notion of monolithic memory for which the flood story stands as paradigm. Noah's ark mythically serves as the first human-supervised record of creation: like Sokurov's Hermitage, an incomplete museum of the world it replaces. I am interested in this vision of a world gathered into one place, a site where creation is ordered, arranged, and made sense of so that it might form a new and improved postdiluvian world where elements of Noah's archive – its apparition of completeness and harmony, its emphasis on order and hierarchy – will be propagated, endlessly multiplied like the children of the patriarch. The ark offers a model for record making and transmission; it shows how an account, vision, proof, or narrative of one world makes it into another. But many medieval representations also underscore the ways in which such transmission remains purposefully and necessarily incomplete: the images that include glimpses of the drowned; the plays that stage a woman who mourns; and the chronicle and romances that speculate about the left behind, digressing over moments of absence and indecision. They thus suggest how the insistent desire for a partition between archive and outside – remembered and forgotten, speaking and silent – can be thwarted by the steady dissolution of these categories in textual engagements with the flood (Chapter 2) and performances of it (Chapter 3). These are works in which the forgotten come inside, if only for a while, and the drowned speak.

3   Brut's Ark

The world Noah archives, then, is only a version of the world, and the medieval chroniclers who similarly endeavor to "discryveþ all þe worlde wyde," as Trevisa phrases it, labor at work that ultimately is both impossible and exclusionary (2:6). In this section, I demonstrate how Noah's ark offers both a starting point and a model for medieval historical narratives that, formulated in its wake, similarly endeavor to organize an always-disappearing past. Some of the narrative consequences of Noah's ark of order can be discerned in medieval English chronicles, whose form suggests an implicit modeling upon that flood-time project. The identity of England as the island in the west, emerging from an encircling sea and reached at last by the hero docking upon its promised shores, suggests an even more precise relationship between narratives of English and sacred history. As Sebastian Sobecki, Kathy Lavezzo, and Lynn Staley have demonstrated, England was not merely an island cut off by a channel in medieval writings, but one placed at the very limit of the world, whose privileged location and potential isolation contributed to its cultural senses of self and to its stories of origin. Though medieval England had two broad founding traditions within which to produce its many chronicles, steeping them either in comparatively sacred or secular events, both traditions required a well-traveled man, a stocked boat, and a breathtaking expanse of open water.

The comparatively secular hero on the shore is Brutus (or Brut, or Bruyt, in its trilingual Latin, English, and Anglo-Norman manifestations). The story of Noah surviving the flood resonates within the structure of the Brut narrative, one of medieval England's most important historical myths, named after the man who first approaches its coasts. The Brut tradition locates England's cultural and genealogical origins in Troy, and even more precisely in the body of Aeneas as he flees from that city's destruction.[44] The basic shape of the story suggests that, years after Aeneas gets to Italy, his grandson (sometimes great-grandson) Brutus, continuing the trajectory set in the *Aeneid*, again sets sail for the west and comes to the shore of Britain, which he empties of giants and inhabits, lending his name both to the island and to subsequent accounts of its founding. Even within this spare outline, several important points of intersection between the Brut and flood stories become apparent. Both are genealogically structured and sea-centered. Noah gathers his sons into the ark where they await the call to repopulate the three known corners of the earth, and the Brut narrative offers a series of ship captain descendants who settle the far-flung regions. Aeneas, like Noah, is a remnant saved from destruction. His genealogy is saved for a new age, saved in order to *begin* a new age, one linked to the past by only the narrowest thread: a nautical rope, say, or a strand of DNA. This narrowness recalls the isolated family aboard the biblical ark; both ships carry a specific lineage whose members will corroborate a single, authoritative narrative of the past. The ship that transports Aeneas's progeny to Britain, just like the ship that takes Aeneas to Italy and the ark that takes Noah into the postdiluvian world, brings with it not just men ready for adventure, but a record of a civilization that will be introduced to the new land exclusively by means of the boat they arrive in.[45]

The idea that the destruction of Troy set into motion the emergence of medieval European cultures thus offers a second story of origins that both echoes and complicates the one offered by sacred history. Chronicles in the Brut tradition participate in the myth of *translatio imperii et studii*, or the fabled westward drift of empire, learning, and culture.[46] Medieval historians, spurred on by the exhortations of Augustine, sometimes wrote adhering to a tradition of biblical narrative, beginning with the events of Genesis, but sometimes they began with this genealogy of Trojan origins.[47] These two possibilities also combine, with different chronicles shifting emphases. Geoffrey of Monmouth's twelfth-century *History of the Kings of Britain*, for instance, begins with a physical description of the island whose perfection is reminiscent of Eden,[48] but then switches immediately to the matter of Troy, forgoing scriptural history. Geoffrey concentrates instead on a different prophetic structure by narrating an episode, reiterated in many subsequent works, in which Brutus, visiting the temple of Diana, learns that he is to travel so far west that he will find a land "sub occasu solis," or beneath the setting sun.[49] Following Geoffrey, other chronicles begin with or prominently include the story of Aeneas, one or two intervening generations, and then the similarly seafaring Brut.

The Brut story also could be fit into chronicles more concerned with scriptural history, where its questions of selection and exclusion map onto Noah's project.[50] The *Flores Historiarum*, for instance, written in the first half of the thirteenth century and associated in its later form with Matthew of Paris, begins with the six days of creation and offers a biblical genealogy from Adam to Noah to an Alanus, the first man of "the race of Japhet" ("de genere Iaphet").[51] Japhet is one of Noah's three sons among whom the world is divided. Alanus also has three sons, paralleling the family of the flood, and his firstborn eventually gives rise to the race of "Britons" (Britanni).[52] But none of this prevents the *Flores* from offering the story of Brutus a few pages later, and describing the island, empty but for a handful of giants, upon which Aeneas' progeny momentously disembarks. Brutus, too, will divide the island among three sons, as John Capgrave's fifteenth-century *Chronicle* also points out, though that work condenses the story to all but its sparest details, squeezing it between events of biblical history.[53] Caxton reverses this move in his edition of the *Eneydos* (1490), when he mentions the events of Exodus as a point of reference for the reign of Ascanius: "And knowe, that from the tyme that the children of ysrahel [Israel] came out of thraldome [slavery] fro the kynge of Egypte, Pharao, whan they passed the red see / vnto Ascanyus tyme, that was kyng of Lombarde [until the time of Ascanius, who was the king of Lombardy], was CCCC.lxvij. yeres."[54]

Around the year 1300, a writer we refer to as Robert of Gloucester temporally locates the founding of England amidst sacred history, in "þe time bi tvene abraham & moyses."[55] He offers an extensive description of Brutus' journey, ascribing to it a number of details that make it temporarily indistinguishable from the story of Noah and the flood. There is the overwhelming sense of an unknown future, the loss of the past, and a grieving wife similar to the role that *Uxor Noe* will take on in the mystery plays. As Brutus prepares to sail from Greece, having reunited with and reconfirmed his Trojan heritage, Gloucester's *Chronicle* turns to his new wife, Innogen. Together, they:

> to ssipe wende
> Hii nuste to wuche londe bote as god hem sende
> Þat deol þat made Innogen no tonge telle ne may
> Heo criede & wep mid sorwe inou & ofte iswowe lay
> Þat heo wende fram al hire kun & fram ech þat heo knew
> & nuste an erþe ʒwderward bote as þe wind blew
> & wuste þat heo ne ssolde neuere aʒen come ne go
> Ne see vader ne oþer kun louerd þat hire was wo
> Brut hire clupte & kuste & confortede hire inou
> Ac he ne miʒte here herte change þat heo to sorwe ne drou.[56]

> . . . wend to the ship; they knew not to which land, except [the one] to which God sent them. No tongue may tell the dole that Innogen made. She cried and wept with sorrow enough and often lay in a swoon, as she was going from all her kin and from each [person] that she knew, and she knew not whitherward on earth they went, but as the wind blew, and she knew that she should never again come nor go, nor see her father nor other kindred lord, and so she was in woe. Brut embraced and kissed and comforted her enough, but he might not change her heart that drew her toward sorrow.

Again, the oracle tells Brutus that they will find a place seemingly beyond the sun, or "a wildernesse vor noman þer inne nis" [a wilderness wherein no man is].[57] The description of Innogen's sorrow and the vision of the world as a new, clean slate evoke the story of Noah's ark; both journeys produce or reveal new worlds that rise up out of the sea and women who lament what is left behind. In *Translating Troy*, Alex Mueller has pointed out the ways in which certain late medieval alliterative romances engage the subject of Troy without participating in *translatio imperii et studii*, arguing that they in fact critique such hegemonic empire building. As Innogen's lament suggests, the chronicles tracing westward-drifting boats also occasionally express hesitations about this historical plot, especially regarding the project of selecting what gets into the boat and what gets left behind.

These medieval histories, written within differing traditions, languages, and centuries, can be drawn together through a conceptual link whose nexus is the ship, whether biblical, Trojan, or Italian. The Brut myth of a traveling empire hinges on a ship that transports genealogical seeds and narrative kernels in order to restart civilization, paralleling and continuing the plot propagated by the biblical flood of a chosen, destined people conveyed across water and time in the belly of a boat. The genre thus links *translatio imperii* to the construction and voyage of Noah's ark, and even equates these monumental preservation projects with the writing of history itself. Classical and medieval poets used the image of a "nautical voyage" as a way of envisioning poetic composition, holding their genius in the "boat of the mind,"[58] and medieval writers of history, each borrowing from a bevy of predecessors, frequently envisioned the work of historiography in terms of compiling an inventory, collecting information of deeds once done and ordering them together in a kind of storehouse.[59] This storehouse, like the biblical *arcae* or classical ships, protects against oblivion and keeps out what must be forgotten. Ship captains whose course is charted for a new world – one beyond the flood or emerging from it – select a past to take forward with them, permitting a sea of forgetting to expunge whatever fails to make it into their portable containers of narrative.

Noah's loading of the ark provides a model for how human events will be written or assembled in subsequent ages, how they will be selected from the world to compose the archive or book, and how they will be transformed from chaotic reality into an authoritative record for later readers. Isidore considers the first historian to have been Moses,[60] whose extensive writings were said to have formed the first five books of scripture, and who loaded the essence of the law into an "arca." But it is Noah who first is confronted with the problem of forgetting, or whose collection is plotted against a backdrop of destruction. Like the patriarch who compiles a sanctioned record within his ark, medieval chroniclers carefully must select and preserve portions of the past within their own holy vessels, leaving aside disruptive alternatives, contradictions, and superfluities, and then marking such absences through the occasional figure of a weeping woman.

The use of Noah's ark as a historiographical model elevates the postdiluvian chronicler whose work is less directly ordained by God, and at the same time it permits sacred history to justify acts of later historiographical exclusion. The central dramatic divisions in the flood story between saved and drowned and remembered and forgotten reverberate violently within the later historical events these chronicles narrate. The shadow the flood story casts across the centuries lends a salvific quality to the non-biblical ships navigating in the ark's generous wake, imbuing historical oblivion with the violence of drowning and raising the stakes for the historian who would write to ward off such forgetting. Robert Mannyng's *Chronicle* provides a good example of a historical narrative at times fixated on the flood, and Mannyng's more pronounced preoccupation with Noah helps to sharpen the focus on the trend when it is manifested more subtly elsewhere. Mannyng's first mention of Noah occurs in the opening description of his project, in which he promises to "schewe fro gre to gre / sen þe tyme of sir Noe" [show from degree to degree, since the time of Sir Noah], the many events that unfurl and the figures who emerge, importantly including "Alle þat kynde & alle þe frute / þat come of Brutus, þat is þe Brute" [all that kind / kin and all the fruit / progeny that come from Brutus, that is, the Brut].[61] Much later, midway through describing King Arthur's preparations to sail to the continent, Mannyng disrupts his plot to look further back into mythic history:

> Queynte he was & right hardy
> & engynous man & sley
> þat first fond schip on se to fare
> & turnde wyþ þe wynd þer he nyste whare
> Lond to seke þat he saw nought
> ne whiderward he schulde be brought[62]

> Wise he was, and very hardy, an ingenuous and savvy man, who first made a ship to fare on the sea, and turned with the wind, where, he did not know, to seek land that he did not see; nor did he know whither he should be brought.

This first sailor sounds like Noah; the basic biography fits, and the *Cursor Mundi* describes the patriarch's aimlessness in similar terms: "þe wind him ledd a-pon þe flodd, / He wist noght wyder-ward he ȝodd" [The wind led him upon the sea / He did not know whither he went].[63] But it also sounds like Brutus, or even like Aeneas, who first starts heading into the western unknown in the *Gest Hystoriale*, a translation of delle Colonne's *Historia Destructionis*: "He not wist, in this world, what wayes to hold, / Ne, what cost, ne cuntre, come vnto laund" [he did not know which way to hold or turn to in this world, nor which coast or country upon which to land].[64] Or Mannyng's figure also simply could be a dreamed up "engynous man," his breathtaking lack of direction given a narrative shape by the adventure of the more famous patriarch. This latter synopsis is how Noah functions in Mannyng's *Chronicle* more generally: elements of his story structure the way other events, including Brutus' voyage, are understood.

The story of the flood imposes a moral framework on Mannyng's text. The *Chronicle* presents a God who directly and spectacularly punishes and rewards human behavior, exacting retribution for the Britons' moral failings just as he did from the antediluvian population. Although a covenant prevents the inflicting of universal disaster, God still exacts enough retribution to frighten those who live in Britain, an island world unto itself, and Mannyng emphasizes how a plot of sin and punishment, or human cause and divine effect, underlie historical events.[65] He is not alone. A number of chronicles work this way; Bede's *Ecclesiastical History of the English People* perhaps most famously links moral failings to historical crises. But Mannyng's ruminations on fluctuating social morality and God's reaction to it seem, at moments, to be specifically plotted onto the story of the flood: it is not just a pattern of sin and punishment that repeats itself over and over again throughout the course of human history, but also a pattern of eras coming to a close and perceptive leaders taking to the sea.[66] When the plague overwhelms England in Mannyng's chronicle, for instance, there are those who sense that God is punishing the island for its iniquity, and who suggest, "it was a vengeance strong; / agayns god þei lyued wrong" [it was strong vengeance; they lived wrongly, against god] (ll.15699–700). Playing out the mythic actions of the patriarch and his chosen few, King Cadwallader goes down to the shore and his waiting ship, taking with him "þe Bretons þat he ches" [the Britons that he chose] (l.15714).

Besides providing a moral framework that structures and rationalizes human history, the flood offers a starting point for historiographical endeavor; the cataclysmic event becomes the explicit or implicit beginning of all subsequent projects purporting to collect and represent present and past, helping further to set a scope and pattern for chronicles. When Laʒamon sets out the parameters for his *Brut*, he suggests that English history begins sometime after the flood. The lapse between the two points is hard to determine, but they occur as if within a mythic time frame, one-after-the-other and very long ago:

> Hit com him on mode. & on his mern þonke.
> þet he wolde of Engle þa æðelæn tellen.
> wat heo ihoten weoren. & wonene heo comen.
> þa Englene londe. ærest ahten
> æfter þan flode. þe from Drihtene com.
> þe al her a-quelde. quic þat he funde.
> buten Noe. & Sem. Iaphet & Cham
> & heore four wiues. þe mid heom weren on archen.[67]

> It came to him in his mind and in his prayerful thought that he would tell of the æthlings of England, who first possessed the English land after the flood that came from the Lord, which killed all the living ones that it found here, except for Noah and Sem, Japheth and Cham, and their four wives who were with them in the ark.

The "æðelæn" or nobility of England, suggests Laȝamon, come "æfter þan flode." In both the history that eventually emerges and in its prefatory synopsis, the time between these events is rhetorically elided, making the emergence of the postdiluvian world a beginning for the chronicler. In Chapter 1, I suggested pinpointing the moment of the fall or the moment in which Adam and Eve pass through Eden's gates as the moment that impels the beginning of history; what comes before exists in a prelapsarian state of timelessness. To think of the flood as the starting point of history shifts the emphasis in this quest for origins from the initial subject of history to the initial historian. Because medieval chroniclers are cut off from that mythic before, they are reliant upon Noah's account of it.

The various historical trajectories that unfurl from this moment of inception importantly take form as genealogical chains, as will the later Brut portions of English histories. The tenth chapter of Genesis and subsequent convention suggest that Noah's sons create a tripartite world – the earth as represented in T-O maps[68] – and that all future generations mythically locate an ancestor in one of the once ark-bound sons. Histories begin not simply at the event of the deluge, but with the family expansion that spreads from the ship. The *Cursor Mundi* deliberately postpones the narration of historical events in order to set out the genealogy that will lend a structure of significance to them:

> þe gode allan suld be for-born,
> Als it in noe flod be-fell,
> Quare of i sal yow siþen tell.

Bot first a tre, ar .i. bigin,
I sal sette hire of adam kin.[69]
Her bigins at noe þe lele
þe toþer werld right for to del;
fiue hundret yeir had þan noe
Quen he had geten his suns thre;
þe first was sem, cham was the toþeir,
And Iaphet hight þat yonges[t] broþer.　　　　　　　　(1622–30)

The good alone should be forborne, as it in Noah's flood befell, about which
I shall tell you next. But first before I begin, I shall set here a tree of Adam's
kin. Here it begins at Noah, the noble, who rightly dealt with (or
partitioned, 'doled out') the other world. Five hundred years old then was
Noah, when he had begot his three sons. The first was called Sem, the other,
Cham, and Japheth was the youngest brother.

The *Cursor Mundi* offers two interrelated conceptions of history: one told in
events, beginning from the flood in which God says he will make "alle in watur
droun / alle þaa bot þi wijf and þe, / þi suns and þair wijfs thre" [all drown in
water / all of those except you and your wife, / your sons and their three wives],
and one told in terms of the "tre" maintained aboard the ark that afterward
will generate further. Capgrave's *Chronicle*, similarly intertwining the propa-
gation of sanctioned narrative with the fertility of one privileged family,
declares that Noah began to work on his "schip" in the "same ȝere" that he
began to "gete childirn," tacitly relating both as projects of transmission.[70]

We might think of the flood as originating two trajectories, then, one in
terms of narrative transmission and the other in terms of biological
reproduction. The sons that Noah disperses across the world promulgate
like the historical account he assembles aboard the ark. Noah creates a
sanctioned version of the antediluvian world to offer posterity, and that
record shuttles through the centuries, spawning additional narratives,
addenda, and new translations that all grow out from their point of origin;
the record he makes engenders a family tree of narrative. Noah becomes the
source of two great lines: first, the genealogical one that, beyond his three
sons, results in Aeneas, Brutus (and/ or Japheth, Alanus) and their many
descendants, passing as encoded history through a chain of bodies.
And second, the chain of remembering, collected into books or arks,
through which historical narrative travels. Noah fathers his historical
account – his record or narrative – just as he fathers Sem, Cham, and
Japheth. Feminist critics have revealed the insidiousness of this patriarchal
underpinning of literary tradition,[71] the father who writes the world into

being, but they have done so largely without turning attention to the flood story and without considering its potential as a narrative model, or as the seminal error in patriarchal canon formation. Medieval chroniclers, however, perpetuate this association between offspring and narrative logically beginning aboard the ark: the name "Brut" itself, referring as it does both to a historiographical genre and to the character whose ancestral tree structures its central story, emphasizes the alignment of texts and people, and of biology and narrative tradition. Again, as Mannyng puts it: "Alle þat kynde & alle þe frute / þat come of Brutus, þat is þe Brute." The "Brut" is fruit and text, progeny and literary production, propagated through family trees and translation.

This interweaving of textual and human genealogies suggests an interweaving of translators and offspring, and of historians and patriarchs, creating that conceptual space in which a chronicler might understand his own work as connected to and continuing Noah's archival project. In certain chronicles, there is the sense that the historian uses his textual ark to perform an act whose dramatically salvific nature specifically resembles the patriarch's. The *Polychronicon*, in an extension of the "dedes þat wolde be lost storye ruleþ" sentiment, suggests that by gathering and preserving a body of learning, a community navigates its way through disaster. It begins with a description of the decline of learning in the contemporary age, a diminishment in the nobility of mankind that might be countered by narrative efforts to preserve art, law, and the "faire manere of spekynge":

> Also now, in our tyme, art, sciens and lawe al were i-falle, ensample of noble dedes were nouȝt i-knowe; nobilite and faire manere of spekynge were all i-loste; but þe mercy of God had ordyned vs of lettres in remedie of unparfiȝtnesse of mankynde.
>
> I praye who schulde now knowe emperours, wonder of philosofres, oþer folwe þe apostles, but hir noble dedes and hir wonder werkes were i-write in stories and so i-kepte in mynde?" (1:5,7)

> Also now, in our time, art, science, and law all were falling away, examples of noble deeds were not known; nobility and a fair manner of speaking all were lost, but the mercy of God had ordained for us letters in remedy of mankind's imperfection. I pray, who should now know emperors, the wonders of philosophers, or follow the apostles, unless their noble deeds and their wonderful works were written in stories and so kept in mind?

An ark of narrative, or sometimes a useful narrative arc, provides the remedy for a society in decline.

It is not, of course, that writing needs the flood story in order to represent itself as something that outlives its age; countless poets have reflected on the longevity or immortality of works written in "eternal lines" without recourse to descriptions of Noah's originary labor.[72] But the important role the flood plays in medieval chronicles nonetheless renders it a fitting model for conceptions of loss and lastingness, and the cataclysmic beginning it provides for human history establishes a pattern for subsequent moments of ruin and survival. The intertwining of textual and human genealogies, or of textual and human incarnations of history, lends a dramatic valence to historical exclusion at the level of plot, intensifying the sense of loss and the non-selection whose result is oblivion. Mannyng at one point uses the figure of Darius (or Dares) to underscore the kind of loss associated with omitted narrative. Dares, like Noah, straddles the categories of historian and historical subject, as medieval chroniclers frequently cast him as a Trojan eyewitness to the fall of his city.[73] For Mannyng, he is a literary predecessor as well as a historical figure, a source and a subject, "a clerk & a gude knyght" (l.147):

> Dares þe Freson of Troie first wrote
> & putt it in buke þat we now wote;
> he was a clerk & a gude knyght.
> Whan Troie was lorn, he sawe þat fight.
> Alle þe barons wele he knewe:
> he tellis þer stature & þer hewe,
> long or schorte, whyte or blak,
> all he telles gude or lak.
> Alle þer lymmes how þai besemed,
> in his book has Dares demed ... "   (ll.145–54)

Darius the Frisian of Troy first wrote it and put it in a book that we now know; he was a clerk and a good knight. When Troy was lost, he saw that fight. All the barons he knew well: he tells of their stature and their hue, tall or short, white or black, all he tells, good or lack. All their limbs, how they seemed, in his book Darius has deemed (judged/described).

Mannyng represents Dares as recording the names of "þe barons" that he knew. The description raises the stakes of the historian's work; it seems, if only for a moment, to place Dares on the field as he records, depicting historical inclusion in terms of a different kind of survival. Further on, Mannyng tells a story that combines images of land and water with memory and forgetting, again acknowledging the historian as the one who saves others from the erasing flood:

Storyes witness it & sais
at a bataile þat þai sette,
at ones Troie & Grece þai mette;
at þat bataile þe Troiens lees
& fled fro þat mykelle prees.
þat myght fle, fled aschore
& Troie destroyed for euermore.
Alle þe world makes ȝitt menyng
how Troie was stroyed for þis thyng.
Clerkes wyse in buke it wrote;
þorgh þer writyng we it wote.
þai wrote þe names of þe kynges
& of all þat oþer lordynges,
whilk were men of most honoure
þat fled fro þat grete stoure.   (ll.712–26)

Stories witness it, and say it was at a battle that they set to, Troy and Greece
met together; at that battle the Trojans lost and fled from that great press.
Those that might flee, fled ashore, and Troy was destroyed for evermore. All
the world yet makes mention how Troy was destroyed for this thing. Wise
clerks wrote it in books; through their writing we know it. They wrote the
names of the kings and of all those other lords, who were men of most
honor, and that fled from that great battle.

Mannyng begins by describing the event from which the "Troiens" flee
"aschore," but then switches abruptly to the scribes who, like him, preserve
this scene ("[c]lerkes wyse in buke it wrote"). The juxtaposed images of
men fleeing "aschore" and scribes writing down names align "shore" and
"memory," as if men not only moved toward dry or safe land, but in fact
scrambled after the writing historian. Those who make it "aschore" are
included in a memorial book and in recorded history; those who do not fail
to find a place in the historical consciousness. As Mannyng writes later still
about the many names and bodies lost to history: "manyon doun was
laied / mo þan any wrote or said" [many were laid down, more than anyone
wrote or said] (ll.4413–14).

The extraordinary length of many medieval chronicles indicates
a compulsion to be exhaustive in record-compilation, to endeavor cease-
lessly after catalogues of the "manyon" otherwise lost. "Fouxul ne worme
forget þou noght" [forget neither fowl nor serpent], warns God in the
Cursor Mundi midway through his instructions to Noah,[74] and the
impressive length of that text implies that its writer works under
a similar injunction. But, as Mannyng points out in his own lengthy
chronicle, some things always must be left out. If this were not the case,

an exhaustive memory might form a record that rivaled creation itself. It is not simply this conceptual deterrent, however, that prevents writers from giving more nuanced accounts of cultures foreign to them, for instance, or, as we will see in the next chapter, that prohibits Noah from allowing his wife's friends to board the ark so that they might continue their drinking songs and lives there. In these historical accounts, the plenitude of the world is excluded not necessarily for lack of capacity, spatial or otherwise, but rather because the desire to record always goes hand in hand with the desire to interpret.

"The things forgotten or not mentioned by history," writes Jacques LeGoff, "reveal ... mechanisms for the manipulation of collective memory."[75] Exclusion – having one's name struck from the book of memory or (seemingly) more passively forgotten[76] – works as a method of narrative control, a means of giving history a shape that corroborates the authoritative narratives of the present. "Defining a nation necessarily involves exclusion," Thorlac Turville-Petre writes in the very first line of his book on English nationality,[77] and thus when Mannyng decides what it means to be English, and what "England" means, he "forgets" the elements that fail to corroborate his vision.[78] Selection and arrangement, the major tasks of Noah and the historian, are counterparts of exclusion, hierarchical structuring, and reinvention; the patriarch who gathers the world into his ark envisions a specific, exclusive reality before embarkation begins, and the postdiluvian chronicle, necessarily predicated on this incomplete history, perpetuates a limited vision, with license to continue such restrictiveness. Noah wields great authority as he guards the portal between old and new worlds, letting only certain parts pass through, indicating on which deck and in which stall each rescued creature might find its allotted berth. Despite this authority, however, he remains incapable of including everything; though chosen by God before all other humans, Noah still is only human, only one human, and a complete account of the antediluvian earth must include multiple, even infinite vantage points, including those that look up from the water.

4   Romance, and a Few Smaller Boats

Though I take up the subject of performance more fully in Chapter 3, I want to look ahead briefly here to the N-Town flood play in order to investigate how a scene that can seem like an awkward interlude relates to the kind of historiographical streamlining described above. The N-Town play features Noah's blind father, Lamech (or Lameth), once a legendary archer whose boasting interrupts the play's central drama. The troubled relationship between historical narrative arcs and forgetting finds an apt metaphor in Lamech's shooting arrow, an image of forward movement and violence that provides one last conceptual link between Noah's adventure and Brutus' legendary voyage to the British Isles. In the play, Lamech insists:

> I xuld nevyr a faylid what marke þat evyr were sett
> Whyl þat I myght loke and had my clere sight.
> And ʒitt, as methynkyht, no man xuld shete bett
> Than I xuld do now, if myn hand were sett aryght (ll.158–61).

> I should never have failed [to hit] whatever mark was set, back when I might look and had my clear sight. And yet, I think, no man should shoot better than I should now, if my hand were set right.

But Lamech does fail, and he shoots Cain, who emerges from the bushes to die at his feet. In anger and shame, Lamech then kills his guide and, certain of the retribution God will extract "seventy times seven," he disappears into the woods, to die then or drown soon after.[79] This lethal arrow, released just before an all-important embarkation, finds a parallel in the Brut story, in which another mistake helps to launch the hero who eventually docks in England. In many versions of the narrative, we learn that, after Aeneas arrives in Italy, his grandson Sisillius and his wife await the birth of their first child. The king assembles his wise men to prophesy what the pregnancy will bring, and the news is grim; in Mannyng's *Chronicle*: "þei said þai fond, as þam was wo, / fadere and modere he suld slo [They said they found, as was woeful to them, that he should slay his father and mother] (ll.839–40).

As promised, the mother dies delivering the child Brutus, and fifteen years later Brutus shoots the fatal arrow:

> When he was fifteen ʒere elde,
> his fadere and he to wod þei wente;
> to venery he gaff his tente.
> A herde of hertes son þei mette;
> at triste to schote, Brutus was sette.
> He ausyed hym apon a herte,
> betuex passed his fadere ouerthuerte,
> & with þat schot his fadere he slouh   (ll.850–7)

> When he was fifteen years old, he and his father went to the wood; he gave his attention to the hunt. They soon met a herd of harts; eager to shoot, Brutus was set. He geared himself toward a hart, but in between passed his father, and with that shot he slew his father.

The similarities are striking: two instances of men shooting other men by mistake in the woods; the shared weight of fate, whose odd components of blindness, prophetic sight, and inevitability mix within the two stories; and a final, violent, ending before that new, seaborne beginning toward which the central plot pushes. There is also a connection between the first and second parts of each of these two stories: the arc of the arrow and the ark on which the hero departs, for both might serve as narrative models. In the *Chronicle* and Lamech interlude, the arc of the arrow rushes forward to wipe out ancestors.[80] But the ark also unleashes a certain violence; its plotted course, across the flood and into the future, helps to transform Lamech and Cain from speaking characters living in an antediluvian wilderness into characters merely referred to by Noah; they become figures relegated to official memory, preserved in the archive of the patriarch's mind as he reminisces, in the York play, from the safety of his ship: "My fadir Lamech, who likes to neven, / Heere in this worlde thus lange gon lende . . . " (ll.15–16).

Pierre Nora has described a process wherein official history eradicates "real" memory; elements from *milieux de mémoire* are conveyed into *lieux de mémoire*, from the world, that is, into the ark, or to a site under the authority of the archivist who lives to tell all tales.[81] The sense is that a reduction takes place, a wrenching away of memory from context, or from the thickness of experience.[82] We can discern components of a similar process of reduction and separation taking place in these stories of arrows and arks. The violence of the shooting arrow suggests a desire to sever worlds, to create a clean break between past and present, or, we might say, between the future and the antediluvian or Italian shore. The archiving vessel sets off and cuts the complex and intertwining ties between its inventory and the shore, manufacturing a narrative less encumbered by troublesome details. The death or departure from ancestors, older heroes, and villains clears space for a new central figure: the archivist, keeper of the treasure-house, the captain who supervises the compiling of his ship's wares and official manifest as his nascent civilization pulls out of port. Both seaborne ark and arrow's arc offer the archiving ship captain greater autonomy over the past; both transform living memory, and the potential cacophony of discordant voices involved, into controlled record. They thus make that thing Isidore of Seville calls "history" ("historia"): the mechanism by which "what occurred in the past is sorted out" [quae in praeterito facta sunt, dinoscuntur].[83]

The more closely a narrative arc is modeled on the arc of the arrows Lamech and Brutus aim, the more controlled, streamlined, and narrow that narrative will be, clear and direct, like the central inked spine of a genealogical tree. The narrative arc that links Adam to Noah, for instance, is forceful and sure; its single-minded purposefulness leaves out everything between the two points not deemed significant. This kind of narrative, like the arrow, and like the ship, moves in a sure, straight line into the future, not pausing for mercy or distraction in whatever form the latter should take: the voices of the dead, the protestations of the left-behind, the weeping wife, the Sirens' song. We might think further of the visual of the rainbow covenant, the line that stretches across the first postdiluvian sky to round off the Genesis episode, with its specific beginning and certain end, a beacon of promise and a charted course from which the saved must not stray. To deviate from the narrative arc would be to invite the chaos abandoned in the antediluvian world: confusion, contradiction, and shipwreck.

But the story of the flood in fact presents two vessels of narrative transmission vulnerable to shipwreck, the ark itself and the human body. These vessels are connected not only by the flood story, but also by language, literary tradition, and exegesis. As we have seen, Latin has the same word, "arca," for Moses' chest of law and Noah's ship, which medieval interpretive tradition further links: "Make Him an ark of the covenant, make Him an ark of the flood; no matter what you call it, it is all one house of God," writes Hugh of Saint Victor.[84] Hebrew, however, links Noah's ark not to the ark of the covenant, but to the basket in which Moses floated downstream into the arms of Pharaoh's daughter: *tevah* is the word for both ship and basket (or cradle).[85] I am interested in the size range of the incarnations afforded the vessel: one *tevah* is a ship built to hold the sanctioned world, and the other is a basket, a cradle that copies the shape of the compact infant. A ship that for a short time becomes the world, and a ship that fits like skin.

When English-speaking poets call the human body a "bark," they conjure up this image of a skintight ship, a body that drifts through or drowns in the currents of the world. And when Capulet (for instance) roars at his weeping daughter: "the bark thy body is, / Sailing in this salt flood," his turn of phrase summons up a narrative trope concerned with the sea- or worldborne body, prevalent (at least) since the Middle Ages.[86] Casting his daughter as ship and the world as sea, Capulet not only suggests the frailty of her own human frame, but evokes the figurative body that floats along in leaky boats or baskets, awaiting the action of providence to shape its adventure out on the water. The trope suggests that providence guides all vessels – ark, cradle, and body – through the world's tempest. This bark of the body, like the ark of the heart, oscillates between resilience and vulnerability; it might withstand the destructive forces of the flood, or it might, as Romeo warns, break apart in an instant ("Thou desperate pilot, now at once run on / The dashing rocks thy sea-sick weary bark!").[87] In contrast to the myth of the single ark, the lone ship sanctioned to ride out destruction and renewal, the number of bodies adrift in creation are countless or, at least, uncounted, transmitting narrative from one bark to another through the unending pattern of birth and death, creations and disasters on a more human scale.[88]

Helen Cooper has examined this story-type concerned with the drifting or drowning human body – "romances of casting adrift" – in *The English Romance in Time*, her study of romance memes linking medieval and early modern traditions.[89] She includes within this genre the journey of the infant Moses, popular medieval romances such as *Émaré*, Chaucer's *Man of Law's Tale* and other versions of the Custance/Constance story, the *Romance of Horn*, stories of Mary Magdalene's apostolic work in France, Shakespeare's *The Tempest*, and "the ultimate ancestral romance," the story of Noah's flood.[90] In her extensive examination of the trope of the body adrift, Cooper emphasizes the importance of ancestry, exploring the relationship between genealogy and nation-formation. The romance emphasis on genealogy complicates attempts to distinguish between that genre and the chronicles,[91] as both combine the desiring (and sometimes undesiring) body with political trajectories, the founding and converting of nations, and the translation of cultures.

In the romances Cooper examines, the bodies loaded onto ships often belong to genealogically significant figures, either young heirs or fertile women, who are sent adrift by those attempting to extend their own power. The forces of providence tend then to intrude, usually interceding on behalf of the reluctant seafarers. The romance of *Horn* offers a nice précis of the trope; toward its beginning, Saracens capture the young, eponymous royal heir along with a group of his friends, and the order is passed down to set them adrift rather than to kill them outright:

> [T]ake one of your old boats and put these boys whom I see here into it. Let them have no oars to help them, no sail nor rudder to guide them. Put into another boat twenty strong men-at-arms who, like good sailors, know how to navigate, to pull them two whole leagues out to sea. Then let them cut the ropes dragging them and leave them there, tossing on the high seas. I am sure you will never hear speak of them more: the god they believe in will never save them, no more than a silly, shorn sheep can.[92]

The command sounds like a gauntlet thrown down to a competing deity, and it sets up a scenario that demonstrates how Horn's life follows a divinely ordained, merciful trajectory. God steps in here as he does in other cases, wafting the rudderless boat toward Ararat or some other miraculous shore.

Cooper describes an interesting distinction between possible plot trajectories of the casting-adrift romances, laying the groundwork for how these arks, barks, and baskets might function as vessels of narrative. She points out that "the outcome of such narratives correlates closely with the point of view from which it is told."[93] That is, if a narrative is told from the perspective of someone who remains on shore, watching the ship depart, then the hapless mariner usually drowns. If, however, as is more commonly the case, narrative perspective accompanies the person in the boat, then that person lives. "Yeres and dayes fleet this creature," says the Man of Law about Custance, "Thurghout the See of Grece unto the Strayte / of Marrok, as it was hire aventure" (*II* 463–5). The reader does not hear of the shore again until the heroine washes up upon it. Narrative stays with, and even *in*, the boat, so that we might think of it as holding the story, transporting it into the future and onto the shore for the next episode or "aventure" to begin. Such vessels seem to hold narrative in the way that Noah's ship – or Brutus' – cradles the sanctioned remnants and sole evidence of a civilization or entire world.

The romance of *Émaré*, a fourteenth-century work whose shipborne heroine is wafted from Sicily to Rome to Gaul and back again, similarly underscores the idea of the boat as a holder of stories. Again, narrative perspective accompanies the heroine in her rudderless ship, following the pattern Cooper discerns. But Émaré also takes something else into the boat: a cloth encrusted with jewels, "[s]tuffed wyth ymagerye," that tells in shining fragments the stories of other romances and histories.[94] Wearing the cloth as a shawl, Émaré conceptually suggests Hugh's vision of a decorated ark: both sport histories inscribed on their casings, stories written across ship hulls and embroidered on the bark of the body. Aboard the ship, of course, Émaré has access to more than just the romances of others. She carries her personal narrative as well, or a catalogue of personal experience. Sir Kadore, who receives the drifting heroine after one leg of her aimless / divinely steered voyage, says she is "the konnyngest wommon, / I trowe, that be yn Crystendom" [the most knowledgeable woman I believe to be in Christendom].[95] Kadore describes her particular kind of knowledge as belonging to the arts of courtesy (he asks her to teach his children), but we might speculate further about the stores of information and memory that she, or any human bark, carries. Émaré has just one cloth; other characters have even less of a material inventory. Horn, Moses, and Apollonius' wife – the latter placed alive into a coffin and then into the sea – have nothing but their own bodies. If a ship holds nothing but a body, then everything must be contained within that human bark; bodies that cross expanses of water without the benefit of objects or artifacts to link subsequent ages must themselves hold what is to be preserved: piety, practical knowledge, behavioral codes, blood, and other, older narratives that necessarily predate the romance or tragedy the exile enacts.[96]

One might, in fact, think of fictional exiles such as Custance or Émaré as merely exaggerating the elements of the most basic narrative of human life. The logic of medieval Christianity suggests that all humans are travelers, pilgrims, even exiles from a state of innocence from the moment the first pair step outside the gates of Eden.[97] Guillaume de Deguileville's *Le Pèlerinage de la Vie Humaine* (c.1331), translated in Middle English as *The Pilgrimage of the Lyfe of the Manhode*, begins with a reminder from the apostle: "but alle, as seith Seynt Poul, be þei riche, be þei poore, be þei wise oþer fooles, be þei kynges oþer queenes, all þei ben pilgrimes" [but all, as Saint Paul says, whether they be rich or poor, whether they be wise or fools, whether they be kings or queens, they are all pilgrims].[98] All "pilgrims" navigate the world within their own human barks, buffeted by fortune and steered by providence. In lieu of a cape embroidered with jewel-encrusted narrative, each bark contains its own woven strands of narrative, the treasure or burden of its individual history. These narratives can take form as embroidered clothing, specific manners, remembered stories, or even genetic makeup, recalling, as Cooper points out, the central importance of genealogy. In the medieval context, this genetic makeup is manifested as genealogical proof: Havelock's birthmark ("kynmerk"), for instance, or the stream of light that flows from his mouth; both verify a lineage that sanctions the narrative trajectory his life next takes.[99] Today we employ a text-based vocabulary to describe genetic coding as a kind of narrative form, maintaining this connection between literary production and reproduction and corroborating the idea of narrative *in* the body (as when, for instance, DNA and RNA undergo "transcription" and "translation"). This adopted vocabulary suggests the idea of the narrative-invested body as an "arca" not only of culture, but also of flesh and blood. Steered shoreward and forward in time, the body is both narrative vessel and narrative link: a connection between one age and the next.

Romances rely on the return of their heroines and young children to provide the necessary links in genealogy-driven narratives. One generation transitions into another through a child returned to shore or the image of a woman's pregnant body, her womb suggesting the belly of the ark, the "barm" filled with new life or the rescued living.[100] But royal families also stand for the realms they rule, and so just as the bark of the body might preserve and transport a dynasty or sacred genealogy, so a larger bark, an actual ship, might transplant an entire culture. This is how the meme of the drifting, providence-guided ship functions not only within private family history, but links up to what Cooper calls a "whole programme of colonial expansion," and to Europe's own ancestral romance of *translatio imperii* and the myth of Trojan culture gradually drifting toward the farthest western islands of Ireland and England.[101] Cooper compares two narrative strands of the founding myth, focusing on the different vessels that each require, and thus combining the human bark of romance with the arks of the chronicles: "Aeneas," she writes, "may have founded a state in Italy after a voyage from Troy in a properly-equipped boat, but Rome itself owed its foundation to twin babies who were exposed on the water in a little basket."[102] Here again we have the *tevah*, ark and basket, the vessel of various dimensions with which one might forge a homeland, Promised Land, or kingdom.

Chapter 3 turns to the ark as it is staged in the flood plays to explore other ways in which the body, particularly the performing body, works as a resource for linking generations and historical epochs.[103] The plays offer the stage as a space of possibility for the memory-relegated and submerged voices of the past, a site where contention, confusion, and protest is transmitted through bodies differently. Ark and stage architecturally and conceptually overlap,[104] effecting a confluence of salvific, archival, and performance space, as the sacred ship becomes the stage upon which the players recall the most violent episode (so far) of sacred history. This hybrid space, I argue, communicates both a desire for preservation and the desire for something new: accumulation and revision, stasis and dynamism. This, we will see, is one way the floating archive is altered, wrested from the control of the archivist-patriarch by the many who would remember.

CHAPTER 3

Uxor Noe *and the Drowned*

The end of Chapter 2 examined the ways in which medieval romance represents the body as conveying narrative through genealogical process. But the bark of the body transmits the past through methods other than biological reproduction, and in this chapter I look at how the mystery plays stage human actors as vessels of memory, permitting performance to work as another means of linking past and present: inviting the "voices of the dead," as Joseph Roach has put it, to "speak freely . . . through the bodies of the living."[1] The past, stored in and memorialized through scripts, bodies, and props,[2] is brought out and made to speak in performances of the flood, but instead of adhering to a master inventory or divinely sanctioned blueprint, it filters through multiple performing and witnessing bodies. The playing space serves as a site where strictures such as patterns and scripts are imposed but the freedom to transgress them still remains. Change happens, even (or especially) in the act of repetition, a dynamic that has become a cornerstone of performance theory,[3] and this potential for change finds fertile ground in the cycling, spiraling annual performances of sacred history.

The events and meanings of sacred history change, purposefully or accidently, as they pass from one performance to the next, variously exacerbated and confirmed by players and audiences. Narrative is transmitted and controlled not by a single authoritative archivist – God, ship captain, state, the patriarch at the portals of ante- and postdiluvian worlds – but moves from body to body, a kind of reproduction that permits transcription, translation, and transformation. This is not to represent the text as rigidly static in comparison to performance, particularly in the Middle Ages, when practices of manuscript transmission could nudge a story into new forms.[4] But the archive of the performing body and the performance space in which that body moves are predicated especially upon this possibility of transformation, a quality and potential always dangerous to the static hierarchy the biblical ship would impose.

The relationship among performance, memory, and the archive has a rich and sometimes contradictory history, with those categories at different moments arranged in both opposition and collaboration. Diana Taylor begins *The Archive and the Repertoire*, a study concerned largely with Latin American performance, by proposing key distinctions between the ways knowledge has been understood as transmitted across time. She aligns the "repertoire" with embodied forms not reducible to transcript, such as gestures and utterance. The "archive" is comparatively textual and conservative, if not sometimes entirely static.[5] These are not reified categories necessarily understood as strict binaries in Taylor's study, but useful poles for thinking through a more expansive understanding of what knowledge is – what *counts* as knowledge, one might say – and how it might be passed on. Taylor argues that text and performance, or the archive and the repertoire, frequently work in tandem, and that critics who would locate one (performance) as anchored to a vanished past and understand the other (text) as better able to endure across time mistake the nature of the interaction between these media. This is important because embodiment and its forms of knowledge historically have been relegated to a second tier of value.

Here, it also can be useful to return to the nautical poetry of Pierre Nora's distinction between the *lieux* and *milieux* of memory, cited at the end of Chapter 2, since Nora is one of the critics whose binaries Taylor wants to nuance. For Nora, the *lieux* are the institutional constructs created or commemorated in the absence of the socially produced, lived, "real environments" of the *milieux de mémoire*.[6] Nora describes these *lieux* – museums, monuments, memorials – as "moments of history torn away from the movement of history, then returned; no longer quite life, not yet death, like shells on the shore when the sea of living memory has receded."[7] Sarah Beckwith has used Nora's formulation to describe the ruins at York against which twentieth-century performances of the mystery plays have been set.[8] But she also suggests that Nora "enacts" the break between history and memory he purportedly seeks merely to analyze,[9] nostalgically writing himself into a reason for nostalgia.

One might say, then, that Taylor introduces the possibility of a more complex scenario, in which – to extend the metaphor swirling through this chapter and the last – the surf offers a contested form of history, one not so emphatically sealed off from memory, nor so easily commodified by the heritage industry that Beckwith's study of the York plays critiques. Performances of Noah's ark, as we will see, collapse even the theoretical poles of Taylor's working distinctions between repertoire and archive, locating performance and archival space – official history and utterances that linger; ark, stranded shell, and teeming ocean – simultaneously upon the pageant wagon stage. Here, text is ever present through the authority of scripture itself; the episodes performed are encoded in the "divine law" of Moses as well as sanctioned by Noah, who instigates archival and historiographical endeavor. But the medieval bodies that perform this scriptural history inflect it with the possibility for dynamism and change, layered, contradictory memories, and potentially new truths about the past discovered through the resources of the present.

It is likely that, in some performances of the flood, the mystery play stage and the ark shared an architecture; that is, that the stage, or pageant wagon, doubled as the ark.[10] If we then think of theatrical space as ark-space, or as archival space, crowded with continuously stored and then divulged memory, we create something of a repeating archival chain: the ark of the heart within the bark of the player's body within a theater of memory, cast as the ark of the flood. The idea of the "memory theater," though anachronistic to the Middle Ages, becomes useful in thinking about traditions of conjuring overlapping mnemonic, archival, and performance space. The early modern thinkers Giulio Camillo and Robert Fludd both worked on projects called "theaters of memory," designs meant to function, at least in part, like Hugh of Saint Victor's mnemonic ark, examined in Chapter 2.[11] Just as Hugh's ark has its strict hierarchies set forth in cubic minutiae, and the antediluvian pillars seal their unchangeable contents in fire- and water-resistant tile and marble casing, so the zodiac-based structuring of the memory theaters suggests permanence on par with the heavens. But the very fact that Fludd and Camillo used theaters as spatial models introduces the possibility of a mnemonic site with a built-in potential for transformation, a site where memory and narrative might be changed through the pressure of performance.[12]

Transformative performance, of course, still might become an instrument of control: one can select which past to perform, or how to re-perform it, in order to corroborate the narratives the present age insists upon. One can, for instance, stage the eventual submission of a wayward wife as a way of presenting human history's founding family, and the mystery plays can (and frequently did) celebrate and reinforce hierarchy. But despite the points of intersection between the stage and the ark, or performance and archival space, these spaces diverge when it comes to the ways in which authority is apportioned. The stage, just like the bark of the body that moves upon it, can function as a ship of memory, but power is more diffuse there than in the ark: the command for transformation comes from all sides, and performances of control often falter. This potential democratizing of memory works against the paradigm of Noah, the patriarch-archivist, and the patriarchal archiving he inaugurates: the model of recording and narrative transmission that stipulates who archives and who is archived, who might remember and who can only hope to be saved, whether in the monumentally compiled chronicles of the historians, in memory, in a ship of memory, or in another form vulnerable to endless recreations in the eye and work of the memory-artist.

This chapter investigates how the struggle between the one who remembers and the one who is remembered gets played out through representations of gender difference. The story of Noah's archive might require numerous acts of exclusion – the ship, after all, crests above a world earmarked for destruction – but the flood plays focus specifically on the power dynamic between Noah and his wife. I examine how the inception of historiography that takes place aboard the ark – the creation of both a new past and a new future – occurs as a power struggle between the two, and how the apocryphal role of *Uxor Noe* relates to larger questions of narrative participation of women in this, the postdiluvian world. I read the domestic bickering and slapstick violence of the biblical pair as a struggle for narrative authority and the right to remember, both within their domestic context and in terms of human history. Noah's archive structures the new world meant to emerge when the flood waters recede, and so his wife's positioning, as co-archivist, as subversive archivist, or as archived human animal, becomes crucial to that vision of an emerging earth.

To approach the relationship between gender, memory, and history, the chapter moves from mythic into medieval and even postmedieval time. It begins with an overview of the figure of Noah's Wife, a woman who flickers faintly across centuries until the late medieval period, when she takes form as a more fully developed and verbose *persona dramatis* in the flood plays, especially in the York, Chester, and Towneley cycles (her role in N-Town is much more subdued). I suggest that her arrival on the scene addresses discomfort with a story about starting over on a global scale, and with the interpretive authority invested so singularly, so exclusively, in Noah. Uxor is able to voice this discomfort from the relative safety of her outsider role as an unruly woman, a figure that traditionally invites correction, and one who rarely accesses authority without dramatic complication. From here, I examine how medieval performances of Uxor's unhappiness resonate with a more modern history of feminist literary criticism, and how they offer an early touchstone for the woman who would endeavor, against various physical and conceptual restraints, to describe her own world and past. Medieval English drama enhances – more or less invents – a character whose unhappiness puts into sharp relief the impoverished methods by which her husband creates his archive, even as that archive mythically becomes an authoritative, divinely sanctioned model for all future ones.

I Uxor Noe

In his groundbreaking discussion of the transition from memory to written record, Michael Clanchy describes various early formations of the archive in medieval England, potentially confusing from our vantage point, but significant to their assemblers: "To the modern eye, an early medieval archive would have looked more like a magpie's nest . . . The best modern comparison might be with an old lady's handbag, which likewise might contain symbolic rings, jewellery, miscellaneous mementos and a few letters and papers."[13] Mary Carruthers has described how the handbag (or rather, the money purse, Latin *saccula* or Middle English *male*) was a potent medieval metaphor for memory, citing Harry Bailey's jubilant "This gooth aright; unbokeled is the male" that celebrates the start of the narrative contest on the way to Canterbury (*I* 3115).[14] The *male, saccula,* or purse is both a receptacle of narrative and a space defined by notions of property. Narrative might tumble out of it, but even more importantly, narrative is contained and owned within: arranged, sorted, and created there. The narrative elements organized in the bag not only preserve a vision of past and present, but structure whatever new world is on the way. Clanchy's characterization of medieval archives picks up on this important metaphor of memory in a handbag. His reference to "old ladies" and "magpies" also gestures toward two wayward figures in medieval versions of the flood story: Noah's Wife and the magpie (read: raven, also family *cordivae*) who similarly errs.[15]

Chaucer makes a joke in the Miller's Tale about the idea of a woman getting her own ark:

> "Hastou nat herd," quod Nicholas, "also
> The sorwe of Noe with his felawshipe
> Er that he myghte get his wyf to shipe?
> Hym hadde be levere, I dar wel undertake
> At thilke tyme, than alle his wetheres blake
> that she hadde had a shipe hirself allone."   (I.3538–43)

In the flood plays, the works most responsible for reconstructing Noah's Wife out of "biblical silence,"[16] the mother of the world to come does *not* get her own ship, or even her own jumbled handbag; she deliberately is made bereft of resources with which to craft and preserve her own memory of the world in which she lived. The plays bristle with implications about the consequences of this denial of a woman's contribution to universal history and the refusal of her participation in the re-creation of her world. Though she is not excluded from her husband's archive, the way in which Noah's Wife is made to enter it helps to shape the models of gender identity, domesticity, and authority that the ark will propagate. Her positioning within the ark positions her also within the archival and narrative project that the disaster of the flood forces into motion.

Genesis points to the existence of Noah's Wife in two phrases: "uxor tua" and "uxor eius," "your wife" and "his wife." Several attempts to fill this silence predate medieval dramatic versions. The arsonist wife briefly mentioned in Chapter 2 – she burns down the ark at least twice in a third or fourth century gnostic work – suggests that a thread of discontent was woven into the story quite early. There was also a steady assault on Uxor's namelessness. In "The One Hundred and Three Names of Noah's Wife," Frances Lee Utley testifies to the tremendous urge to name the nameless woman, mother of the whole world that followed. Of course, this desire might simply have been part of a larger medieval desire for encyclopedic knowledge, often appropriately focused upon the original vessel of systematic recording, the ark itself. "What was the name of Noah's Wife?" was hardly the only question posed and answered about the ship. "What about the amphibians?"[17] went the others; "Were sirens, unicorns, or phoenixes given berths?"[18] "Could a ship with such un-seaworthy dimensions float?"[19] Eagerly posed and answered across the centuries, these questions invited much flood-centered analysis and speculation. But the question about the nameless Uxor seems not to have participated simply in the medieval theological or early modern natural philosophic patterns of inquiry that drove so many of the others. Perhaps a different desire is involved: the impulse to throw many compensatory names on the woman who has none; to contextualize her through suggestive ones (Eva, Bathsheba, Semiramis, Venus, Mama . . .);[20] to heap narrative after narrative upon her as she participates in the one belonging so unequivocally to her husband.

An unhappy and even angry Uxor, wholly absent from the Genesis account, begins to acquire her own narrative in the flood plays at York, Chester, and Towneley. Trouble brews also in the non-cycle Newcastle Flood play, which features a conversation between Noah's Wife and the devil,[21] and in images in the Queen Mary Psalter (early fourteenth century), which further hint at that association.[22] These instances, together with Chaucer's joke, the description of the arsonist from the lost gnostic account, and more than a hundred names bestowed in solidarity, scholarly endeavor, or through the need to know that fuels invention, help to recreate the role of Noah's wife, a woman who definitively breaks with her silent, canonical counterpart by speaking.

In the flood plays, Uxor delivers many of her lines in the throes of her domestic disputes, the central dramatic conflict around which the disaster of the flood swirls. These calamities are firmly connected: the spouses fight *about* the ark, and they do so until the waters begin to rise. Scholars have pointed out the link between these domestic disturbances and the bad weather that compels the two into the ship together. The chaotic world God sends the flood to destroy finds its remnant and resonance in Noah's Wife; Noah therefore must tame and bring her into the anti-chaotic fold, fitting her into the hierarchical structure that attempts to eliminate chaos. V.A. Kolve argues that the hierarchy and stability of Noah's ship are a microcosm for the new, improved world about to be born:

> Just as fallen man is rebellious to his master, God, so too is the wife rebellious to her husband, and only when the proper human relationship is re-established does the universal order begin to reconstruct itself anew. When all have finally entered the ark [in the Towneley play] it is a new Mrs. Noah who speaks, in a voice chastened in tone and moving to a graver rhythm.[23]

Noah's houseboat sets the pattern for domestic relations, and these, in turn, create the microcosmic rules of behavior the rest of the larger world follows.

Kolve suggests that the domestic disputes eventually lead to a clarification and confirmation of accepted order, reading the protestations of Noah's Wife as participating in a familiar narrative arc of rebelliousness and return to order. The implication is that the plays affirm the corrective bent of this narrative shape, and that they conclude with a return to the accepted chain of authority (God, Noah, Uxor, animal) that structures the new world about to take form. "[A]ll things exist in their proper degree," writes Kolve of this vision of stability; "God is greater . . . than the angels; the angels, in turn, are above man, man is above woman, human beings above animals."[24] Noah and Uxor must fit into their assigned roles because, as Kolve suggests, the cosmic hierarchical structure corresponds to their domestic pattern, perhaps even depends upon it. Who knows what new chaos would ensue should Uxor demand a different role? Robert Mannyng offers a prescient glimpse of the catastrophe of the authoritative woman in *Hanndlyng Synne*, his early fourteenth-century devotional work, written before the *Chronicle*, suggesting that such a scenario makes a woman into a "shrewe":

> And ȝyf she þe maystry onys wynne,
> Al newe lawes she wyle begynne,
> For þan makyþ she hyt al newe
> And begynnyþ to be a shrewe.[25]

> And if she wins mastery once, she will instate all new laws, for then she makes it all new, and begins to be a shrew.

Moreover, if Uxor's rebellion goes unchecked, it potentially calls into question the entire hierarchy proposed in the plays of the flood. If Uxor successfully challenges Noah's work, it seems possible that Noah, too, might become something other than the loyal deputy who precisely carries out divine instruction. Transgression at one point in the chain of command introduces the possibility for it at others.

Uxor's movement from unruliness to submission, arcing in the form of conversion narratives, surely resonated with medieval audiences eager to return to the fold and be counted among the saved. But some critics resist the emphasis on closure such an elegant narrative arc demands. In "Women on Top," Natalie Zemon Davis points out that the unruly woman was a "multivalent image," difficult to constrain within stories about conversion or correction.[26] Although women invested with unruly power might cause witnesses to such power to crave a return to order, temporary alterations are not always so easily or permanently erased. Even after correction, memory lingers. Jane Tolmie, looking specifically at the flood plays, describes Uxor's "recalcitrance" as "present and persistent even when it is disapproved and defeated."[27] In *Gender and Medieval Drama*, Katie Normington speculates about audience members particularly positioned to respond to Uxor's recalcitrance, exploring the new constraints being imposed upon women during the late medieval period in which the plays were performed.[28] Stressing the forced nature of Uxor's eventual silence, she proposes that the plays document "important economic transitions which faced working women in the late Middle Ages," especially their loss of authority within the textile industry and the emergence of an urban economy increasingly wont to characterize them solely as wives and mothers.[29] This loss of economic independence and agency, Normington suggests, corresponds to the loss of authority Noah's Wife experiences when her husband forces her aboard the ark. Both are scenarios of a changing world, a space making new rules in order to reaffirm its patriarchal ordering. Aboard the ark, whose "hierarchical design . . . silences women," Uxor is "domesticated and stripped of her personal power"; in the Towneley play, she is made to abandon her distaff, the "emblem of her working status."[30]

Because of my interest in Noah's ark as archive, I want to approach Uxor's diminution of authority in terms of her relationship to the organization of history. Normington rightly characterizes the distaff as an emblem of the workingwoman, but it also conjures a cluster of metaphors connected to the related arts of weaving and spinning, activities long associated with narrative production. Perhaps the most powerful example of this within the medieval context is the iconography and exegetical tradition of a Virgin Mary who sews, as Gail McMurray Gibson points out, both the human skin and death shroud of her miracle baby, encompassing his life and human history in her handiwork, carefully spinning a son (*filium*) out of thread (*filum*).[31] But Noah's wife is associated with the distaff or spindle not in order to suggest a connection between her and that other mother, but rather because many unruly women were; several medieval and early modern depictions place unruly women within reach of the distaff.[32] Unlike Mary, these women do not produce children whose lives structure a sanctioned narrative trajectory; instead, they speak in a way that threatens to disrupt sanctioned narrative.

Eve is our earliest example of the wayward spinning woman with an impulse to narrate. She was supposed to have taken up or even invented spinning when she left Eden, and certain traditions also associate her with the emergence of writing. In Chapter 1, I looked at an image that showed an aging, humbled Adam and Eve in need of a scribe to record their extraordinary lives. The *Canticum de Creatione* describes an Eve also in need of a scribe, but invested with more narrative authority; she instructs her children to write on the clay that will fill those antediluvian pillars encased in marble or tile.[33] The scenario suggests that a woman who spins also might supervise the construction of official record. Critics have noted the flood plays' association between the two troublemakers Eve and Uxor,[34] and this connection between ante- and postdiluvian mothers is strengthened by the link that might be forged between speaking and spinning in their respective extrabiblical stories. Each thread spun out through their hands subversively suggests narrative input, the risk of a stray or unsanctioned mark encased within the pillars, and the troubling capacity to alter a story meant to last.

The Towneley play is most invested in the importance of Uxor's identity as a textile worker. Here, Noah and his wife quarrel when she refuses to board his newly built ship. Her reluctance stems from a number of things:

she is loath to leave her community; she is angry with him; and she would prefer to spin. "Sir," she says, to the patriarch's evident frustration:

> for Iak nor for Gill
> Will I turne my face,
> Till I haue on this hill
> Spon a space
> On my rok.[35]

> For Jack nor Gill will I turn my face until I have, on this hill, spun a space / spun for awhile on my rock.

"Spon a space" works as a reference to time, as in "spun awhile," but it also suggests geographic space. Noah's wife desires to have a space, a "rok" separate from the realm of her husband's ship, on which she might spin her yarn, or transform her experience into narrative. Bad weather and Uxor's refusal send Noah into a panic. He begs her to look at the cataracts in the heavens; he worries that the planets will whirl out of their "stall" and that "halles and bowers, / Castels and towers" will crumble, providing a tantalizing glimpse of a soon to be drowned civilization (ll.500, 504–5). The daughters-in-law join Noah in his exhortations, begging Uxor to board the ship as the skies threaten rain; they call to her from the ship deck, offering a compromise:

1 MULIER:	Good moder, com in sone,
	For all is ouercast,
	Both the son and the mone.
2 MULIER:	And many wynd-blast
	Full sharp.
	Thise floodys so thay ryn;
	Therfor, moder, come in.
UXOR:	In fayth, yit will I spyn;
	All in vayn ye carp.
3 MULIER:	If ye like ye may spin,
	Moder, in the ship. (ll.512–22)

WOMAN 1: Good mother, come in soon, for all is overcast, both the sun and moon.
WOMAN 2: And many winds sharply blast. These floods rain down so; therefore, Mother, come in.
WIFE: In faith, I will continue to spin; you speak all in vain.
WOMAN 3: If you like, mother, you may spin in the ship.

If Noah's Wife acquiesces to her family's exhortations, her narrative-production henceforth will occur exclusively under the auspices of her husband and within the safely contained space of the ship. The ark, a kind of proto-church and realm of patriarchal control, will impose unknown strictures upon the stories that she spins. Noah's Wife perhaps will begin to think and speak like the numbered women begging her to join them, the daughters-in-law who confirm the necessity of the project Noah supervises and whose voices already have been appropriated into its service. The entranceway to the ark becomes something of a gangplank, promising a certain loss of narrative authority in exchange for the preservation of life. Nonetheless, if Noah's Wife shuns entry and stays where she is, perched precariously on that antediluvian "rok," she will drown.

The compromise shouted by Uxor's daughters-in-law introduces the dilemma of the woman who would narrate from within the patriarchal order, a concern rigorously investigated by early phases of feminist literary criticism. Though many critics since have turned from the problem of the writing woman to interrogate how gender itself is discursively constructed, the story of Noah's Wife might be used to think through questions underpinning multiple waves of feminist and gender theory, offering a way for their central questions to be thought of together, rather than in opposition. I want first to investigate the episode in relation to the conundrum of the writing woman, and then to consider how categories produced under duress – archival organizing in the biblical storm – might relate to understandings of the construction of gender identities.

Mary Jacobus succinctly articulates the first paradox in her essay "The Difference of View" (1979), which reaches back in time no further than Mary Wollstonecraft, and yet precisely summarizes Uxor's crisis:

> The options [for women writers] polarise along familiar lines: appropriation or separatism. Can women adapt traditionally male dominated modes of writing and analysis to the articulation of female oppression and desire? Or should we rather reject tools that may simply re-inscribe our marginality and deny the specificity of our experience?[36]

This latter option, Jacobus points out, risks aligning the feminine with "a yet more marginal madness or nonsense";[37] as the logic of the flood story insists, it is the decision that places Uxor underwater. The scenario frees her narrative production from the controls and resources of her husband's sanctioned space, but, like all things that "escape" the ark, it too then must sink into silence. By boarding the ship, however, Noah's Wife relinquishes the ability to have the "specificity of her experience" contribute to the narrative that posterity will construct from what has been preserved in her husband's boat. This "specificity of experience" could be lost in a number of ways: her voice could be erased or co-opted, and the narrative she tells either expunged or made to fit into the master narrative sanctioned by her husband.

I do not want to draw the connection between Uxor's plight and the one investigated by feminist criticism simply to castigate further the obvious misogyny of certain medieval texts, and I am wary of referring to such plays as participating in a kind of "protofeminism," lest, to turn to Dinshaw, the term positions them as "mere prefigurations of what we now appreciate as the robust feminism of modernity."[38] The story of the flood, however, establishes Uxor's conundrum as one that underlies *all* postdiluvian narrative production, and that, according to the schema of salvation history, means all narrative production, as Noah's archival project mythically formats the world we now inhabit. Uxor boards the ark in the book of Genesis and in every reworking (that I know of) thereafter, and so turns our focus onto the woman who narrates from within the space of the ark and the world later arranged to its design. The flood plays dramatize the disappearance of Uxor's narrative perspective, representing it as coinciding with her loss of the right to remember the world from which she departs. Stepping from drenched land to ship, she undergoes a loss of subjectivity, of interiority, of the capacity to lay claim to an "arca cordis," or an ark of the heart, that might modify or challenge the ark docked in the world without. An ontological shift takes place when Uxor steps onto the gangplank of salvation; she begins as a potential narrator, a spinner who might encode in text or textile the series of events she both witnesses and experiences, and then, aboard the ship, she becomes netted in the narrative of another.

Several of the flood plays foreground this shift from potential archivist – one endowed with the authority to compile and interpret – to inventory: from narrator to narrated, active commemorator to passive memory-object, shepherd to animal. In the Towneley play, Noah speaks as the ship loading begins:

> Now ar we there
> As we shuld be;
> Do get in oure gere,
> Oure catall and fe,
> Into this vessell here,
> My chylder fre   (ll.469–74).

> Now are we there, as we should be. Do get our gear, our livestock and possessions, into this vessel here, my free/ noble children.

Noah's "fre" children load the livestock and possessions, leaving his wife to wonder into which category this new enterprise will place her. The Chester play offers one answer through a communal reading of the ark's inventory. In this play, Noah, his wife, his three sons, and their wives load the ark together, reciting the names of a seemingly exhaustive catalogue of animals. Lisa Kiser has pointed out how these recitations organize the ship's animal inventory into specific categories, distinguishing, for instance, between wild and tame and between those associated with traditionally masculine and feminine activities.[39] But, as Kiser points out, when Noah's Wife contributes to this expanding catalogue, with its taxonomies proliferating far beyond the scriptural divisions of clean and unclean, she lists animals that fail to adhere to orderly groupings. In keeping with the unruliness that characterizes her role in this play and in others, Uxor offers a jumbled list, recklessly juxtaposing creatures from different categories, disrupting the order and hierarchy on which the project of the cataloguing ark is based.[40] She brings aboard an unregulated multiplicity, muddling what is meant as a model for the new and improved postdiluvian world, a world in which, according to God's injunction at York, animals in all their variety and differing degrees must not "blende" (l.126). The long list compiled at Chester establishes a further taxonomical precedent, one relating to the categorical difference between human and non-human. After his wife's disordered contribution and the more careful inventory taken by his children, Noah speaks up: "Wyffe," he says, in what I think we should understand as a continuation of the inventory, "come in. Why standes thou there?"[41] Uxor explains that unless Noah includes her "gossips" in his ship, he can "rowe forthe" without her (ll.201, 207). The family engages in a spirited exchange until, it appears, she is herded onto the ship by her son ("whether thou will or nought," says Sem).[42]

   This conflation of woman and animal inventory, explicit in both the Chester and Towneley plays, has a disorienting effect upon Noah's Wife. Once corralled aboard the ark in the Towneley play, she laments to her husband:

> I was neuer bard ere,
> As euer myght I the,
> In sich an oostré as this!
> In fath, I can not fynd
> Which is before, which is behynd.
> Bot shall we here be pynd,
> Noe, as haue thou blis?   (ll.475–81)

> I was never before barred, as I swear to you, in lodgings such as this. In faith,
> I cannot determine which is before and which is behind. But shall we here
> be penned, Noah, as have thou bliss?

Uxor, "barred" and "penned" in, cannot tell "before" from "behind," front from back, perhaps tomorrow from yesterday. Disorientation is a natural enough fear when all landmarks are sinking fast, but Noah's Wife is the only one to voice it in the play, and she importantly associates her disorientation with the architectural specificity of the ark and all of its organized compartments, not with the unchartable sea outside. It is in the holy vessel, the only remnant of light and promise left in the world, where she suddenly feels most in the dark.

The inability to distinguish demarcated space and chronology herald Uxor's transformation into *something* narrated from *someone* who once herself could use space and time to structure narrative. Here again Uxor intersects with the dilemma of the writing woman; her articulated sense of entrapment resonates with the ways in which feminist critics have described the entrapment of women within patriarchal textual production. Noah's Wife claims to feel "barred" and "penned" like livestock; in the same year that Jacobus' essay came out and roughly five hundred years after that Middle English lament, Susan Gubar and Sandra M. Gilbert write:

> As a creation "penned" by man, moreover, woman has been "penned up" or
> "penned in." As a sort of "sentence" man has spoken, she has herself been
> "sentenced": fated, jailed, for he has both "indited" her and "indicted" her.
> As a thought he has "framed," she has been both "framed" (enclosed) in his
> texts, glyphs, graphics, and "framed up," (found guilty, found wanting) in
> his cosmologies.[43]

Similarly to the ways in which patriarchal literary tradition might be understood to frame "woman," Noah the archivist pens his wife into his floating museum and into his account of the antediluvian earth, framing her as a character and indicting her as a transgressor in his narrative of a world whose other witnesses are submerged. The story of Noah's Wife thus dramatizes the imprisonment of woman not just within "patriarchy and its texts," but within patriarchy's mythic seminal archive: Noah's Wife is penned in the prison of the ark, the blueprint for a narrative of the new world, and for the narratives that new world in turn will propagate. When Noah's Wife leaves her position of potential authority to cross an ontological divide, she becomes inventory, object, or "character," an entity imprisoned within the ark belonging to her husband. Penned into history, locked up in the houseboat, and carefully formatted to a vision of the new world.

"It is thus," writes Derrida in "Archive Fever," "in this *domiciliation*, in this house arrest, that archives take place."[44] Those afforded "the hermeneutic right," he argues, can only be undermined if their inventory should come alive again, if, that is – and he articulates the scenario without conviction in its plausibility – "the *arkhē* appears in the nude, without archive. It presents itself and comments on itself by itself."[45] Derrida makes a shift to archeological terms to follow Freud, the opening of whose house-museum in 1994 provided the occasion for "Archive Fever." Freud, writes Derrida, wrote of archives and psychoanalysis as "scenes of excavation":

> Each time he [Freud] wants to teach the typology of the archives, that is to say, of what ought to exclude or forbid the return to the origin, this lover of stone figurines proposes archaeological parables. The most remarkable and the most precocious of them is well known, in the study of hysteria of 1896. We must once again underline a few words in this work to mark what is to my eyes the most acute moment. A moment and not a process, this instant does not belong to the laborious deciphering of the archive. It is the nearly ecstatic instant Freud dreams of, when the very success of the dig must sign the effacement of the archivist: *the origin then speaks by itself.* The *arkhē* appears in the nude, without archive. It presents itself and comments on itself by itself. "Stones talk!"[46]

Of course, to *be* stone, or to be as stone, implies that a shift already has taken place: becoming inventory means passing into an ossified state from a prior, more dynamic one; this is the process potentially reversed *in a moment* in the dream of archaeological success. And this becoming-inventory means transforming from a prior state in which various qualities exist and matter, into being a part of someone's collection, where the aspect of belonging takes over as the defining feature. "It is," wrote Benjamin, "the deepest enchantment of the collector to enclose the particular item within a magic circle, where, as a last shudder runs through it (the shudder of being acquired), it turns to stone."[47] For stones to speak would require a second shudder, stones becoming flesh once again, breaking free of the magic circle of acquisition and control.

This dream of eschewing archival structures that mediate objects of memory or collection might be transferred from its psychoanalytic context and resituated within a more general context of one's relationship to the past. What if ruins might reconstitute themselves, as Freud fantasizes, the rubble regenerating into lost palaces and columns, "halles and bowers, / castels and towers"? What if women, become objects of study, even stone – Lot's Wife, examined, in Chapter 4, in her calcified backward twist – should speak *through* the interpretive frameworks in which they are penned, endeavoring to escape such mediation? We stumble upon two related problems. First, the speaking stones that would efface the archivist still require, according to the logic articulated above, archeologists, geologists, and workers to "interpret" and "translate" their encoded meanings in order to restore, reconstitute, and recreate their former identity. A "laborious deciphering" can only ever be replaced by a slightly less laborious deciphering; the "ecstatic instant" remains a dream. It is a commonplace that the past exists only through mediation, and thus that "history" refers both to the past and to that genre of mediation. Likewise, there are no mythic characters without mythmakers: no Noah's Wife to say something different when she steps back onto dry land, and no Lot's Wife ever to return to flesh. And then, for Uxor, a second prison exists beyond this ontological one. Returning to the dilemmas articulated by Jacobus, Gilbert, and Gubar, and moving into the fictive frame of the myth itself, how is Noah's Wife to employ language within her suddenly circumscribed world? How is she, as woman, the half of the human pair denied an ark of the heart and thus resources with which to shape the arc of structuring narratives, to speak from within the patriarchal prison of the ship? If a mythic, prepatriarchal language, long since abandoned on the antediluvian "rok," proves useless, and patriarchal discourse threatens to re-inscribe oppression, how can Noah's Wife speak within the reality of her textual world, let alone through to another?

One way of envisioning the continuation of Uxor's narrative contribution is to think of her as speaking where the logic of the performance places her: on the threshold, the line where ship gives way to water. The flood narrative emphasizes the idea of boundaries: the saved and the drowned, the ark and the sea, the stage and the watching crowd. This is how some earlier feminist critics characterize the possibilities of women's writing, in which transgressive differences are "played out within language, across boundaries."[48] It is the transgressed and transgressable boundary that is the object of Uxor's desire: a rift that does not sink the ark, a miracle that offers salvation *and* authority, life *and* speech. A permeable boundary would seem to be the ideal, one without bars or locks, or a ship that lets in more of the world and yet does not sink. This is the desire that Virginia Woolf describes in reverse, contemplating the situation of the professional woman writer in the early twentieth century: "I thought," she wrote, chased off the lawns at Oxford and denied entrance to the library, "how unpleasant it is to be locked out; and I thought how it is worse perhaps to be locked in."[49]

But we must also assume that a permeable boundary is the state of affairs against which Noah must struggle. There would be no need for the violent establishment of the boundary line were the categories of saved and damned easily identified and relegated into separate groups, and no need for the insistent confirmation and reassertion of that boundary were it not continually threatened with transgression, if the rest of the world did not threaten always to seep onto the ark and into the story. Uxor mourns her drowned gossips, conjuring them back from beneath the sea. Medieval iconography includes the corpses drifting up beneath the hull, brushing against the wood, visible to those on the ship deck. The drowned are always present, in one way or another, and it is these always present whom Noah must work continually to exclude and re-exclude, to forget again and again.

Noah's Wife, safely aboard the ship but speaking of the dead – perhaps standing at the very edge of the medieval stage – becomes a symbol for this boundary-dissolving mode of writing. But importantly, she does not pose as the mother of an alternative history, the woman at the root of an exclusively women's literary canon, or a figure who might have had, as "hende Nicholas" jokingly suggests, an ark of her own. Placing her at the center of this project would risk the errors Toril Moi, writing not quite ten years after *The Madwoman in the Attic*, ascribes to Gubar and Gilbert's work. Moi distills the essence of Gubar and Gilbert's formulation of "alternatives to the authority" of a patriarchal literary tradition as essentially suggestions for a new tradition formed from old elements, a women's canon still founded on humanist and thus patriarchal values. Such an interpretive model, suggests Moi, locates "the woman writer as the *meaning* of the texts studied," thereby mimicking a patriarchal literary tradition, one not far from the myth of "fathered" texts examined in the previous chapter, where both text and hero might be called *Brut*.[50]

I do not then argue for positioning Noah's Wife as an ur-woman who generates a mode of narrative, a canon entangled in biology like the chronicles clustered around the seafaring Brutus. We might understand her, rather, as a sign of possibility, a woman on top, or at the edge, whose eventual correction does not erase her ghostly presence and transgressive position; she laments the existence of the boundary while standing on it herself. Her marginality, to follow Moi, means that she is neither quite inside nor quite outside. She disturbs the all-important hierarchy, the careful architecture, the rows of divided stalls, and perhaps even eludes the narrative net after all. The properties of ambiguity and illegibility ascribed to women within the context of the patriarchal order find resonance in the story of the flood, especially in the performances that represent Noah's Wife as shoehorned into a specific place (stall, category) in her husband's archive and in his account of history. At Chester, Noah's Wife is assigned a place in the ark ("Wyffe, come in ...") to neutralize her unknowableness, to retrieve her from a chaos whose most frightening quality is its illegibility; Noah attempts to recreate her as a category that might be inventoried so that the illegibility she harbors can be erased.

This is how the flood plays also might find relevance within the new trajectories gender studies has taken since the modes of inquiry mentioned here: the medieval performances not only dramatize the denial of a woman's narrative voice, they perform the reification of the category "woman," an identity that supplants and effaces the potential for a subject to have a less easily categorized identity, to be, in the term crucial to feminism since at least Simone de Beauvoir, always "becoming."[51] Tara Williams has written about late medieval attempts to explore "what it meant to be a woman," especially after new, postplague economic opportunities began to emerge, bringing new questions: what *is* a "woman" when she cannot be identified as virgin, wife, or widow, or when those designations are unclear? What is "woman-hood," when it is not an entity contextualized by relationships with men?[52] The term was used widely during the later medieval period,[53] during the centuries when Noah's Wife (played by a man) was forced into the ark and made into a creature that might be archived, recreated as a category exemplar in the inception of a newly static, codified taxonomy. The continual attempts to pull Uxor back from the boundary – the place from which she hesitates to embark and afterwards from which she watches the sea – are efforts to situate her as a knowable entity inside the world of the ark. Her transformation from human to memory-object is also a transformation from that which cannot be archived to that which is tamed into legibility and catalogued neatly within.

The fact that this transformation is staged offers the crucial caveat. Because the performances of the flood dramatize the codification of hierarchies – the reification of gender identities and inequalities already afoot in the scriptural drama being played out – they implicitly unsettle the perception of such divisions as natural. They stage, moreover, a heavily protested loss of a woman's right to remember and to narrate with authority. The plays represent the transformation of Noah's Wife neither as necessarily natural nor as matter-of-course; in fact, we might think of ourselves as invited to view it as part of the universal catastrophe they perform. The destabilizing potential of performance challenges the con-ception of an archive that operates as a site of house arrest. Staging the flood presents an opportunity for medieval writers, players, and audiences to critique Noah's archive and to participate in its re-creation as a more fluid site of mediation between past, present, and future. Elizabeth Grosz has suggested that we think of history as being about "the production of *conceivable futures*," futures that do not simply follow from the present in which the order of the past remains latent, but that have the potential to unfurl otherwise, unrestricted by that order.[54] The flood plays perform this continually ongoing production of possible futures, representing how the interconnectedness of repetition and transformation shake loose a static inventory, offering up voices that, year after year across this unwinding and ephemeral present, protest the rigid cataloguing of a penned-in menagerie.

2   Uxor's Co-Mothers

To close this chapter, I want to turn briefly to other stories, names, and bodies not quite erased by the flood. Their mentions are short, fragmentary, and enigmatic. The first example returns us to the genre of history writing, with which this chapters-long exploration of the ark as archive began. In *The History and Topography of Ireland*, written toward the end of the twelfth century in the service of Henry II, Gerald of Wales tells the story of Cesara, Noah's granddaughter, born before the flood:

> According to the most ancient stories of the Irish, Cesara, the granddaughter of Noah, hearing that the Flood was about to take place, decided to flee in a boat with her companions to the farthest islands of the West, where no man had ever yet lived ... All the ships in her company were wrecked. Her ship alone, carrying three men and fifty women, survived. It put in at the Irish coast, by chance, one year before the Flood.
>
> All the same, in spite of her cleverness, and, for a woman, commendable astuteness in seeking to avoid evil, she did not succeed in putting off the general, not to say universal, disaster.
>
> ... But since almost all things were destroyed in the Flood, one may reasonably have doubts as to the value of the account of these arrivals and events that has been handed down after the Flood. Let those, however, who first wrote these accounts be responsible. My function is to outline, not to attack, such stories. Perhaps, as in the case of the invention of music before the Flood, *a narrative of these things had been inscribed on some material, stone or tile, which was later found and preserved.*[55]

Gerald visualizes an extraordinary scene: a world covered by water, a smooth, glassy surface interrupted only by the ark and *possibly* by inscribed debris, pieces of wreckage *possibly* narrating the otherwise lost story of Cesara, allowed to last like music.

This is a vision of alternative history: narrative that escapes submersion and voices that outlast the flood. The story of the antediluvian pillars, found in the *Polychronicon* and the apocryphal lives of Adam and Eve, lacks the ever-present, instructing deity so essential to the construction of the biblical ark; there is no heavenly message divinely micromanaging the cubic dimensions of each tower. Cesara's story takes this independence to a new level, almost to one of defiance; she attempts to sail her thirty ships beyond a realm structured by salvation history, to avoid the fate of her antediluvian community and to preserve an alternative history separate from official record. This history, however, remains just as lost as those sunk definitively in the flood. The existence of Cesara's inscribed tablets remains unconfirmed, only dreamed of, and its contents are inconceivable. We cannot know what a history that does not adhere to Noah's looks like; we can only recognize the desire for one. Gerald's own meta-commentary regarding his historiographical task suggests a desire for inclusion without interpretation: "Let those, however, who first wrote these accounts be responsible. My function is to outline, not to attack, such stories."

Such stories reveal curiosity about lost narrative trajectories. In his essay on utopia and medieval cartography, Daniel Birkholz considers the signs of desire for difference, proposing that the twisting pillar of Lot's Wife on the Hereford map functions as a "monogram of a possible alternative history," inviting us to imagine "the world another way."[56] She is a sign of choosing otherwise, Birkholz suggests, or of looking in a different and unsanctioned way, and in this he explicitly links her to Uxor Noe, also visible on the map.[57] In the flood plays, Uxor works as a portal to the many histories lost; she becomes not just a discordant voice that the plot of each play silences, but a persistent sign, the first in a chain of remembering. If Noah is invested with the official task of recording, then Uxor subversively commemorates.[58] Other bodies participate in this chain, or in the web of memory set in motion by a single backward glance, a single question, posed at York: "But Noye, wher are nowe all oure kynne / And companye we knewe before?" [But Noah, where are now all our kin, and the company we knew before?] (ll.269–70). Husband might rebuke or correct his wife's mention of the dead, chastising her fixation on the water and even insisting on her silence ("Dame, all ar drowned – / late be thy dyne" [Dame, all are drowned, let be your din]), but in each instance this pattern of appeal and reproach casts even more attention onto those meant to be forgotten (l.270). The dead continually brought up (brought forward, brought stage-center) to be punished with oblivion render that punishment ineffectual, and those left behind in the antediluvian world re-form a ghostly chorus in front of the watching medieval crowds.

   Noah's Wife mourns for her lost companions out of sorrow and compassion, but also as a way to ward off the forgetting her husband's ark
would accomplish. "My frendis that I fra yoode / are ouere flowen with
floode," she laments and reminds in the York play [my friends that I went
from are flooded over with the sea] (ll.151–2). Uxor's curiosity about her
drowned community – those whose inclusion necessarily would have
nuanced Noah's archival account – has the immediate result of leading
to a further streamlining of that account ("late be thy dyne"). The flood
narrative, however, requires the troublesome presence of this lost community, the always just-recently-lost, in order to make sense. Memory of the
dead might derail the project of the ark, that is, the creation of a new,
iniquity-free world to which Noah's archive will bequeath an equally new
past. But the story, as textual, dramatic, and iconographic representations
suggest, has less coherence and power without it.
   In *Cities of the Dead*, Roach writes that gossip often is the best "hedge
against amnesia,"[59] and the flood plays, as if in response to the massive
performance of forgetting they enact, have actual personifications of gossip
march forth to hamper the spread of oblivion. The Good Gossips, filling
the sea around the ark like Cesara's scattered tiles, emerge as caveats to
Noah's authoritative record. They are mentioned by Noah's Wife in the
Chester and York plays, where she requests berths or mourns the lack of
them for her gossips, cousins, and "co-mothers," and in Chester, they
actually parade across the stage. In York, defeated, Uxor admits ruefully to
Noah: "My commodrys and my cosynes bathe, / Tham wolde I wente with
vs in feere" [Both my co-mothers and my cousins, I would that they went
in together with us] (ll.143–4). In the Chester play, she protests their
exclusion more spiritedly:

> But I have my gossips everyechone,
> one foote further I will not gone.
> They shall not drowne, by sayncte John,
> and I may save there life.
> The loved me full well, by Christe.
> But thou wilte lett them into thy chiste,
> elles rowe forthe, Noe, when thy liste
> and gett thee a newe wyfe.   (ll.201–8)

> Unless I have my gossips, each one, I will not go one foot further. They shall
> not drown, by Saint John, if I might save their life. They loved me full well,
> by Christ. Unless you let them into your chest/ ark, row forth, Noah,
> when you like, and get yourself a new wife.

Uxor, of course, is too important to release to the flood; her presence is required to form the balanced family, leader-husband and obedient wife, meant to structure the rest of human relations, and even, as Kolve suggests, the cosmos. The ark has room for a "converted" wife, but no space for the gossips who must find room in the sea and in the unofficial and unsanctioned space of Uxor's "arca cordis," her own "chiste," or the ark of her heart. When the soon-to-be-drowned women speak in Chester, they, like Noah's Wife, appear as multivalent figures; they are both raucous, purportedly confirming the justice of the cataclysmic weather, and afraid, eliciting, perhaps, compassion or a sense of the familiar from the sea of spectators crowded beyond the salvific space of the ark/stage:

THE GOOD GOSSIPS: The fludd comes fleetinge in full faste,
one everye syde that spredeth full farre.
For fere of drowninge I am agaste;
good gossippe, lett us drawe nere.

And lett us drinke or wee departe,
for oftetymes wee have done soe.
For at one draught thou drinke a quarte,
and soe will I doe or I goe.   (ll.225–32)

The flood comes fleeting in fast, on every side that spreads so far.
For fear of drowning, I am aghast; good gossips, let us draw close.

And let us drink before we depart, for often times we have done so.
For with one draught you drink a quart, and so will I, before I go.

The drowned members of Uxor's community, drinking and reveling en route to the sea floor, appear, even more so than the long dead chosen family, as ghosts: unsaved but not forgotten, unsinkable glitches in Noah's archival project and in the performance of salvation. This spectral realm beyond the borders of sanctioned history – the sea of specters and spectators that the flood plays create – has lasting power similar to the antediluvian pillars or Noah's archive. Even after the dove returns with the olive branch, plucked somewhere from new dry land, a sense lingers that the world-sea, strewn with corpses and Cesara's lost tiles, lasts, like the Ararat-docked ark, forever. And unlike the patriarch's architectural masterpiece, constructed obediently from divine plans, the sea roils with possibility, unfinished stories, contradiction, chaos, illegibility, subversion. Among the bodies and alternative histories, it holds, perhaps, an apparition of Eve, in the water where Adam, in the apocryphal lives, once commanded her to stand, with the Tigris up to her chin and her hair "spredde abrod" on the surface, so that she too might experience a flood, be baptized *avant la lettre*, silenced ("of þy mouth let no word reke" [from your mouth let no word issue]).[60] We might imagine this ghost, too, as crowding into the ocean of time Uxor still commemorates as she speaks through the medium of modern poetry, acknowledging Hugh of Saint Victor's description of the sea within and claiming once and for all that she, too, has an "arca cordis," filled with desire and memory:

> I can't sit still these days. The ocean
> is only memory, and my memory as fluttery
> as a lost dove. Now the real sea beats
> inside me.[61]

CHAPTER 4

Infernal Archive

After beginning with an ending in the form of Judgment Day, and then moving chronologically through episodes of sacred history, from divine creation through fall and flood, this book finishes with two chapters on the Harrowing of Hell, an event associated more with its function as a central pivot – a hinging moment in a narrative middle – than with any kind of salvific finality. There are several reasons for this, beyond, admittedly, a vague reluctance to feel one's own research ushered along by the aggressive momentum of sacred history. First of all, the archive resists an ending, or, rather, the ending of the archive – its completion, fulfillment, and final wholeness – signals the end of history. Such completion opens onto an eternity that obviates the need for inventory, appraisal, or organization; even the fever for origins subsides, as all times are one. One might say that time has ended, and without time, we are without either need or capacity for the archive. The complete inventory of Judgment Day, with which this book began, offers a limit case; this is the moment of full accounting before all records and worlds dissolve into something else, a new heaven and earth, and the end of time as we know it.

The episode of the Harrowing of Hell, however, is weighted with time. It almost seems to have too much of it, and part of Christ's salvific work, I argue, is to disentangle and set into a clear hierarchy the temporalities competing for value in the vexed space between hell and earth. This is salvific *work*, an endeavor toward prophetic fulfillment, and not full salvation itself. The Harrowing is situated still in the messy middle of things, balanced between a look backward toward the beginning of time, variously anxious and yearning, and the anticipation of the culmination of time. In the *mean*time, or in that middle time, attempts to narrate and perform this central episode can be understood to comment on the struggle to assemble history and then look back at it without being temporally overwhelmed. The Harrowing presents a continual chronological push and pull, the effort to move toward the end of a story and the need to look backward as that culmination looms, and to draw a specific authorizing past forward into the future.

The chapter on the earthly paradise investigated desires bound up with the fever for origins, and the chapters on the ark concentrated on issues of inventory selection and narrative authority. These chapters on hell turn on the problem of archival access and the temporal complexities understood to inhere in recording the past and then revisiting that record. They ask how one opens the archive without being toppled by it, or without sensing the importance of one's own historical present becoming superseded by the always-increasing material and narrative bulk of the past. To address these questions, I turn to stories of infernal descent, centrally though not exclusively those concerning the Harrowing of Hell, and investigate how representations of that underground space comment upon imagined access to the past and the dangers that attend such chronologically disruptive contact.

Such underground space – whether termed hell, the under- or otherworld – consistently is equated with the past and figured as a realm of capacious, almost overflowing history. For while representations of Noah's archive emphasize tragic undercurrents of selection and exclusion, looking into the classical otherworld or medieval hell, at least up until a specific moment in Christian sacred history, reveals a realm into which *everything* eventually descends, into death and into record, accumulating as the centuries pass. There resides the entire past, shades from every century, sometimes organized in exacting circles, sometimes jumbled, and sometimes trying to get out. The desire associated with such infernal inventory thus has a different trajectory than that attending the inventory Noah compiles; infernal inventory yearns for escape, not for the kind of salvific collection afforded by the ark.

And, as we will see, infernal escape occurs. Hell frequently is exposed as having problematic leaks out of which its records seep. In some images of the Harrowing, hell is depicted as a kind of architectural vault – several plays refer to it as a "logge" – intimating a storage space much like representations of the ark, but also with the features of a formidable fortress; the infernal threshold takes form as a kind of grand entranceway, with armed guards at the ramparts (see Figure 3). But even with this imposing architecture, the inventory of hell still manages escape; the architectural threshold frames Christ pulling Adam and Eve through a collapsing doorway, flaunting the weakness of such stately, ineffective fortifications. "Helle logge," announces Abraham in part two of the N-Town Harrowing, "lyth vnlokyn" (l.39). Whether represented as majestic, crumbling gates or merely as a burning gap in the surface of the earth, hell "logge" struggles to maintain that which it

Figure 3. The *Harrowing of Hell.* From the *De Lisle Hours.* England, 1316–1331, MS G.50, fol. 080 r, at the Morgan Library.

houses, especially when those in the present (Christ, reaching for Adam) gaze back into it.

As other examples will demonstrate, cosmic voyagers frequently put pressure on the borders between hell and earth, and the permeable condition of these borders spreads beyond that singular, central moment of the Harrowing. The porous nature of the partition between hell and earth suggests not only the redemptive power of Christ, who can overturn the crises of history, but also the tendency for cosmic realms consistently to intrude upon one another, and for their associated temporalities to interpenetrate. Geographic breaches between hell and earth, whether taking form as stately, yet broken doors, holes in the terrestrial crust, a gaping infernal maw, or secret portals adorned with breakable locks, indicate the difficulty of containing the ever growing past and of relegating it as separate – geographically, chronologically, ontologically – from the present.

The growing importance of purgatory, moreover, whose status as a "third place" the church made doctrine in the thirteenth century, also weakens the physical borders of a punishing otherworld by softening perceptions of perpetual damnation; the introduction of a realm of suffering from which the dead eventually might depart alters understandings of both time and cosmic geography.[1] This in-between realm, whose very design encourages movement and solicits intervention from both heaven and earth, prevents one from thinking of the past as over and done with, or as definitively sealed off. Instead, embodied by the shades that wait and work in a vast purgatorial in-between, the past continually shifts, as parts of it are remembered or absolved. Despite the doctrine that attempted to clarify ideas of purgatory, long-standing geographic and conceptual confusion about the nature of perpetual and temporary punishment persisted in the medieval period;[2] this confusion sometimes made it seem as though one could languish in purgatory as in hell, and emerge eventually from either.

In the first part of this chapter, I examine the episode of the Harrowing of Hell through its various versions in Middle English poetry; I then move on to other narratives explicitly describing infernal descent or more obliquely evoking it, in genres ranging from romance and visionary poetry to biblical paraphrase, in order to sketch out more broadly the verbose and crowded nature of the medieval underworld and the permeability of the partition between that world and earth. Chapter 5 then will investigate the episode of the Harrowing as it takes form in the mystery plays. That said, it is difficult fully to divide poetic and performance versions of the

Harrowing, in part because it is not always clear from textual records which works were performed or thought of as suitable for different kinds of performance. A poetic Middle English version of the Harrowing – the Middle English *Harrowing of Hell* – sometimes assigns parts to speakers, for instance, but there remains uncertainty about what kind of performance tradition it might have belonged to.[3] Rather than making strong claims about how to go about separating these works according to their form and function – rather, that is, than making the argument about whether a work is a play or a poem – I instead want to focus on the different strategies for accessing and regulating the past that might be discerned in the texts and performance records that we have, including those we think might have been associated with actual productions.

Harrowing episodes situated in long Middle English poetic translations of the *Gospel of Nicodemus*, or the standalone *Harrowing of Hell*, both a poem and apparently a dramatic dialogue, reveal poetic strategies for corralling and taming the particular past that they conjure forth. This chapter considers those strategies, as well as the moments in which they are shown to falter. I look at how narrative framing, ostentatious revision, and syntax intimate the ways in which infernal inventories – the voices and bodies of the past – variously are enclosed, willingly released, or lost. When, in Chapter 5, I turn to the mystery plays of the Harrowing, which belong to the same performance tradition as the plays of the fall and flood, I investigate how the medium of performance and the resources of medieval staging additionally complicate this endeavor to summon forth a usable past in a manner that does not overwhelm the present.

1 The Harrowing of Hell

Much of the basic plot of the Harrowing of Hell is concise enough to fit within the Apostle's creed, where it is initiated and concluded within the space of nine words: "Credo ... descendit ad inferos, tertia die resurrexit a mortuis" [I believe [Christ] descended into hell, [and] rose from death on the third day]. But the feat of descent accumulates a number of important additional details as it passes through the centuries, and a more full-bodied narrative takes shape around the handful of allusions to descent and underground shadows thought of as encoded in the Vulgate, the great source text which in fact offers an even vaguer notion of Christ's Harrowing than it does of hell itself. According to the logic of Christian sacred history, before the Harrowing of Hell, an infernal collection grows in steady proportion to death in the world above. The fall of Adam and Eve prevents human access to paradise, both terrestrial and celestial, and so the infernal cavern, created by the fall of Lucifer, begins to fill. This great underground gradually compiles a complete record of earth's erstwhile population, just as classical models of the underworld collect the dead.[4] And though some parts of hell are more comfortable than others, again as in classical models, all of the dead, even those apparently in the "bosom of Abraham," are denied the kind of joy proximity to God affords.

The event of the Harrowing changes that. When he breaks down the gates of hell and wins the debate with Satan (or, in some poetry, Satan and Lucifer) over who has better rights to the dead,[5] Christ not only liberates the patriarchs and prophets imprisoned there, but also opens up new possibilities for all of humankind who will die between that moment and Judgment Day. Virgil describes the event and its consequences to Dante in the fourth canto of the *Inferno*, one of the most famous medieval poems of infernal descent, adding that he, Virgil, also belongs to those unfortunate shades who lived before Christ and thus before the possibility of salvation.[6] Right after he took up residence among the other poets in limbo, Virgil explains, a momentous change occurred:

> "... I beheld a Great Lord enter here;
> the crown he wore, a sign of victory.
>   He carried off the shade of our first father,
> of his son Abel, and the shade of Noah,
> of Moses, the obedient legislator,
>   of father Abraham, David the king,
> of Israel, his father, and his sons,
> and Rachel, she for whom he worked so long,
>   and many others – and He made them blessed;
> and I should have you know that, before them,
> there were no human souls that had been saved."   (4.53–63)[7]

Virgil offers an eyewitness account of the Harrowing that saves certain souls; the rest of the poem makes it clear that after that moment of select redemption, hell continues to function as a repository for unrepentant sinners. However, those who, like Dante and unlike Virgil, are born *after* this pivotal episode of descent and redemption might hope to find space in paradise or purgatory. Dante figures the latter realm as a terraced mountain around whose winding paths the shades slowly climb, their gradual progress indicating a crucial difference from the stasis of hell, which imprisons the dead perpetually within its circles of punishment.

The Harrowing finds its most important source in the *Gospel of Nicodemus*, whose Latin translation dates from the fifth century.[8] Though widespread and well known during the medieval period, the episode, unlike the fall and the flood, is not canonized as a component of official scripture. It is an interesting difference, especially since one of the meanings this episode offers has to do with the instability of the past, and the idea that even written history might be made to shift around. The extrabiblical episode, which gets translated and transformed across multiple centuries and through numerous vernaculars and media, supplies the crucial pivot point for sacred history, opening up new possibilities for the Christian afterlife. In late medieval English and earlier iterations, the story's key elements are as follows: the crucified Christ rises from his grave and descends to the underworld, calling "attollite portas" [lift up your gates], a line lifted from the twenty-third psalm. He argues with Satan over a set population of the dead, crucially including Adam, Eve, Moses, Isaiah, David, Jacob, and Rachel, and implicitly the other worthy patriarchs, wives, and prophets of the Hebrew Scriptures, as well as John the Baptist. The prophets joyfully confirm Christ's presence as the fulfillment of their own scriptural prophecies and fall down on their knees to worship him. Then Christ takes Adam by the hand or, in much of the iconography, by the wrist. According to a fifteenth-century, Middle English poetic version of *The Gospel of Nicodemus*:

> By þe hand our lord has Adam hent,
> with Michael he bad him ga;
> þai toke þe way with gud entent
> vntyll Paradyse full thra.
> Michael resayued þam sone
> þat war to him bikend,
> In blys he has þam done
> þat lastes withouten end.[9]

> By the hand our lord has taken Adam, with Michael he bade him go; they took the way with good intention, all the way to Paradise. Michael received them right away, those that were promised to him. He has taken them to a bliss that lasts without end.

The major figures of the Hebrew Scriptures, refigured as the Old Testament by supercessionary, typological practice, at last are admitted to paradise. Chaperoned by the archangel Michael, they leave their savior behind on earth, in some versions for as long as forty days, a wait that parallels his sojourn in the wilderness.

Medieval poetry, visual art, and the mystery plays revel in these elements of the Harrowing: the broken gates; Christ and Satan shouting questions and answers across the cavernous wastes of hell; the prophets' verbal confirmation of fulfillment; and Adam's hand in Christ's, the linking of testaments and the blurring of temporalities as the one pulls the other across the threshold dividing hell and earth, past and present, and across religious narrative traditions.[10] These engagements with Christian sacred history celebrate the pivotal event of descent and redemption, its suggestion of mercy, its depiction of triumph, and its poetic balance. The symmetrical perfection of the poetic economy takes form as an assurance that the descent and redemption occur exactly as they should. "Qui per lignum et diabolum et mortem damnati fuistis, modo uidete per lignum damnatum diabolum et mortem," narrates a Latin *Nicodemus*, describing the neat reversal that vernacular translations and other poetry will poetically delight in.[11] The tree that connects transgression and the cross will take form, in the liturgies and the mystery plays, as the staff with which Christ bangs on the doors of hell when he demands access to the infernal collection of the dead. His presence, armed outside the soon-to-be-crashed gates, becomes a mechanism of reversal, tricking Satan, who long ago tricked Adam and Eve in the garden. In versions of *Nicodemus* and in the Middle English plays of the Harrowing, the prophets and patriarchs offer recitations and new exegesis of the Old Law with which they are associated, affirming that their liberation by Christ has been foretold by their own prophetic writings and lauding the descent of the redeemer and the reversal he initiates: "laus tibi cum Gloria" [Praise be to you, with glory], sings Adam at the close of the York play.

Just as frequently as the fortified, turreted threshold, a pair of monstrous jaws frames the infernal portal through which Christ passes, widening as he leads the patriarchs, prophets, and many others ("e altri molti," in Dante's words) out of the inferno. The iconographic tradition suggests a number of things that will be important to this chapter and the next. Like the broken door, the open mouth implies that the partition between hell and earth is permeable; the mouth becomes a breach, opening wide to permit movement in either direction; the lost go in, and the saved come out. This fanged rupture between hell and earth invites the viewer to think of time in spatial terms. To be drawn or swallowed into hell is to be relegated to historical record, to the past; to emerge from hell is to undergo a different temporal transition by crossing physically from one realm into another: to move, in the manner of ghosts, from an underground past into an above-ground, ephemeral present. This possibility of resurrection, redemption, or infernal escape presented by the Harrowing unsettles the idea of the static past and the security of historical record. If an infernal inventory can shift around, be lost, or redeemed (rejudged, reconsidered), then the past cannot be held in place: it is spoken out anew, and perhaps differently, between the parted teeth.

How, then, do we know what is past? If Christ can descend into hell, in which the voices of the Old Testament prophets, long dead, still resound, then it would seem that the "past" cannot be separated definitively from the present. Not only confusion, but also a certain ethical slipperiness inheres in the idea of the past as I am using it to describe that which Christ releases from the infernal archive. This is because the idea of "pastness" works on several levels. The texts with which the Old Testament patriarchs and prophets are associated predate the gospels by almost a millennium, but the episode of the Harrowing of Hell also endeavors to depict Jewishness and Judaism, the cultural and religious traditions associated with those texts, as finished. When Christ fulfills the prophecies of those in hell, an act that includes the redemption of their souls, he ushers their narrative toward closure. Older scripture is represented as finished, not because the patriarchs and prophets are in hell, but because they are *let out*, their prophecies completed and their resurrected bodies spirited away to the silent eternity of heaven. The Old Testament is represented as encountering its own completion and obsolescence at the moment of Christ's act of redemption. In this way, Judaism, too, becomes relegated to a hermetically sealed and superseded past, a phase of history that has ended.[12] Kathleen Biddick describes this medieval Christian "temporal logic" as dividing a "Jewish 'that was then' from a Christian 'this is now,'" a schema that reduces understandings of temporality into the reductive "binary of past and present."[13] Such an interpretive maneuver, she suggests, worked to deny historicity, and thus the promise of futurity, to medieval Jews.[14] They have only a past, and it is firmly concluded. They *are* past.

I turn to a fuller exploration of how the Harrowing of Hell uses supercessionary typology to frame the relationship between these two religious traditions in Chapter 5, but I want to clarify here that, by examining representations of past and present in various versions of the episode, I do not want to perpetuate the reductive temporality that Biddick describes. Rather, I want to examine the representation of that reductive temporality in the Harrowing and to show how a focus on repetition and time, in both poetry and performance, foregrounds its insufficiency by complicating the relationship between past and present. I will continue to use the word "past" because that is how the patriarchs and prophets are represented in the Harrowing, as belonging to another, almost or about to be superseded time. But at its root, the story of the Harrowing of Hell suggests the impossibility of sealing that past off from the present and the anticipated future in any lasting or meaningful way.

Versions of the Harrowing present this always-imperfect attempt to seal off one time or space from another in a variety of ways. They emphasize ideas of uneasy confinement in geographic, temporal, and narrative terms, as well as both a desire for and an anxiety about possibilities of infernal escape. A vocabulary of locking and unlocking, binding and rupture, breaking loose from and maintaining contracts permeates the plays and poetry. All three closely related versions of the Middle English *Harrowing of Hell* consistently employ the language of imprisonment, in which the corralling of physical space and the binding of bodies happens in two stages.[15] First, Satan keeps all of the prominent Old Testament figures infernally imprisoned, and then, upon their release, Christ in turn binds Satan. When the prince of hell seeks to prevent the loss of his most valuable souls, he protests, in the Auchinleck manuscript, that he is meant to "haue & hald" them forever:

> "Par ma fay! ich hald mine
> al þat ben hereinne;
> wiþ resoun wil y telle þe
> Þat þer ogain may þou nouȝt be,
> Þat me bihoueþ haue & hald
> & wiþouten ende wald"[16]

> By my faith, I hold as mine all those who are in here; I will explain to you with reason, and you cannot be against it; it falls to me to have and hold and to rule over them without end.

Satan repeats the sentiment a few lines later: "lat me haue þat ich halde" [Let me have what I hold] (l.111), doubling up his verbs of maintaining as if to ensure his capacity to keep the dead. But the Harrowing inevitably permits that privileged segment of Satan's population to escape, while he in turn is secured in place, even more tightly: "so fast schal y binde þe" [I shall bind you fast] Christ threatens him (l.133). And once past the broken gates, Christ does just that, announcing: "fare þou seþþen whare þou may, / fare þou seþþen ware þou fare [fare from now on where you may; fare from now on where you fare] (ll.154–5). Even the verses describing Satan's new restriction twist back upon themselves, fastening down words that otherwise indicate roaming. Satan will "fare" nowhere at all; he will "fare" where he "fares" and "haue" what he has: right here, in a new stillness where even language coils back upon itself, seþþen and forever. Such infernal binding, locking, and holding also takes form as a "holding off," a dynamic in which the confinement of bodies corresponds to territorial restriction. In the same poem, when explaining his rights to the dead, whom he believes are contractually given to him to keep, Satan articulates a desire to keep the realms and populations of hell and earth strictly separate. He says to Christ: "heuen & erþe weld þou þe, / þe soules in helle lat þou be" [Heaven and earth you take charge of; let the souls in hell be] (ll.81–3). Satan wants to divide hell and earth along with their populations, and he asks that there be no confusion about where one kingdom ends and the other begins.

The *Gospel of Nicodemus* also indicates a desire to keep these realms clearly divided, but here the desire is not only articulated by Satan, but also enacted through the structure of the narrative. Instead of physical chains, the *Gospel* creates a narrative frame to partition hell from earth, and to hold in place, paradoxically, the very souls who are released. A narrative frame literally circumscribes what otherwise threatens to emerge as uncontrollable history, reinforcing the geographical borders of hell with a formal device and locking in place the older story with which the redeemed Old Testament figures are associated. The strategy works as an attempt to contain what goes on underground and to neutralize the intensity of infernal narrative when eventually it gains an earthly audience.

In the *Gospel of Nicodemus*, the event of the Harrowing filters through the testimony of two witnesses, the brothers Carinus and Leucius, sons of Simeon, the man who receives Christ in the temple in the Gospel of Luke (2:25). Carinus and Leucius, whose redemption Christ secures, remain on earth after the Harrowing in order to describe and then write down the miraculous event they have witnessed. The *Gospel* thus describes the process of its own inscription, shifting the audience away from hell itself and its celebrated Old Testament speakers – men such as King David, who composes and sings, and Isaiah, who prophesizes – by foregrounding two new narrators in the form of Simeon's sons. The brothers' testimony frames the events that occur in hell: listeners inside the text, gathered around the brothers, and readers *of* the text are held off from the infernal site of action; both groups are made dependent upon the words of Carinus and Leucius. The brothers provide the details of the descent and redemption to a small gathering of witnesses, in front of whom they also write their experiences down on parchment. In a Middle English translation of *Nicodemus*, the brothers request their writing materials:

> "Lordynges," þai said withouten lyte,
> "'Tak vs parchemyn & pen;
> þe preuetese we sall yhow wryte
> þat we for sothfast ken."   (ll.1153–6)

"Lords," they said without pause, "get us parchment and pen. These secrets we shall write for you, the ones that we truthfully know."

At the end of their account, having related the speeches of the patriarchs and prophets, the debate between Christ and Satan, and the ascension of the redeemed, the brothers conclude their testimony:

> Þat Caryn wrate he it bitoke
> Till Nichodeme and Annas,
> And Lentyn allso gaf his boke
> Tyll Ioseph and tyll Cayphas;
> Togyder þan þai gan þam luke
> þat serely wryten was,
> And þat one wrate noght a letter note,
> Bot euen als þat other has.
> when þe Iewes had of þam tane
> þa rolles þat wryten ware,
> þai vanyst oway onane,
> Of þam þai saw no mare.   (ll.1633–44)

What Caryn (Carinus) wrote, he took to Nicodemus and Annas, and Lentyn (Leucius) also gave his book to Joseph and to Caiaphas. Together, then, they began to look at them, those that individually were written, and what one wrote not a letter differed, but was just as the other one had it. When the Jews had taken from them those rolls that were written, they vanished away at once. They saw no more of them.

Each brother records the event of the Harrowing in a separate book, and Nicodemus and his small company see that the accounts coincide exactly. They receive the new text and the scribes vanish, making their delayed ascent to paradise.

The framing device of the scribal Carinus and Leucius means that the patriarchs and prophets deliver their speeches from within a double enclosure. David, Isaiah, and the others speak from within the geographic confines of hell, as well as from within the framing device of the narrating brothers. The narrative frame works to shore up the uncertain, leaky container of hell, as the voices of the redeemed are placed into a text about to become the *Gospel of Nicodemus*. The nature of this narrative transmission, in which Christ's scribes relate the familiar, prophetic speeches of David and Isaiah, enclosing their words in the new gospel written on earth, increases the control that the voices of the present are afforded over those of the past. Carinus and Leucius, narrating the new gospel to the still-living men assembled around them, introduce any number of modifications and adjustments upon the scripture the infernal prisoners recite. The words of the dead are altered both by the linguistic pressures of Middle English poetry and by the demands of the Christian project of typological, supersessionary interpretation. The process of the brothers' narration and inscription frames the words spoken by the patriarchs and prophets, and also appropriates them in a way that partially recalls Harold Bloom's description of *apophrades*, or "the return of the dead," in which later poets seem to usurp the voices that precede them. Carinus and Leucius "station the precursor," David or Isaiah, so that:

> particular passages in *his* work seem to be not presages of one's own advent, but rather to be indebted to one's own achievement, and even (necessarily) to be lessened by one's greater splendor. The mighty dead return, but they return in our colors, and speaking in our voices.[17]

Of course, the earlier prophets *also* are understood to presage the advent of Christ, but in the *Gospel of Nicodemus* and the Harrowing plays, they reannounce such prophecy from within a frame of Middle English Christian poetics, their words purportedly subsumed by its greater splendor. The brothers speak out the prophets' words, which we might imagine as sounding, deep in hell, already like a haunting echo of an original scriptural quotation. Isaiah or David speaks through the mouthpieces of Simeon's sons and the meter of our medieval poet; the prophets' voices filter through new mouths to new ends, and into a new religion. The words the brothers speak seem almost to shed their association with past texts, their initial source of authority, by gaining new traction in the gospel given to Nicodemus.

The poetry of *Nicodemus* encloses, displays, interprets, and controls the voices of its "strong poets" and precursor dead, lest, perhaps, those voices sound louder, too insistent, alluring, or hauntingly familiar. The aggressive vocabulary of confinement in the poetic *Harrowing of Hell* and the strategic device of the brothers' testimony in the *Gospel* acknowledge and attempt to counter the potential of resounding, infernal voices; they work to keep listeners at a safe distance from hell and its speakers. Such efforts suggest the uneasy acknowledgement that one cannot release the past without risking it overwhelming the present. Treatments of the Harrowing offer a moment of redemptive triumph, but they also present hell as a dangerously imperfect and impermanent container, with its many infernally archived narratives capable of bursting out through the gates of the underground storehouse to spill onto the shared ground of the present. The threat is that this "past" will not stay in place, and that it will arrive, like a ghost story, to filter onto the earth, the many ruptures between cosmic geographies wearing away the ordering of temporal divisions, inviting past and present to collide.

2 Poems of Descent

The rest of this chapter looks at moments of poetic confusion between past and present as well as the physical porousness between those categories when they are spatialized as hell, purgatory, and earth. Despite the importance of the Harrowing of Hell, I do not want to suggest that this fraught and anxiously mediated relationship between past and present is exclusive to the extrabiblical episode, or that the Harrowing presents a unique conception of a hell out of which the past might escape. Other medieval narratives also contribute to the notion of the otherworld as a crowded but easily compromised container, a realm filled with important inventory, yet with open doors and porous borders. In this section, I look at Dante's *Inferno*, the medieval lai *Sir Orfeo*, and the legend of Saint Patrick's Purgatory, all works that also treat ideas of stored history, divulged stories, and the relationships between the present and the past, or between the living and the dead. Ultimately, I want to trace out a context for understanding the temporal dynamics of the Harrowing episode and the tendency for hell and purgatory to be seen as holding pens of an unstable past. I am interested in how the extrabiblical fulcrum of sacred history both informs and is informed by other instances of cosmic travel between the otherworld and the earth, whether this takes form as redemption from sin, escape, a kind of didactic, infernal tourism, or as visionary experience.

Medieval vernacular literature contributes to a tradition, established far earlier in classical works and in patristic writings, which emphasizes the facility with which one might negotiate the geographic divide between the living and the dead. In the *Dialogues* (c.593), Gregory the Great proposes that sinners might acquire visual proof of hell through volcanoes, suggesting that, in select portions of the world, the inferno is so close that those still capable of repentance might gaze into its fiery landscape. Gregory even suggests that the portals between hell and earth are widening, inviting passage and revealing evidence of other worlds.[18] Centuries later, Mandeville will report on these impressive "swalghes in þe erthe alleyway brynnand" [always-burning swallows or gaps in the earth] which some say are "þe entreez and þe ȝates of helle" [the entrance and the gates of hell] (31). But of course, those who believe in hell long have known how effortless such a descent into it might be; "easy – / the way that leads into Avernus," the sybil warns Aeneas, who follows in the steps of Ulysses, "But to recall your steps . . . that is the labor."[19]

The round-trip voyage to the otherworld perhaps better indicates the permeability of the partition between hell and earth; one must be able not only to descend into that place, but also to get out again. Orpheus, the poet who, in classical literature, goes down to Hades to retrieve Eurydice, only to lose her again before gaining a foothold on solid ground, functions as one of these travelers. The classical myth undergoes its own metamorphosis in Middle English romance in ways that suggest the influence of Christ's descent in the Harrowing.[20] In the late medieval version of the story, the musician-king Sir Orfeo actually *succeeds* in bringing his dead wife back from the otherworld, and both are permitted to depart from the land of the shades in order to return to their kingdom. The poem suggests that the barrier existing between worlds might be rendered entirely traversable through the desire of an earnest husband or through his careful music.

Orfeo first enters the otherworld by following Heurodis/Eurydice and her unearthly companions through a cleft in a rock. This ghostly host apparently makes the cosmic journey often, crossing from the kingdom of the dead into a more earthly wilderness whenever they want to, and even on horseback. The poem never explicitly calls this otherworld "hell" – in fact, it compares it once to paradise – but the confusing space is filled with bodies, some of them holding uncomfortable positions that recall their violent deaths. Orfeo enters a kingdom that seems like a museum of the dead, even though its inhabitants might not all, in fact, be dead:

> þan he gan bihold about al
> & seiȝe liggeand wiþ-in þe wal
> Of folk þat were þider y-brouȝt,
> & þouȝt dede, & nare nouȝt.[21]

> Then he began to behold all about and saw, lying within the wall, folks that had been brought thither, and were thought dead, and were not.

Some bodies are frozen in positions of drowning, others in their childbirth beds. Time has stopped, and given way to static record, though it would appear that time stops at a *different* moment in the case of each of these statue-like bodies, some of whom are indeed dead ("Sum ded & sum awedde [mad]") (l.400). The frozen figures, garish in their stricken immobility, testify to the once fluid passage of time that has left them as its victims, depositing them here in this kingdom. But if they are not all dead, the stasis cannot be complete. Some just might begin to move again, and what time would it be then?

Orfeo plays his harp for the king of this underworld, who, disgruntled but fair, grants him his boon and allows him to take back Heurodis, no notorious strings attached:

> Take hir bi þe hond & go:
> Of hir ichil þatow be bliþe!"
> He kneled adoun & þonked him swiþe.
> His wiif he tok bi þe hond
> & dede him swiþe out of þat lond,
> & went him out of that þede;
> Riȝt as he come þe wey he ȝede.   (ll.470–6)

"Take her by the hand, and go – I wish you to be glad of her!" He knelt down and quickly thanked him. His wife he took by the hand, and betook himself quickly out of that land, and went out of that place; right as he came, that way he went.

Orfeo departs from the otherworld kingdom the same way he entered it, that is, rather effortlessly. He takes his wife's hand in his, a visual echo, perhaps, of images of Christ grabbing Adam's wrist and pulling him out of the hell mouth. The punishment for looking backward, so central to Ovid's version, never gets mentioned; in this poem, Hades permits, if begrudgingly, the turning back of time and the waking of the dead. The medieval romance sanctions and even rewards the mourning that Ovid's version of Orpheus characterizes as debilitating and doomed, and for which the angry, neglected Maenads eventually tear the mythic poet to pieces. The *Metamorphoses* seems to suggest that onward, in the physical, historical, or narrative sense, is the correct direction; it is the path upon which the poem progresses, from Eden to Caesar; the way mourners move on from loss; and how poets are supposed to look ahead to new subjects. In Ovid's poem, Orpheus, like Lot's doomed wife, suffers for turning around. But in the medieval *Sir Orfeo*, the sense of moving forward is not necessarily in contradiction to looking back. The return to the past, in which Heurodis still lived, and the return of the dead to the world of the living, gets superimposed upon the forward passage of time and the metrical path of poetry. The journey to the otherworld authorizes Orfeo's return, from the wilderness and from his madness, and back to his kingdom, harp and wife in hand.

Sir Orfeo announces itself as a lai toward its beginning, explaining that it belongs to the genre performed by those who "token an harp in gle & game" [took up the harp in entertainment and in game] (l.19).[22] The very first lines of the poem begin with a description of how such songs became written poems: "We redeþ ofte & findeþ [y-write,] / ... Layes þat ben in harping . . ." (ll.1, 2). A few lines into *Sir Orfeo*, the narrator announces that he or she also will "tel" one of these "auentours" if the lords gathered round will "herkneþ" (ll.21–3); the narrator then immediately introduces the hero, who "mest of ani þing / Louede þe gle of harping" [most out of anything, loved the entertainment of harping] (ll.25–6). A thread runs through these three intimations of music, all present within the song of the poem: there are the lais performed long ago, in some past, Breton world; the one about to be reanimated by our narrator, sung as coterminous with the fictive frame of the written poem; and the kind of music in which Orfeo so excels that earth seems like paradise and hell relaxes its grip on the dead.[23] The songs and music are split into separate registers of reality, weaving the different ontologies of the lai into a haunting kind of harmony, offering a narrative record of what was, even as they endeavor to unsettle it. To put it another way: the song of the poem offers a record of what has happened, but the music within the poem – the harping by which Orfeo makes the king of the underworld relent – demonstrates how what happens is never irreparable.

When Orfeo returns from his long exile and his trip to the otherworld, he enters his own kingdom disguised by what the years have done to him. To test his steward, who fails to recognize him, Orfeo says the familiar harp he carries belongs to a man who has died. Grieving for his dead king, the steward falls to the floor, and the assembled barons hasten to revive him, reminding him "it nis no bot of mannes deþ [there is no remedy for the death of man]" (l.552). But this statement is precisely contrary to the truth the poem offers.[24] Though Orfeo's harping sometimes creates the effect of ethereal stillness (among the courtiers who experience it as they would the "ioies of Paradis" [l.37] and among the birds and beasts that gather around in the wilderness), the music *also* manages to unstick Heurodis, one of the sort-of dead, from her frozen posture of repose. In this sense, Orfeo's harpsong *is* the "bot" or cure for "deth," or at least it reanimates the curious inbetween: Heurodis, who perhaps is only sleeping, and Orfeo himself, thought dead, whose familiar face emerges from its ravaged features, eventually recognized as the owner of the harp.

James Simpson argues that the medieval lai "Sir Orfeo" models a theory of recognitional reading. Our interpretive process, he suggests, depends upon looking for the familiar (typically in the sense of generic convention) and recognizing it anew: we turn back and see a dearly known face, but as if for the first time. "Sir Orfeo," Simpson argues, is conservative in that it brings everyone home again (to a reconfirmed aristocratic marriage no less), but it is also reformist, as opposed to reactionary or revolutionary.

This reformist quality comes from the "as if for the first time" force of recognition that then propels one into the future.[25] Simpson writes:

> Understanding text is dependent on recognition of the text's long prehistory, compacted into the deep coding of genre. At the heart of our reading practice, that is, stands not the revolutionary discovery of the never before known, but rather the reformist recovery of the somehow already known.[26]

Simpson describes several moments of recognizing the "already known": recognition in terms of generic convention, but also the moving exchange of glances as the ghostly Heurodis rides with her host through Orfeo's wilderness, or the steward's eyes falling upon the harp in the hands of his disguised king.[27] This last example, the steward's recognition of the harp, would seem to work in a slightly different manner than the initial moment of mute recognition shared by Orfeo and Heurodis. On one hand, it corresponds to our own crucial act of recognition as readers in a very practical way. We, too, recognize the harp; it means that, despite the changed place names and ever so slightly altered personal names, the addition of a court and parliament, and even a wife who makes it out of hell, this indeed is Orpheus, the mythic musician, divinely gifted and associated, however variously, with a sad story about the underworld. But unlike the recognition of a familiar, beloved face, whom one might recuperate and return with to the way things were, newly committed to the familiar, the harp is an instrument capable of making more and different music, and so of extending and altering a tale. This powerful instrument, which can resurrect the dead, also can make a new work of art, and change even an old story made legendary in the past.[28]

Orfeo's music unseals what seems like irreparable past, the state from which there is no "bot" or "amendement" (l.200). But at the same time, the lai that contains that music also is inscribed as lines of poetry, etched in adamant, as Chaucer might write, and so unchanging.[29] It is as if two different forms, superimposed one upon another, offer competing conceptions of the past: a song sings of a past that can be altered by music, and the inscribed version of that song (the poem) insists, through the permanence of its ink, that some things cannot change. Inscribed text contains disruptive music, holding it still, even while it displays as its central plot point the disruptive force of that music. The layered time of composition – purportedly song, then poem – reflects the temporal dynamic encased in the work that is *Sir Orfeo*, in which past and present work upon each other, that is, in which the living intrude into the realm of the shades, and a shade returns to the realm of the living.[30] This poetic revision of a much older tale suggests that other pasts, too, might be revised, and that those imprisoned in the otherworld, "sum ded & sum awedde," might get out. The past cannot be kept in place, no more than Hades can hold onto Heurodis as she leaves with her husband and his harp.

In the Auchinleck manuscript, in which "Sir Orfeo" and a poetic, Middle English *Harrowing of Hell* appear, a poem about Saint Patrick's Purgatory describes another portal, this time to a Christian otherworld that one might visit and then depart from.[31] Henry of Sawtry composed the frequently copied *Tractatus de purgatorio Sancti Patricii* in the late twelfth-century; three Middle English versions of the story, including *Owayne Miles*, the poem in the Auchinleck, take the *Tractatus* as their source. The story describes a hole or ditch in the east wall of an abbey founded by Saint Patrick in Ireland, through which living beings might journey to the otherworld and then come back again:

> In þe est ende of þe abbay
> Þer is þat hole, forsoþe to say,
> Þat griseliche is of siʒt
> With gode ston wal al abouten,
> Wiþ locke and keye þe gate to louken,
> Patrike lete it diʒte.
> Þat ich stede, siker ʒe be,
> Is yclepyd þe riʒt entre
> Of Patrikes Purgatorie:
> For in þat time þat þis bifelle,
> Mani a man went in to helle,
> As it seyt in þe storie,
> And suffred pein for her trespas,
> And com oʒain þurth Godes gras[32]

> In the east end of the abbey, there is that hole, to tell the truth, that is fully dreadful to see; Patrick made it ready with good stone walls all around, with lock and key to lock the gates. That same place, assuredly, is called the very entrance of Patrick's Purgatory. For in the time that this befell, many men went into hell, as the stories say, and suffered there for their trespasses, and came back again through God's grace.

The vision of such traffic – the "mani" who visit hell and then return – contributes to the wearing away of the partition between cosmic realms, confirming and marking points of porosity. Saint Patrick is anxious that the portal be carefully guarded and regulated by ecclesiastical authority, and a strong hint of bureaucratic procedure hovers about the careful rules he makes:

Seynt Patryke lette make ryght well
A dore bow[n]den wyth iren and stele;
Lokke and key he made þerto,
That no mon shuldę þe dore vndo.
The key he betoke þe pryour
And badde hym lokke hyt as tresour,
And euur close þe entre so,
That no man myȝth þeryn go.
But ȝyf hyt were þorow þe assente
Of þe pryour and þe couente;
Of þe bysschop he most haue a lettur,
Elles hym were neuur þe better.[33]

Saint Patrick had it well made, a door bound with iron and steel; lock and key he made for it, so that no man should undo the door. The key he took to the prior and bade him lock it up as if it were a treasure, and always close the entrance so that no man might go in there unless it were by assent of the prior and the convent. He must have a letter from the bishop, or else it would avail him nothing.

Patrick has the door physically secured and invests the ecclesiastical estab-lishment with the authority to supervise it. When, centuries later, the knight Owayne Miles arrives in Ireland to test out the passage, the saint's rules still stand, and the knight requires a letter from the bishop, who "seled hyt wyth hys owne sele" [sealed it with his own seal].[34] A procession of clerics escort Owayne to the door, and he ducks inside "a pryue entre; / Hyt was yn a depe dyches ende" [a private entry; it was at the end of a deep ditch].[35] *The Vision of William of Stranton*, a fifteenth-century prose work that narrates another trip through this same portal, suggests a similar amount of clerical supervision and the initial, slightly awkward passivity of the traveler: "I was," writes William, "put in by þe prior of Seint Mathew."[36] Beyond the locked door of the abbey, Owayne Miles (and later, William) will encounter a realm filled with the dead, who suffer various punishments and are divided into sections according to their sins, as they are in Dante's *Inferno*.

But unlike in the *Comedy*, the departure scenes described in accounts of Saint Patrick's Purgatory are concerned with physical logistics and bureau-cratic procedures; they lack the stately beginning of that more famous trip to hell, when Dante, single file behind his legendary guide, embarks on the "steep and savage path" (2.142). They also lack the clarity of the infernal road map Dante provides, with its clear and ominous warning inscription on the gates. In the *Comedy*, the pilgrim knows when he has entered hell and when he has gotten out of it. Hell and purgatory are less easily demarcated in accounts of Saint Patrick's Purgatory, despite the name. For instance, some of the sinners Owayne encounters seem to be in a realm of punishment for perpetuity, but others appear to be in the process of the kind of painful, spiritual cleansing associated with purgatory, one with a promised efficacy and bent toward paradise. Owayne and William (like Dante) both make it to the earthly paradise after passing through these uncertain regions of punishment, and when it is time to go back to earth, both pilgrims turn with difficulty away from that place of pleasure. In the Cotton version, Owayne's reemergence takes form in a rather matter of fact way, as if he merely were returning to England from Ireland: "A redy way anon he fonde / Ryȝth ynto hys owene londe" [a ready way he soon found, right into his own land].[37] The Auchinleck puts it a bit more spectacularly; the prior of the abbey comes to the portal with his procession to see a light: "And riȝt amiddes þat ich liȝt / Com vp Owain, Godes kniȝt" [and right in the midst of that same light, up came Owain, God's knight].[38]

Despite the gleam of light in which Owayne reemerges from the ditch and door, and despite the miraculous visions of demons, the dead, and the earthly paradise, what I find most intriguing about descriptions of Saint Patrick's Purgatory is its comparative ordinariness. The pilgrimage that becomes the *Comedy* could only happen to Dante; although he is neither Aeneas nor Paul, Beatrice chooses *him* specifically, and he quickly senses his own privileged place among the great poets of limbo. Sir Orfeo, too, is rewarded for being able to produce the kind of music that makes even the wild animals gather around him and hold still, listening. But it appears that anyone might go through the door in the east end of Saint Patrick's abbey, as long as they have the right paperwork and carefully follow stringent bureaucratic, ecclesiastical procedure. The locks on the door and the need for correct documentation evoke the sense of secrecy that Isidore attributes to the "arca," linguistic root of the archive: part of its meaning, he suggests, derives from the fact that it prevents easy disclosure, holding secrets "from which other people are fended off" ("unde ceteri arcentur") (XX.ix.2). Owain does not need to be an exemplary harpist or poet, but he does need a letter of recommendation to gain entrance to this place where he will learn about the past, in the hope that it will change his future.

The bureaucracy around the door in the wall is in place for a more communal reason as well: the infernal visits, when well reported, redound beneficially upon the church and increase its flock. In the beginning of the poem, Patrick has a revelatory dream in which Christ reveals the portal to the saint as a resource for his doubtful parishioners. Their initial spiritual reluctance requires a spectacular remedy, as they themselves note:

> And al þai seyd commounliche,
> Þat non of hem wold sikerliche
> Do bi his techeing,
> Bot ȝif he dede þat [sum] man
> Into helle went þan,
> To bring hem tiding
>
> Of þe pain and of þe wo
> Þe soulen suffri euermo,
> Þei þat ben þerinne[39]

And they all said in common that none of them truly would adhere to his teaching, unless he made it so that some man went into hell to bring them tidings of the pain and woe that souls, those that were in there, suffer forevermore.

In Patrick's vision, Christ suggests a way in which one pilgrim's very physical journey, complete with iron locks and awkward crouching into ditches, might assure those who stay behind about the otherworld whose presence they doubt. The voyager who discloses the record of the dead educates the living. Even though Owayne journeys alone, and even though the clerics carefully rebolt the door behind him, the otherworld revealed to him finds a large audience in the congregation who gather around him when he returns, looking upon the one who looked upon the dead, ready for the stories he will tell, and ready to commit them to poetry. The infernal visit produces narrative for the living.

Visionary experience also permits pilgrims to embark on different kinds of otherworld visits in order to produce persuasive, didactic narrative. The entrance to hell might be down a volcano, past a locked gate in Ireland, or through a cave with the help of the sybil, but it also might take form through visionary ecstasy, dreams, or rapture, a method perhaps most influentially modeled by Saint Paul, whose experience occurs "whether in the body, I know not, or out of the body, I know not."[40] The *Revelation of the Monk of Eynsham*, for instance, a twelfth-century Latin account of a vision of purgatory and paradise, translated into Middle English prose in the fifteenth-century, suggests that the eponymous monk lies prostrate on the floor of his chapter-house *while* visiting the otherworld. That journey, the monk clarifies, occurs while he is "[r]apte in spyryte" [raptured in spirit].[41] With Dante's dark wood in mind, we also might consider how these methods of travel sometimes are represented as working in combination, or how a passage between hell and earth can exist somewhere in between the categories of geographic trek and ecstatic dream, particularly in the case of those writers who eschew framing the experience as merely one or the other.[42] Both kinds of cosmic travel produce an account of that which is seen and experienced, offered up as proof of the otherworld briefly encountered.

But, as I have suggested in the section on the Harrowing of Hell, the under- or otherworld also is well stocked with its *own* stories, the ones belonging to the dead it houses. Cosmic travelers bring back tales not only of their own miraculous experiences, but also reports suggesting that the infernal archive already is packed with words, images, and voices, stories that might be transported and translated *out*. The often-verbose dead are only too eager to share their stories with the living pilgrims who manage to descend, and these stories, like the repeated prophecies of David and Isaiah, then seep out to the land of the living, back into the present, as it were. In the organized compartments of Dante's inferno, the shades are laden with personal histories and animated with frantic protestations; the underground space fills with their voices. When the poet-pilgrim enters through the infernal gates, he encounters resounding noise:

> Here sighs and lamentations and loud cries . . .
>   Strange utterances, horrible pronouncements,
> accents of anger, words of suffering,
> and voices shrill and faint, and beating hands –   (3.22, 25–27)[43]

Hell pulsates with noise that wants to get out. The closer to these gates, and so the closer to the border between infernal and earthly worlds, the louder the voices are; the shades seem to want not only Dante to hear them, but to be heard by an aboveground audience as well.

The cacophony that first greets Dante issues from the shades whose names are lost to the world above; this earthly silence, the absence of fame or memory of any sort, is the very thing they so loudly lament. Next come the poets, who cluster in stark opposition to this reputationless state: "the honor of their name," Virgil explains to Dante, "echoes up above within your life" (4.76–77).[44] Across the circles, hordes of sinners enthusiastically offer up their biographies, passionate feuds, self-justifications, and ardent memories. They are desperate to have the passing poets listen; many of them, like the Florentine Ciacco, want Dante to carry word of them back to earth: "I pray," he pleads, "recall me to men's memory" (6.89).[45] It is only deep down in hell, toward the frozen epicenter, where sinners begin to disdain the prospect of their fame spreading up and out. In circle nine, when Dante promises the uncooperative Bocca degli Abbati, named by another, to put "your name among my other notes,"[46] the half-frozen

shade claims to want "the contrary" ("contrario"); he would rather be left
alone to lapse into silence (32.93–4).

The shades of *Inferno*, locked in their circles and repetitive patterns of
punishment, note the disruption of Dante's corporeal presence with keen
interest, listening to his words, asking for news, noting the way his body
disturbs their infernal terrain. He embodies a potential for change, for
difference: a new plot twist for the dead. His descent and passionate
interactions with different shades threaten the stasis of infernal record,
unsettling the stories the dead remember and *how* they remember, just as
his body shifts the infernal geography that the incorporeal wraiths apparently leave untouched. Dante's encounters with the shades he knew permit
further conversation, more questions and answers, new perspectives and
regrets, inviting one to ask: what if infernal descriptions take a form
different from the earthly events they sometimes memorialize? What if
not only Dante learns something, but also the dead themselves begin to
change, to speak differently? What if this place offers not only record, but
also the potential for counterfactual history? Dante often seems to foreclose
this possibility by making the dead stubborn, still blind to their sin and
what they have lost. But conversation can be a tricky thing, hard to keep
safely in place, particularly when driven by tercets and shaped by words put
into the mouths of the angry dead and somber poets.

It is, moreover, important to remember that poets themselves – figures
indicating the potential for proliferating infernal narrative – inhabit the
underworld. Aeneas discovers Orpheus plucking at his lyre; Dante encounters that ring of limbo poets; and in Milton's hell the fallen angels extricate
themselves from the lake of fire in order to begin composing the epic of
their own exploits. In the Harrowing of Hell stories, the prophets and
patriarchs speak as writers and poets, as composers of prophetic scripture
and as psalmists. David and Isaiah recall their own textual history, repeating fragments of their prophecies in language passing through Hebrew,
Latin, vernacular poetry, and, in the plays, Latin and Middle English
woven together. A bustling realm of narrative, translation, and transformation exists just beneath the surface of the earth: on the other side of the
cave, across the river, beyond the wood, past the gates, down the ditch,
through the mouth of hell. In these texts, the underworld collects and
stores narrative to create an infernal repository that operates as an alternate
world humming just below or beyond the world we know. This is a world
of record, but, in the manner of the Garden of Eden discussed in Chapter 1,
it is also a space that challenges neat divisions between record and reality,
archive and world. If the past is not static, if the infernal poets continue to

make poetry, if figures reperform and renarrate their legendary deeds but one day make a misstep, then the infernal realm of narrative might overflow its archival frame and archival status, might spread out, gain ground, and become a dynamic reality that rivals the one playing out on the stage of the earth above. The stories of the dead might begin to shift, like those upon the spiraling terraces of Dante's purgatory, slowly winding toward redemption. The divide between hell and earth, which textual and iconographic traditions suggest might be transgressed with or without a golden bough or accommodating guide, effects a scenario in which the voices of the dead might leak out of their imperfect infernal containment to resound in the world above, where other, newer narratives unfold upon the surface of the earth.

3 Looking Back

There are, then, a number of ways in which the past might be released from its status as record in hell, and ways in which what is thought to be over and done might become reanimated or made susceptible to change. Sometimes the dead resurface to inhabit the earth in the flesh, as in the Harrowing or with the medieval Eurydice; sometimes more ordinary retrospection makes them loom. The latter does not necessarily require pilgrim-poets or messiahs, but occurs in more quotidian ways, such as by turning back the page, or by using memory to write the book that will remember in turn. Retelling a story is a form of looking backward, of opening a portal between temporal realms, one that *might* permit traffic in either direction. This kind of retrospection continually invites us to reconsider the past, but it also invites the past to intrude upon the present, that always-moving moment in time continually losing ground to history and memory on the one side, and prophecy and anticipation on the other. Both those who literally descend to hell and then reascend, and those who look back onto hell from the vantage point of the earth and the present, negotiate space and time, traveling back and forth on history's timeline, encountering the past, and then returning to the present that endeavors to replace it.

Looking back upon the past is not identical to descending into the otherworld, of course; only one requires keys and ditches. But the actions carry different degrees of similar risks; sometimes it is hard to distinguish one from the other, and sometimes one is used as a figure for the other. Ovid's Orpheus fatally turns to see a disappearing wife, dissipating again into the gloom of hell; Lot's Wife gazes upon the ashes of her city in the moment before turning to salt; and even Noah's Wife is chastised by her husband for looking back upon a sinking world. A sense of danger attends the act of remembering, of looking backward, even when the physical descent into hell is not required for it. In the *Historia Scholastica* (c.1169–1173), Peter Comestor suggests the risk even of sacred historical paraphrase. Comestor links literal and figurative backward glances – the gaze into hell and the gaze into history – in his recapitulation of the biblical past. Telling the story of Lot's Wife, who dared disobey God and look backward upon the destruction of her city, he writes: "And Lot's Wife, looking back behind her, was turned into a pillar of salt, which Josephus says he saw and which still remains now."[47] Comestor characterizes the nature of the first-century writer Josephus' labor – his research and com-position of *The Antiquities of the Jews* – alongside the biblical transgression of Lot's Wife. Josephus and *Uxor Lot* converge in a tableau of backward gazes focused upon destruction and punishment; the crystallized wife twists toward the burnt-out cities, and Josephus, looking upon that tragic, still-standing pillar, takes up a posture of risky retrospection that matches hers. Comestor's insertion of Josephus' testimony links the early historian with the biblical transgressor, and the dangerousness of the wife's venture momentarily permeates Josephus' project of recording; the subversion of the one act of memorialization bleeds into the other. Comestor, of course, also implicates himself in this chain of history, drawing as he does upon Josephus, looking backward upon that source text. The danger understood as attending an iconic look into the past and into a kind of hell seeps into the act of looking backward as it relates to narrative recapitulation more generally.

In this danger, however, also resides considerable power and narrative authority. Looking into the otherworld of the past or of the inferno precedes and underpins the action of narrating that past. "To narrate," Carlo Ginzburg writes, "means to speak here and now with an authority that derives from having been (literally or metaphorically) there and then," to have been to the beyond and returned, or to have gone to hell and back.[48] This is the narrative authority that Saint Patrick's parishioners crave in their spiritual guides; that inflects Sir Orfeo's music when he passes across that otherworldly threshold and into earth again; and that produces the *Divine Comedy*, whose lines Dante swears by as he would swear by scripture, in part because his poem is underpinned and confirmed by knowledge of the otherworld.

The next and final chapter returns to the story of the Harrowing of Hell to investigate how the medium of performance and the cosmic symbolism of the stage might further illuminate competing kinds of authority:

between old and new, dead and living, and past and present, all of which merge between the bared teeth of the mouth of hell as it opens onto the mystery play stages. Augmenting poetic strategies, the architecture of the stage helps to realize physically the permeability between earth and under-world, and the bodies of the players demonstrate how one realm might spectrally haunt the other.

CHAPTER 5

The Harrowing of Hell: Closure and Rehearsal

Chapter 4 ended with Carlo Ginzburg's assertion that the journey to a "beyond" authorizes narrative and that world-traversers accrue such authority. In an essay written over a decade after *Cities of the Dead*, Joseph Roach also investigates a world-traverser and, through him, the relationship between the present and the past. This time the cosmic journey does not offer a "matrix for all narrative," as Ginzburg suggests,[1] but a touchstone for performance; Orpheus's classical descent and return from Hades, Roach argues, suggests the continual oscillation between past and present inherent to that medium. In "The Blunders of Orpheus," he writes:

> The action that the Orphic plot imitates – moving forward while glancing back – recapitulates the risky act of performance itself, for the performer typically feels the urge to look back, despite the prohibitions and costs, because performance always seems to be authorized by something prior, even when it isn't.[2]

Investigating the relationship between text and performance, and through them, literary and performance studies, Roach describes both the risky frisson of the performer's search for an authorizing past, often an authorizing text – something "back there" in the shadows of the past and hard to discern – and the danger or despair of becoming permanently severed from it.

But, as we saw in Chapter 4, when the *medieval* Sir Orfeo leaves the otherworld, he brings his dead with him. Hand in hand with his recovered Heurodis/Eurydice, the minstrel-king mirrors Christ's salvific exodus with the redeemed patriarchs and prophets, the spectral dead who recite their authorizing, scriptural texts as they step out through the mouth of hell, toward the redeemer who has turned back for them. The problem or "cost" that "Sir Orfeo" treats, then, is not the crisis of irreparable loss, disclosed by the performer-poet who glances backward toward a shadowy something

136

that might not be there at all. Rather, it is the question of what to do with the past that the moment of performance cannot shake free of, the past that variously burdens and enriches the present, or the "now" that is the time-frame of performance.[3] If we replace Orpheus with the medieval Sir Orfeo as a way to think about performance, a new set of questions emerges: What happens when the look backward neither effects nor reveals loss, but rather discloses overwhelming accumulation? What happens when turning around exposes a past that does not necessarily disappear, but rather metamorphoses before one's eyes and beyond one's control?

These are the questions that this chapter pursues through a considera-tion of the mystery plays that stage the Harrowing of Hell, the medieval story about the resurrection of the dead with which the previous chapter began. The cycles associated with York and Chester and the Towneley and N-Town manuscripts all include a Harrowing of Hell play (in N-Town, split into two parts). In the following section, I examine these plays alongside late medieval iconography of hell, particularly centered on the hell mouth, in order to consider the effect of narrative loosed from an infernal "logge" and spoken out through bared teeth.[4] I then turn to a consideration of performance strategies for accessing, displaying, and releasing the past, and look at how spectrality and repetition, constitutive features of performance, complicate efforts to maintain control over its return.

1 The Speaking Mouth

In the previous chapter, I argued that medieval journeys from hell to earth might be understood in both spatial and temporal terms, as movement from the past, housed in an infernal otherworld, back into the present, which takes place upon the surface of the earth. Within this dynamic, the past seems more easily locatable: it is "back there" or "down below," in a "logge" with "yendles yatis" (endless gates), "barres and bandis," and "watches on the wall,"[5] from within which figures lament their carefully fortified imprisonment. The present is harder to find. It would seem to be where one is: the contested, earthly ground upon which one is situated and encroached upon by past and future, or from which one attempts to influence the layered histories represented by the waiting rooms of purga-tory. It is the spot upon which, in the manner of Lot's Wife and Orpheus, one makes a slow and momentous pivot, knowing that the turning will change what comes both before and after, back there and up ahead upon some future ground.

In the Harrowing of Hell, Christ the redeemer supervises what occurs as both temporal change and geographic journey, facilitating and negotiating the logistics of his own infernal access and the departure of his scriptural predecessors, or those whom he has newly claimed as such. In iconography of the Harrowing, he looks back into hell and pulls figures from scriptural history (Adam, Eve, Abraham, Moses, Isaiah, David, . . .) out of what frequently is figured as a gaping mouth. The stage directions from the Chester play unceremoniously summarize: "Hic extrahuntur patriarchi. (Here must God take owt Adam)."[6] Here, also, he must drag the past forward in time – in the plays, literally toward center stage – briefly permitting Adam and the rest of the figures that emerge from their long confinement to take up their story once again.

Multiple generations, centuries, and books of scripture are included in this reemergent history; disparate phases of the past all are compressed into one single moment of present redemption. The crowded generations surge forward together to encounter Christ and earthly light, even while approximating themselves into a rough chronological line, beginning with Adam: "I xal hem brynge," says Christ in the first part of the N-Town Harrowing, "reknyd be rowe / out of here purcytorye" [I shall bring them, reckoned by row, out of their purgatory] (ll.47–8). "Reknyd," or "reckoned," can mean to guide, to narrate, to produce or access an account of something, as in the reckonings offered up at Judgment Day. In this moment, Christ guides the newly visible past forward in a neat row, making an account and narrating an old story, as the inventory and elements of that story stream out of hell. Recapitulated history, carefully ordered and supervised by the redeemer, spills out of the mouth to start once again with its remembered beginning: the first human crossing a momentous threshold (see Figures 3–5).

In much of the iconography, when Adam stretches his leg over the bottom lip of hell to set his foot upon the earth, the redeemer grabs his wrist. In a phrase mined by medieval and performance studies, Christ at this moment "touches the past," embodied here by Adam, as well as by the emerging figures, crouching and blinking, arrayed behind him. The encounter between past and present has been described in affective, even visceral terms. Carolyn Dinshaw characterizes it largely as positive opportunity, a way for marginalized figures to recognize one another across a temporal divide in the formation of queer communities.[7] Performance theorists similarly posit various flashes of recognition that might take place across large gaps of time and space. "[T]imes touch," writes Rebecca Schneider in her study of historical reenactment.[8] The experience of the

Figure 4. *The Harrowing of Hell*. From the *Fitzwarin Psalter* (Psalterium ad usum ecclesiae Sarisburiensis). England, fourteenth century, Latin 765, f.15 r, at the Bibliothèque Nationale.

Figure 5. *The Harrowing of Hell* (image at top). From an English psalter. England, first quarter of the thirteenth century, Arundel MS 157, f.11 r, at the British Library.

body permits one kind of knowledge to take form even as it disrupts another; it accesses a past that it reaches for, conjures, touches, and shapes, while it, in turn, inevitably is touched and shaped by the past. But such an interpenetration of temporalities, instead of forming a rich, instructive, benevolent confluence, also might take the more dangerous form of mutual dependency. For Michelet, famously inhaling the dust of the dead in the reading rooms, as described in the Introduction, the past could be all too present and overwhelming, a reality that crowded out the needs of the present. Employing the bodily and digestive metaphors used in medieval descriptions of remembering, Barthes writes that, for Michelet, the past was both a body and a kind of warmth to reach for; the earlier scholar consumed – *devoured* – history, as it consumed him, destroying his health and upending the claims of the present for primacy in his life.[9]

But not all temporal encounters are reciprocally *balanced*, whether in positive or insidious relation. The Harrowing of Hell presents a struggle between past and present, (partially) disguised as the former's confirmation of the latter. Although the iconography of this redemptive moment traditionally illuminates the Harrowing as salvific event, the monstrous, fanged jaws also signal danger and disquiet, suggesting an uneasiness attending this story of descent and redemption, an uneasiness about the power of the past to speak beyond the invitation of the present, or to exceed the script meant to guide it. And so, when the Old Testament figures exit their infernal confines – emerging as bodies and "a warmth" to reach for, bodies warmed by almost five thousand years in hell – Christ reaches for Adam. He takes him by the "riȝt hond," a prose Middle English version of *Nicodemus* specifies, though its full description of such touching evokes the more frequent iconography of the grabbed wrist: "I heere þe Lord, for þou hast fonge me . . ." says Adam, using a verb that means "collected" or "taken up."[10] It is different from an embrace. Adam does not touch Christ; Adam is touched, taken up by him, ordered and "reknyd." For one of the dangers of the always-open mouth of hell, it seems, is that it will speak erratically or out of turn, with a force that threatens to overwhelm rather than merely to authorize, and that it will make the past seem to matter more than the present that reaches out to touch it. That is why the past needs to be not only touched, but also firmly, cautiously grasped, *fanged*, by a redeemer at times as aggressive as the infernal maw.

The hell mouth, which widens to permit movement between the earth and the underworld, takes many forms in the medieval period; it is inked on parchment, shaped in stone, pieced in glass, and sometimes used as a dramaturgical device in the mysteries. It is always wide open: gaping, fanged, swallowing, yawning, or screaming, situated in a face part sea-creature, part feline, and all monster. Frequently, it emerges out of the ground or from an unspecified below, its jaws unhinging to frame two possible scenarios. When illustrating Judgment Day or the death of a sinner, men and women are drawn into it, prodded by devils with pitchforks or by some other invisible, inexorable force that makes them step, half unsuspectingly, backward into a gaping abyss. In a famous image from the Winchester Psalter (c.1150), for example, the hell mouth gapes so widely that its disembodied face threatens to split in two; demons torment the newly dead between the even rows of teeth as the bodies tumble into the darkness. Smaller hell mouths frequently lurk in the bottom curves of the rondelles of *bibles moralisées*, parting to taste the foot of the sinner fearfully stepping back upon them. In a late, dazzling complication of the basic design, the hours of Catherine of Cleves (c.1440) offers a page with an entanglement of mouths: one hell mouth swallows another (the eyes look out from an inner pink, fleshy lining), which in turn swallows another; towers rising above the first infernal face vault yet another set of yawning jaws skyward.

But, as we have seen, in the Harrowing of Hell a trail of scriptural figures processes *out* of the mouth, crouching among the teeth, stepping over the bottom lip, waiting down further in the throat for an opportunity to exit through the anatomic portal. Adam and Eve exit first, sometimes still wearing fig leafs and crouching low; a few bodies after them, Moses sometimes can be picked out by a pair of horns. Behind them, the recognizable or partially recognizable redeemed form a loose train of bodies, and, in some cases, crowds of unidentifiable figures, suggested by indistinguishable faces, wait further down toward the back of the hell mouth's throat, implying a considerable though vague population still waiting to get out into the open air. In one late fourteenth-century English manuscript, these figures fade into mere silhouettes, almost hastily drawn heads, as if to intimate the extensive crowds still waiting impatiently below.[11] In many images, the mass exodus appears to make the infernal jaws open uncomfortably wide, as if the mouth were vomiting or screaming.

This tableau of Christ, ushering or pulling a procession of Adam, Eve, and the rest of the redeemed out of the open mouth, comprises a train of embodied and infernally archived, mostly Old Testament narrative, at last redeemed and let out through an open mouth, accessed and reassessed.

The bodies and the texts with which the figures are associated form an authorizing past and a usable history, a scripture upon which Christ can look backward as he moves forward, an older *something*, part body and part text, to sanction the fittingness of the new world that he establishes. This infernal inventory takes form as narrative realized through bodies laden with backstories, bodies carrying or quoting text, and text recalled through suggestive gesture (hand holding fig leaf in place). Sometimes, a familiar story is specifically rearticulated in the admission of regret: "A, lorde, we were worthy / Mo turmentis for to taste," admits Eve at York (ll.357–8). The exit of Adam and Eve out through the infernal jaws immediately recalls the eaten fruit that led to the loss of paradise, for they again stoop in that iconic pose of departure, the bent form assumed at Eden's gates. It is as if they are passing through the mouth in order to begin a familiar story all over again.

The emergent figures insist on their relationship to text in the plays. Some figures quote text, some bodies seem to stand in for the texts with which they are associated (e.g., David for his psalms, Isaiah for his prophecies), and some perhaps even clutch material codices: in the York Harrowing, David says, "That may thou in my Sawter see, / For that poynte I prophicied" [that you can see in my psalter, for that point I prophesized] (ll.187–8). At Chester, Simon suggests one might check that the words he now quotes in Latin accord with the passage featuring him in the Gospel of Luke; they are words, he affirms, "that men may fynd in booke" (l.48). In York, Isaiah recalls that his prophetic "poynte" about redemption is "puplisshid," and both Isaiah and John the Baptist describe themselves as "rehears[ing]" their lines in the Chester play (ll.31,71). The word is a clever aside to the actor's labor, but also – emphasized through the switch to Latin – a reminder that the scripts they rehearse borrow from older materials. The player-Isaiah rehearses his lines as his script rehearses the *Gospel of Nicodemus*, which in turn rehearses the Book of Isaiah.

Along with this tumble of bodies, then, comes a religious and textual tradition. The hell mouth spews out the bodies of Adam and Eve and, by association, speaks the stories of Adam and Eve, and, following that pattern, the histories and prophecies connected to the patriarchs and prophets who come after the bent-over pair, regurgitating and retelling with wide-open mouth episodes of the Old Testament (as well as two from the gospels, carefully interpolated and linked up with that older text). These voices, raised in eager reminiscence and recapitulation, carefully provide the textual authorization that the present craves. At York,

Isaiah paraphrases his prophecies in order to show how Christ's descent fulfills them:

> Adame, ȝe schall wele vndirstande,
> I, Ysaias, as God me kende,
> I prechid in Neptalym, þat lande,
> And Zabulon, even vntill ende.
> I spake of folke in mirke walkand
> And saide a light schuld on þame lende,
> This lered I whils I was leuand,
> Nowe se I god þis same hath sende.   (ll.49–56)

> Adam, you will understand well; I, Isaiah, as God called me, I preached in Naphtali, that land, and in Zebulon, until the end. I spoke of people walking in darkness and said a light should shine upon them. This I taught while I was living; now I see God has sent just that.

In the same play, David quotes in Latin from Psalm 15, a text ascribed to him and later reprised in the Acts of the Apostles (2:27):

> Als I haue saide, ȝitt saie I soo,
> Ne derelinquas, domine,
> Animam meam [in] inferno [. . .]   (ll.373–5)

> As I have said, yet (again) I say it: do not, Lord, leave my soul in hell.

David annotates the scriptural verses in Middle English, so that even the cross-lingual rhyme seems to affirm that the old lines link up in precise ways with new requirements, continuing to signify across testaments and languages. At York, Christ suggests that *all* previous text is significant in relation to his work in hell, or rather that his work in hell makes such previous writing newly and now fully significant. The Harrowing of Hell is where the words of David and Isaiah and the experiences of Adam and Eve will find their ultimate (as in most important *and* final) meaning: "ilke trewe prophettis tale" [each true prophet's tale] announces Christ, "Must be fulfilled in me" (ll.273–4).

As these Old Testament figures emerge onto the stage, one-by-one stepping across the threshold widened by Christ's redemptive work, dramaturgical features overlap with those of sacred cosmology. Heaven, most likely constructed with scaffolding, hovers above hell, corralled beneath the stage or else off to the side, and the stage itself serves as the earth, the main ground for the performance of the central actions of the unfolding drama.[12] Adam, the first man, thus enters the stage of the earth before a spiriting away to the scaffold of heaven, with hell left behind or below: his very fleshly foot touches the staged ground, his body at last reencountering the clay, as if to signal that scripture begins again at the moment of his reintroduction to the earth.

No matter how cosmologically distinct, however, these realms cannot be sealed off from one another practically in the context of the plays. Christ's command to unlock the gates – "attollite portas, principes" – resounds through hell, alarming the demons who clearly can hear it. Noise also passes from the below- or backstage inferno to filter onto the stage of the earth. Peter Meredith points out that, in the case of plays that begin with a view of the infernally imprisoned, "hell must be seen as closed . . . while at the same time the souls within must be both visible and audible."[13] His point suggests how the necessity of seeing and hearing wears away at the attempted state of enclosure; the acoustics of hell are staged as uncontainable, and voices pass through to an earthly audience listening above. Just as the narrative frame could not quite contain the potency associated with older prophecy in the *Gospel of Nicodemus*, the physical limits of the stage cannot muffle the voices sounding from the backstage or below-stage hell. In fact, one of the defining qualities of infernal space on the medieval stage seems to be the cacophony that issues from it. Not only the scriptural recitations of the "populus qui ambulabat in tenebris" [people who were walking in darkness[14]] leak out (the demons at York call it an "vggely noyse") (l.101), but often a more riotous, indeterminate shouting, intimations of thunder, and banging on pots and pans (the Harrowing was the Cooks' and Innkeepers' play at Chester).[15]

Medieval stages could incorporate the hell mouth as an apparatus not only to provide a portal for bodies between the earth and the underworld, but also to conceptually filter these sounds and voices. It is possible that actors entered and exited the playing space through or near a mouth-like threshold, creating a visual effect similar to the iconography in which the patriarchs and prophets step out through the jaws.[16] Pamela Sheingorn suggests that in the plays, the entrance to hell "was most frequently represented as the gaping jaws of a beast,"[17] and Clifford Davidson has unearthed records for the cost of repairing hell mouths in late medieval productions. One particularly impressive sounding fifteenth-century version at Rouen is described as "made like a great mouth opening and closing as is needful."[18] REED provides numerous accounts involving the costs associated with hell mouths for plays now lost, money paid for "kepyng of the wynde and hell mowthe"; "kepyng hell hede"; and "paynting of hell mowthe."[19] And Gary D. Schmidt points out that even though most records of hell mouths as stage devices date from the sixteenth-century onward, texts nevertheless make specific references to them in the fourteenth century.[20]

But even when the stage did not incorporate a spectacular, three-dimensional mouth, medieval audiences still might associate more subtle portals to and from the underworld with the iconic, monstrous jaws. Sheingorn stresses the "accessibility of this image" of the mouth and its familiarity to the laity as public art.[21] Frequent depictions of the hell mouth in visual art made it easier for an audience to associate the entrance to hell with the gaping jaws, even when a toothy threshold participated less ostentatiously in the architecture of the stage. This is helped by the fact that doors and mouths seem to be conceptually linked from time out of mind. Sheingorn takes the title of her essay on the hell mouth, "Who can open the doors of his face?" from the Book of Job's description of the Leviathan (40.5), and Isidore of Seville addresses the link between mouths and architectural portals with another etymology:

> The mouth (*os*) is so called, because through the mouth as if through a door (*ostium*) we bring food in and throw spit out; or else because from that place food goes in and words come out.[22]

Words, writes Isidore, come *out*. And although Sheingorn writes that the hell mouth, when "disembodied," might imply "unidirectionality" – sinners are swallowed *down* or *into* hell – images of the Harrowing and the logistics of actors processing onto stage also suggest that things must come *out* of the mouth.[23] The complex hell mouth from the hours of Catherine of Cleves presents this possibility of opposing trajectories by means of a smaller, monstrous mouth in its margin; set directly beneath the repeating hell mouths that swallow sinners, demons, and other hell mouths, this marginal maw has scrolls inscribed with the seven deadly sins spilling out of it. Or perhaps "spill out" interprets too far; these scrolls are, of course, static on the page, balanced halfway in and halfway out. They might, after all, be on their way belly-ward, like the book ingested by the prophet in the Book of Ezechiel (the book that gets lodged in the bowels), but they also might be tumbling outward, spewed from the mouth in the visualization of the vomit-metaphor attending speech and narrative production in various works potentially familiar to medieval audiences.[24]

The Middle English *Gospel of Nicodemus* captures the idea of this infernal spout or megaphone by equating the mouth of a very verbal Satan with the hellish jaws that open onto earth. When, immediately prior to Christ's descent, Satan calls out a psalmodic "qui est iste" to determine the identity of his visitor, "hell a voice vpkast[s]": the question travels from Satan's lips, up through the infernal regions (l.1386). "Hell" itself is given a voice; the monstrous chute approximates a megaphone. Certain images further depict the two apertures – Satan's mouth and hell's mouth – as linked; in the de Lisle Psalter (c.1310) and in an earlier thirteenth-century English psalter (Figure 5), Christ attacks Satan's mouth with a staff as he pulls Adam up out of the jaws. The positioning works to remind the viewer that both apertures are mouths, both fearsomely articulate, both capable of "upkast" voice, and that both are vulnerable in Christ's presence.[25] Words come out of Satan's mouth, and words come out of the hell mouth. And these "upkast" voices, rumbling through the bowels of hell, suggest the presence of more words and more voices that threaten to reverberate out through an infernal megaphone.

It thus matters that the portal of hell takes the form of a mouth because it suggests the activity of speaking; narrative, in the form of bodies, texts, and voices, emerges from it, rumbling up from the belly of hell, anatomy also strongly suggestive of one of the places where one holds memory. Ambrose allegorizes "venter" as the "belly of our souls," viscera filled "with the word of God."[26] In the *Confessions*, Augustine describes how information once stored in the belly of memory might be brought forth or up once again: "Perhaps then, just as food is brought from the stomach in the process of rumination, so also by recollection these things are brought up from the memory."[27] Whatever is in the infernal belly of memory might be recollected, brought forth through the mouth speaking out to the earth above. The suggestive anatomical structure of hell – its resemblance to a monstrously verbal creature, all mouth and stomach – implies a cavern full of words that might spill forth from an infernal belly of memory.[28]

But the mouth of hell not only speaks, it speaks *again*; this moment of renarration emphasizes the inextricability among access to the past, repetition, and alteration. The image of the open maw implies a measure of instability, an uncertainty of just what will come out and what will be said, despite the familiarity of the scripture it regurgitates. Recall, for instance, that Adam and Eve are the first to depart from the gaping mouth. The gnashing teeth through which the pair step remind one of that initial sin so firmly tied to transgressive apple-eating, but then later associated with transgressive female speaking in an exegetical confusion of errant mouths.[29] The gaping jaws through which Eve still shamefully, delicately steps, covering her body with leaves or her own hair, recalls that supposedly even more sinful orifice with which a story about eating fruit stubbornly associates her. Nutritional disobedience slides into a more salacious trespass, becoming aligned with unsanctioned speaking and the incessant tongues of subsequent, almost always-female gossips.[30] Even Eve's moment of redemption, framed between open lips, prevents her from escaping the damning associations of her own original sin, and thus from shedding her story. History sticks to her, but that history itself links up with transgressive speaking. It conjures both the idea of a story that one cannot shake free of, but also one that threatens always to tell itself differently, to speak, in a moment of transgression, beyond the bounds of what has been handed down as law.

The orderly parade of exiting Old Testament figures attempts to neutralize the force of the many characters imagined as imperfectly contained beneath the porous surface of the earth, characters whose voices previously could have been cast upward at any moment, blaring through the cosmic partition that, as we have seen, is punctured in so many places and far from soundproof on the stage. There is always something *going on* in hell: the soliloquies and arguments of Dante's sinners; the demons' debates in the plays; the quiet conversations among the poets; the cooks and inn keepers with their pots and pans; the prophets' rehearsal of their scripture; the long, noisy period of waiting underground as the years – thousands of them – tick by. The mouth of hell becomes a spout for these unruly guts of memory, a megaphone that blares out a history that is usable, but also overwhelming, one made up of bodies and voices stored and restless in the underground viscera, capable of speaking in ways that might unsettle what is supposed to be over and done.

2 Touching the Spectral Past

The mouth of hell opens to form a threshold between the saved and the savior, hell and earth, the dead and the living, present and past. It frames the relationships between these categories and, widening to permit passage in multiple directions, suggests how one might blur into or overwhelm another. As Biddick points out, Christian exegesis attempts to relegate the Hebrew Scriptures, along with their associations of Jewishness and Judaism, to a superseded "past," in part to prevent the risk of the present being overwhelmed. The interpretive process fuses typology to a supersessionary schema, so that one figure (i.e., Isaac) foreshadows another figure (Christ); the latter completes the prophetic overture and supersedes the importance of the former. In medieval Christian exegesis, Christ always fulfills Old Testament prophecy, rather than the other way around; typology follows only one chronological trajectory. Biddick suggests that in this way supersessionary thinking works to "ward off the shattering threat of typological reversibility," or the potential for typological readings to coil back upon themselves, switching the positions of shadowy promise and fulfilled truth.[31] The hell mouth opens up upon this danger of reversibility, widening to reveal a voluble past that threatens to detract from what comes next. In the crowded space between the teeth, Christ must reassert, even insist upon, a specific content and narrative direction. The traditional orderliness of the iconographic departure works to counter an anxiety about the tendency of worlds to blur together, and for clear, supersessionary chronology to be lost: the threat of what is understood as an older world, religion, law, and narrative intruding into, haunting or otherwise disrupting the new world Christ inaugurates. The Harrowing iconography suggests a desire for shepherding the unruliness of an un-containable past into order, into a narrative that can be "reknyd on rowe" so that it leads, inevitably, inexorably, toward the present. The neat processional, the serene Christ, the safely, staff-struck mouth, and the firmly grasped wrist of Adam all work together to control the risk of disorder inherent in a story about the return of the past.

Like Biddick, Steven Kruger has examined medieval Christian exegetical efforts to hold a superseded Jewish past in place, and in *The Spectral Jew*, he points toward the ways in which the study of performance might shed light on how these exegetical practices falter. Kruger borrows a key part of his theoretical model from Derrida's *Specters of Marx*, which in turn uses the Ghost of Hamlet's father to illustrate an understanding of spectrality: a kind of haunting presence, or a past that does not end, even when (especially when) its culmination determinedly is pronounced. Performance long has been associated with haunting, ghosting, or spectrality, resources for theorizing and enacting the wary relationship between past and present, and for thinking about how the past might come to life, revoiced and reanimated through living bodies. Marvin Carlson writes that, "the theatre has been obsessed always with things that return, that appear again tonight … Everything in the theatre, the bodies, the materials utilized, the language, the space itself, is now and has always been haunted."[32] And though he argues that performance need not take the return of the dead as its plot in order to suggest just that sensation – "every play," he writes, "might be called *Ghosts*" – he nonetheless turns to *Hamlet* as a touchstone in his book, calling it "the most haunted of all western dramas."[33] It is a play frequently invoked by theorists contemplating the relationship among the past, performance, haunting, and hell, and it shares a number of important features with the Harrowing.

Through his specific use of spectrality, Kruger wishes to examine ideas regarding Jewish embodiment in the Middle Ages and the conjured nature of a "fantasy construction" that takes shape through an accretion of stereotypes deployed to distinguish medieval Jews from Christians. Kruger argues that, in the attempt to represent the end of Judaism and the culmination of the usefulness of its associated scriptures, medieval Christians paradoxically must bring Judaism into focus, thereby fusing "dependence" with "erasure":

> Even as it is made to die, to disappear, Judaism comes to occupy our field of vision. It is this dynamic in medieval Christian thought – a dependence upon the Jewish ancestor that is simultaneously an erasure – which I hope the book that follows helps us more fully to understand ... Jewishness is a *spectral* presence.[34]

Kruger writes that the "Christian incarnational reorganization of history," a belated schema that makes older narrative conform to the Gospels through typological interpretation, attempts to "put Judaism to rest, to kill it off ... phantasmatically," even though this attempt always is complicated by an "ambivalence" and "a need to preserve the Jews."[35]

This is the ambivalence, or the wavering between invitation and eradication, that Derrida illustrates through the opening scene of *Hamlet*, when the Ghost first appears, already "again to-night." Derrida describes how the present attempts to manipulate the voices of the past (to "reckon them by row," we might say, or to stage manage their communication, making the past simultaneously stop and speak), as when Horatio and the wary sentries of Elsinore encounter their dead king:

> And in French, in fact, "I charge thee" is often translated by "je t'en conjure," which indicates a path where later we will see injunction crossing with conjuration. By charging or conjuring him to speak, Horatio wants to inspect, stabilize, *arrest* the specter in its speech: "(For which, they say, you Spirits oft walke in death) – Speake of it. Stay and speake – Stop it Marcellus."[36]

Horatio, Derrida suggests, desires the Ghost to present itself, but he also wants to contain that presence, to order and regulate the emergence of the spectral past. However, Derrida continues, "one cannot control its comings and goings" because the specter, the reembodied past, in *Hamlet* and elsewhere, always "*begins by coming back*."[37] Specters rumble forth, finding momentum in the authority of the past, and they speak in voices neither exclusively their own nor fully controlled by the present that summons them. This return recalls the very nature of performance, whose critical discourses, Elin Diamond points out, find their traction in the rhetoric of "re," in *re*embodying, *re*inscribing, *re*configuring, *re*signifying, and we can add, with the Harrowing of Hell specifically in mind, in *re*demption, that is, redeeming and redeciding about the past.[38]

Though he notes its investment in the potential multiplicity of times and temporal directions, Jonathan Gil Harris has suggested that Derrida's insistence on a disruptive past that takes only spectral form – his "hauntology" – fails to account for a multitemporal materiality: the kind of temporally composite stuffness belonging to and evocative of several centuries at once.[39] In a similar vein, Rebecca Schneider argues that Derrida under-emphasizes the inevitable *body* of the actor playing the Ghost, and that his reading of the haunting return does not fully acknowledge the corporeality of performers.[40] To be sure, Derrida reads a certain elasticity of form into the specter, from which it derives its capacity for resiliency and diffusion; haunting, in this sense, is all about being unburdened by the finite body. But elsewhere in *Specters of Marx*, he seems more reluctant to give up the "paradoxical incorporation" of the one who haunts – "the becoming-body, a certain, phenomenal and carnal form of the spirit . . . neither soul nor body, and both one and the other"[41] – a description that recalls, for me, the physically-suffering specters of Dante's *Inferno*, or all the shades who frequently, in Christian otherworlds, seem to flicker between corporeality and shadow, retaining the features of their ageless bodies and clutching psalters in their weightless hands.[42]

What better way to approach this paradoxical embodiment than in medieval performances of Christian redemption? In the Harrowing, the prophets and patriarchs are literally remembered: given hands, feet, and fig-covered bodies as they process out of the mouth and, in the mystery plays, onto the stage, resurrected by both performance and the progression of sacred history, though fully controlled by neither. For the performer, much like the specter, is, as Kruger puts it, positioned "between life and death, conjured up but not therefore necessarily in the full control of the conjurer."[43] Like Horatio's encounter with the Ghost, the episode of the Harrowing suggests a desire to control the communication of that which appears as revenant, and to contain its presence and demand for memory within a careful narrative or theatrical frame and a highly controlled system of stops and starts. The episode illustrates the paradoxical effort Kruger describes: the effort to begin and to end, to preserve and destroy, to look back and yet to move forward. It simultaneously offers a redemption *and* a conclusion in the form of prophetic fulfillment: a "saving" of the past that salvages it for new ends, even as it purports to provide an ending to its otherwise on-going duration. Evidence of the desire to control the past – Christ grabbing Adam's wrist, say – also indicates the difficulty of such a task. This difficulty only is compounded on the stage, where the inherent instability of performance, which always threatens to exceed the script imagined as authorizing it, threatens also to transform repetition into the production of something new.[44]

The Harrowing of Hell plays employ a medium that self-consciously shuttles between past and present in order to perform a story built upon a similar action. The "theater," by definition populated with ghosts, stages a particular set of them stepping out of the wings, through the mouth, and into the light. This connection between performance and haunting – between actors and ghosts, or between enacting and resurrecting – injects instability even into plays ordered and controlled by scripts, guilds, rehearsals, and over a millennium of narrative tradition. Ghosts and performers introduce a quality that resists containment: their ethereal, unstable substance passes up through the ground and in between walls, or slips out of the narrative and structural containment of scripts, escaping the underworld or whatever familiar, restrictive shape fails to keep them. At the moment of the Harrowing, Christ turns back toward an accumulation of text, the scripture about to spill forth from a speaking mouth; his access releases it, conjures it forth, and invites it to overwhelm him in the moment before he confirms it as over, fulfilled, ended, an attempt at closure equally undermined by both the nature of performance and his own need for such figures.

The Harrowing of Hell thus stages the return and reappraisal of a story whose culmination it also requires. It returns the patriarchs and prophets to the earth and to the present, frames them in the very center of a pair of gaping jaws, and then has them escorted to heaven. The first component of this scenario illustrates Kruger's description of "dependence" on an authorizing past and narrative. In the next section, I consider how the second part, the redemption and celestial ascension, produces the "erasure." For the Harrowing, I argue, presents an effort not only to redeem and control the past, but also to clear it out: to open the infernal archive so that it releases the important voices that have been humming just underground, or just backstage. Christ liberates his scriptural predecessors, whose bodies are vomited out through the mouth, and authorizes their collective ascension to paradise, a realm of eternity, beyond narrative and history. He attempts to clear away an ongoing past, still rumbling down below, in order to make space for a new narrative unfolding in the present. The monstrously wide-open mouth suggests the *difficulty* of this narrative closure, as well as the frightening, exhilarating, open-ended, and unending nature of the archive. It also reveals the incapacity of even the most Christ-like of historians to manufacture a story's beginning and end. The episode foregrounds the complexity of circumscribing and regulating the space in which times touch, suggesting how the infernal archive continually is on the verge of blurring into and overtaking the present: times touch, but between frightening, parted teeth, in a mouth threatening always both to swallow and to speak.

3 The Rest Is (Celestial) Silence

The moment in which Christ and his claimed scriptural predecessors share the space within or just beside the yawning hellish jaws signals the transformation of one world into another. The main characters of one text ascend heavenward to make space for the new world, a renewed earth structured according to new rules: "all þat liste [desires] noght to lere [learn] my lawe," begins Christ's warning in the York Harrowing, "þat I haue lefte in lande nowe newe . . ." (ll.314–15). Attempting firmly to end the unsettling dynamic in which infernally archived voices threaten to disrupt or detract from a new, belated narrative unfolding on the earth above, the Harrowing of Hell presents the hell mouth as speaking out scripture for the last time, and as emptying the archive specifically of those important, powerful dead. Christ empties hell of its most precious inventory by sending the Old Testament figures into the scaffold of heaven, a world beyond narration and a realm without leaks. In all of the Harrowing plays, the end of the performance means the entry of the redeemed into heaven. The Chester play emphasizes the eternal nature of this final step:

> To blys nowe I wyll you bringe
> there you shalbe withowt endinge
> Mychaell, lead these men singinge
> to blys that lasteth ever   (ll.209–12)

> I now will bring you there, to bliss; you shall be in it without ending.
> Michael, lead these men, singing, to bliss that lasts forever.

The Christ in the Towneley Harrowing play offers a similar message, noting that the redeemed will "pas fro payn, / In blys to dwell for euermore" (ll.247–8).

This celestial "euermore" contrasts starkly with the nature of hell. Heaven lacks both the cacophony of the underworld and its noticeable passing of time, the latter a resource that both permits narrative and occasions it; the patriarchs, when they speak in hell, speak about time and their long wait through it. The infernal calendar, or Adam's arithmetic of waiting, originates at the departure from Eden, and he carefully numbers the millennia that separate him from a promised homecoming: "iiii ml. and vi c yere" [four thousand and six hundred years] he says in the Towneley Harrowing, "Haue we bene here in darknes stad" [we have been here in a place of darkness] (ll.27–8). The plays employ the dramatic calculation of infernal time to emphasize their wait underground, the duration of the incarcerated presence of those just beneath the earth or stage. We might even speculate that the audience's experience of the daylong or days-long performance cycle enhances this sense of duration, that the crowd remembers the initial barring of the gates after the loss of Eden, and that they feel the weight of the hours that have intervened between then and the Harrowing. At Chester, David says, kneeling to soften the insistence:

> Come, lord, come to hell anon,
> and take owt thy folkes everychon,
> for the yeares be all comen and gonne
> sythen mankynd first came here.   (ll.93–6)

> Come lord, come to hell right away, and take out each one of your people,
> for the years are all come and gone since mankind first came here.

Though hell traditionally threatens the earthly sinner with endless punishment, these descriptions of the portion of hell where the patriarchs and prophets await their redemption suggest a purgatorial temporality. It is a realm of long and arduous waiting for a heavenly ascent, an underground with a clock or calendar on the wall, marking the moments to a prophesied redemption, a place where, as Gervase of Tilbury suggests in the thirteenth century, day and night might alternate, rolling steadily toward some kind of promised happening;[45] indeed, in the Chester Harrowing, Adam says he has been waiting "nighte and day" (l.15). These intimations of counting ascribe purgatorial features to hell, again confounding the difference between the realms. In the Middle Ages, purgatory was not just a place where time existed, it became almost a figure for time and counting, a place wherein earthly intercession affected purgatorial duration and encouraged, to the dismay of some, a kind of "arithmetical thinking" about sin and redemption:[46] so many prayers reduce a sinners' time of suffering by so many years, days or moments. These are units of time that perhaps elude true quantification, or quantification that we might easily equate with earthly numbers, but, as Dante learns on the terraces of Purgatory, they are durations that might at least be compared: some sinners need more time to be purged of their transgressions, some need less.

Heaven, however, has no more need for waiting and counting, and without waiting, there is no narrative, which requires a chronology along which events might be placed, ordered, and set in relation to one another. The realm of heaven belongs to eternity and tranquility; in the plays, there is no cacophony there, and very little speaking. Occasionally a voice issues forth from paradise, but this is the voice of God or a deputized angel, one that neither transgresses nor haunts the earthly realm, but rather gives it shape and purpose, creating, establishing covenants, occasionally regretting the past and making corrective plans for the future. The N-Town manuscript is unique in its inclusion of a play called The Parliament of Heaven, which takes place entirely within that celestial realm. In it, the trinity and a number of allegorical characters (Contemplation, Mercy, Justice, Truth) acknowledge the unrest in hell and discuss what should be done down there, where "man" has been waiting, rather loudly, "fowre thowsand, sex undryd, foure yere" (1.1). God the father says that those who wait in hell clamor for release: "My prophetys with prayers have made supplicacyon / My contryte creaturys cryse all for comforte" [my prophets have made supplication with their prayers; my contrite creatures all cry out for comfort] (ll.53–4). The play ends (or phases into Gabriel's Salutation to Mary) with God-*Filius* expressing his "hast to be man thore" [haste to be man there] and taking his own fall into action (l.201). The earthly and infernal regions demand actions, plans, and change; it is their voices to which heaven's citizens must respond.

There are a few other moments when God speaks from heaven in the plays, with the actor located in some impressive upper mansion "or in the clowdes, if it may bee."[47] And very occasionally, even other characters get to chime in; Lucifer declaims his own majesty from heaven, and in Chester, the patriarchs and prophets encounter Elijah, Enoch, and the good thief there. They all identify themselves and relate their stories and when the good thief, the last to speak, finishes his lines, Adam says, "Nowe goe wee to blys," and exhorts his companions to sing (l.273). The stage direction reads: "Tunc eant omnes, et incipiat Michaell 'Te Deum laudamus'" [Then they all go, and Michael will begin, "We praise you, O God"]. Otherwise, however, voices in heaven tend to sound only when that realm intersects with another: when Lucifer speaks the words to precipitate his long fall into the inferno below; when Christ promises to follow him to earth; or when Adam and Eve first enter paradise after their long wait underground.

Interruptions from hell or earth – the intrusion of hellish or earthly things, such as the loud counting down below that the heavenly parliament acknowledges – create narratable events in heaven: introductions and explanations before songs of praise and eternal "blys" are renewed. It is not that nothing happens in heaven, but rather that happenings mostly occur at points of cosmic intersection. In heaven, narrative is an interruption, something eventually to be subsumed into eternity and an endless *Te Deum*. Emphasizing this contrast between realms, the Chester Harrowing ends not with Adam's heavenly song of praise, the voices of the saved lifted in bliss "euermore," but with a return to hell, still bustling down below.[48] A new sinner, another talking woman, arrives at the close of the play: she is "a taverner, / a gentle gossippe and a tapster," and she takes up infernal residence for her many indiscretions committed above ground (ll.285–6). The lines are assigned only to MULIER (WOMAN), who says:

> Therfore I may my handes wringe,
> shake my cuppes and kannes ringe.
> Sorrowfull maye I syke and singe
> that ever I so dalt   (ll.299–301)

> Therefore I may wring my hands, shake my cups and ring my cans,
> sorrowful will I sigh and sing, that I ever dealt in that way.

The conclusion of the play presents two divergent songs and two kinds of "euermore." In hell, rattling cups and cans accompany whatever anger or lamentation the woman chooses to "singe," and in heaven, voices offer up the *Te Deum*, a hymn of praise. In one realm, there is endless suffering, in the other, eternal bliss.

These visions of endlessness are not equal in their relation to narrative. Despite the brief scenes staged in paradise, and despite an actor-God who occasionally utters promises, plans, and commandments from his heavenly scaffold, the Harrowing plays, and even the larger drama of sacred history within which they are situated, work to present paradise as an eternal realm beyond narrative. Hellish music and hellish narrative suggest a *different* kind of "euermore": one that continually threatens to last forever and thus proposes the temporal quality of endless duration; it is not, in the manner of paradise, an eternity that is the simultaneity of all time, an indivisibility akin to the in-gathering Dante perceives in the cosmic book that cannot be separated into separate pages. The cosmic book suggests the timelessness Boethius terms eternity in the fifth book of the *Consolation of Philosophy*, where he distinguishes it from the perpetual, ongoing duration that might be used to describe the timeframe of the world or, more punishingly, the underworld. "Eternity," Boethius argues, gathers all times into the present, and the "perpetual" continually, doggedly manifests the present as it moves through time.[49] Purgatory, in some texts, would seem to be somewhere in between, occasionally keeping its souls in a vice grip indistinguishable from hell and sometimes permitting them to ascend toward celestial eternity.

Though these understandings of heavenly timelessness and infernal time without end might seem to resemble one another, representations of how humans experience them diverge considerably. First of all, time in hell is imagined in the form of continual punishment and monotonous occupation: by Dante, who describes the thief who turns to ashes, reconstitutes like an infernal phoenix, and catches fire once more;[50] by the classical poets, who have Tantalus stoop waterward again and again to mark the passing of time like a human metronome; and by the tavern-keeping woman at Chester who, understanding her fate, picks up her cups and cans to beat out an endless but rhythmic song. Here, duration is marked and noted; the sinners count out stretches of endlessness through the infliction of wounds, conflagration, and with their sad songs. This marking of time only intensifies in the case of the patriarchs and prophets who count out centuries in their special portion of Abraham's bosom, a pocket of hell imagined to have qualities similar to those eventually ascribed to the great waiting rooms of purgatory, where the promised ascent to heaven potentially draws closer every moment.

Conceptions of time just seem to attach more easily to hell. In the *Confessions*, for example, Augustine fields the question of what God did before creation. He offers two answers: a good one and (according to him) a bad one. He will not, he writes, answer as someone once did "to evade the force of the question. He said: 'He was preparing hells for people who inquire into profundities.'"[51] Instead, Augustine suggests that the difficulty of formulating a direct answer arises from the fact that God simultaneously invents time *and* creation; the one does not exist before the other, and so the question of a "before" is inherently flawed: "But if time did not exist before heaven and earth, why do people ask what you were then doing? There was no 'then' when there was no time."[52] Augustine's first, facetious response – that God creates hell before the rest of creation in order to house those who ask unanswerable questions – lingers even after Augustine dismisses it for its facetiousness. "Hell" stubbornly remains as a response to the quandary of eternity. The answer "hell" fills the space otherwise occupied by the non-articulatable response that questions about eternity solicit; it replaces the lack of an answer about a "before" with an answer that nonetheless insists on temporality. The vision of God making hell supplies a narrative in the place of the narrative-defying explanation Augustine offers. Hell is adamantly linked to chronology and to narrative; it becomes the space imagined by those who refuse to (who are unable to) move beyond the bounds of narrative.

The effect of these competing visions of timelessness manifest on the stage during the Harrowing of Hell plays, when Christ releases his pre-cursor figures from a space of narrative and sends them to a space beyond narrative. He redeems them in order to permit their ascension to a space that exists beyond the end of their story, and beyond the possibility of narrative in general. Christ does not immediately accompany these Old Testament figures on their ascent to heaven. In York, he gives instructions to Michael to take them while he prepares to resume his grave:

> And Mighill, myn aungell clere,
> Ressayue þes saules all vnto þe,
> And lede þame als I schall þe lere
> To paradise, with playe and plenté.
> Mi graue I woll go till,
> Redy to rise vpperight,
> And so I shall fulfille
> That I before haue highte. (ll.390–6)

> And Michael, my bright angel, receive all of these souls unto yourself, and lead them, as I shall instruct you, to paradise, with play and plenty. I will go to my grave, ready to rise upright, and so I shall fulfill what I promised before.

Although the end of the patriarchs' and prophets' waiting, and so the end of their story, brings them into eternity at the end of the Harrowing, the same is not yet true for Christ. Still enwrapped in his humanity, and so still in the midst of his story – in its rich meantime – he has the resurrection and the witnessing of that resurrection yet to come. Christ remains on the stage of the earth, avoiding eternity so that the narrative whose center he occupies might continue. The N-Town Harrowing play especially empha-sizes this idea, concluding with a promise and description of the savior's next act, along with a harsh note about the contemporary "Jewys," made to take up a position in a story from which biblical Hebrews have receded. The last lines of the play are:

> Now wele I rysyn flesch and felle,
> þat rent was for ʒoure sake.
> Myn owyn body þat hynge on rode,
> And, be þe Jewys nevyr so wode,

It xal aryse, both flesch and blode.
My body now wyl I take. (ll.67–72)

Now I will rise, flesh and skin, that was torn for your sake. My own body
that hung on the cross – and though the Jews be never so mad – it shall arise
both flesh and blood. My body I will now take.

This body, both the human body taken by Christ and the body of Christ
taken on by the medieval player, would seem, for however brief a time, to
remain alone on the earth and on the stage, the precursor portion of the
infernal archive cleared out from beneath him, and heaven silent, or else
resounding with the eternal *Te Deum*, above.

The Harrowing of Hell thus stages an invitation for the hell mouth to
speak out its last of scripture; it represents Christ as emptying the infernal
archive of his scriptural predecessors and silencing the voices that might
otherwise filter through the unruly portal of the mouth of hell. The
emphasis is on closure, because finishing or fulfilling the narrative rumbling underground clears the stage so that Christ might stand on it alone,
free from the specters of interruption waiting just beneath him or off to the
side, that memory of older narrative that threatens always to intrude or
overwhelm his own. Once the prophets and patriarchs ascend, he commands both earth and stage, remaining behind in a temporal realm to act
and to be witnessed.

The Harrowing, however, also explores the difficulties attendant upon
that project of clearing the stage, page, or hell of the important voices of the
past. The narrative closure effected by the ascent of the redeemed into
paradise is represented as nothing if not impermanent, annually performed
and re-presented as it is in mystery play productions, and continuously
retranslated and reworked in text and image. The very etymologies of
"harrowing" suggest just such a recursive impulse,[53] a desire literally to
return to earth. The "harrow" was a blade that cut into the ground,
furrowing soil in an agricultural context before piercing the more daunting
crust of the earth, as when Christ descends to redeem that which has been
deemed "past." ("Plowing," writes Vance Smith, "suggests both erasure
and inscription, both beginning and rebeginning."[54]) The episode of the
Harrowing is not an ending, but a return so that one might begin again:
a "rehearsal," to which its etymologies also link,[55] that the prophets continually perform and reperform, a pivot that launches those previously
doomed toward salvation, even as it discloses the inherent recursivity in the
larger sacred narrative it so centrally punctuates. Because broaching the
subject of the past unsettles its containment, access requires delicate

balance between opening the archive and regulating its inventory: redeeming and directing, or, as Derrida puts it, "conjuring" in order both to invite and to enjoin. Iconography suggests the care with which Christ breaks the gates of hell to combine those actions, the edge of his toe stepping warningly upon the bottom of the gaping maw, and his right hand pulling out the cautiously resurrected.

This wavering between reopening and fulfilling/finishing the past, or opening and closing the door to Ginzburg's exhilarating, authorizing "beyond," marks out the path of narrative in the always-circling present of the great middle of sacred history, the phase during which narrators continually return to older narrative even as the inexorable path of prophecy impels them forward. Balanced between the desire to finish and the desire to perform in a way that does not finish – to name and to erase – the ambivalence of the Harrowing creates specters that cannot be controlled, haunting the stage of the earth, calling out "remember me" from an imperfect infernal containment,[56] or from that brief touchdown on the stage of the earth. It is this invitation to remember, resounding from the infernal holding pen whose powers of containment can at times be weak, that the plays stage as both a necessary part of the unfolding present of sacred history *and* as a threat to the centrality of the gospel in the new world that the gospel inaugurates. The nature of the confirming speeches the prophets and patriarchs make – always carrying that persistent subtext of the Ghost's unsettling refrain – as well as their inevitable ascension to paradise, work to control or to modify the invitation to memory, and to coax the remembered into a heavenly realm without doors or mouths, a place where eternity obviates the need for active collection and storage. But in the *mean*time, the medieval Christian reorganization of history continues as ongoing effort, remaining always an attempt performed from the circling middle of a perpetually enduring story, and never a finished or fulfilled act. The archive remains open, continually inviting the living to remember even the problematic dead, an inventory that, when viewed, seems to move forward in time toward the viewer, rather than dissipating, disappointed, into shadow.

Epilogue

We shall sleep-out together through the dark
the earth's slow voyage across centuries
towards whatever Ararat its ark is steering for.
Our atoms then will feel the jarring and arrival of that keel.

Charles Tomlinson, "Ararat"

The medieval people who attended performances of the mystery plays were immersed, at least for a moment, in a swirl of time: that of the festival that suspended the quotidian rhythms underpinning ordinary civic life; the liturgical calendar on whose eschatological spiral the feast of Corpus Christi annually located itself; the performed sacred history divided into biblical ages, or into old and new; and the kind of time that exists within the zone of performance itself. This last category might be apprehended in a number of ways. There is the time during which a play is performed and then reperformed, according to the processional, reiterative nature of cycle drama, and the time that performances of sacred history flexibly evoke: emerging out of nothing and then proceeding toward eternity. Or there is the rushing across centuries as the pageants skip from one biblical episode to another, from fall to flood, say, or from the girlhood of Mary to the birth of Christ: "Tyme sufficyth not to make pawsacyon," apologizes *Contemplacio* in the play that prepares for that latter elision of years.[1] Hewing to the quality he embodies, the allegorical figure narrates the rush of time he stands stalwart against, holding still and beholding. And finally, there is the time between the plays, in which all of those things described might converge, or disrupt one another, as players and audience themselves contemplate, relax, laugh, listen to pageant wagons creak, drink, eat, applaud, disperse, and *wait*. Perhaps in these interstices, roaming spectators listened to voices from different moments of sacred history resounding in their civic spaces, the grief of one disrupting the joy of another understood to exist centuries later, and the trumpets of the angels mingling with the hubbub of the city.

And then it would end, or try to make an ending. In the York Doomsday play, with which this book began, *Deus* announces: "nowe is it tyme to me / To make endyng of mannes folie" (ll.55–6). It is a nod both to the finality of a day that heralds the end of history, and to the packing up of the pageant wagons. As the angels gather all the souls who ever lived together to make a final and complete reckoning, the medieval people at York perhaps would prepare to disperse and return to the more ordinary rhythms of their lives. Again, *Deus* says that he will send the angels to sound their trumpets, so "þat all may here / The tyme is comen I will make ende" (ll.63–4). But he cannot keep those two words, "time" and "end," apart. Their inextricability in his concluding verses emphasizes the representational difficulties of eternity in this play, the only one set in the future, where time works just as it does in the present and the past, holding off the advent of eternity. Time underpins the meter and the very syllabic divisions of God's avowal that all folly – both history and performance – is nearing an end. The progression of the lines both articulates and gives the lie to the end of time.

It is difficult to know what it might have felt like. We can attend reenactments of the mystery plays today, or other performances more in keeping with our aesthetic familiars, or even take part in processions, religious or otherwise. Or we can go to the archives, to find records associated with the Mercers, who put on those lavish Doomsday plays, to help us imagine what the bedecked wagons might have looked like, or to hear, in at least one instance, about the irreverent laughter of a mocking crowd, to the chagrin of players who were eager to inspire devotion.[2] Or we can read the thoughts recorded by a certain bishop Abraham, who watched similar religious plays in Italy and described the logistics of the pyrotechnics and the flying angels, and who expressed his awe at witnessing them: "the appearance of the machinery is amazingly wonderful, even to grown men."[3] But these strategies for knowing how something was, what it was *like*, are only ever partial. The full bulk of the past eludes us; textual records, new performances, and reenactments offer only tantalizing glimpses of a past that, even in its own moment, could hardly be perceived in its entirety. And if it is difficult to perceive one's own age in its entirety, efforts to encompass all of history also surely must falter. As we have seen, Borges locates his "inconceivable universe," containing all of space and the infinite things inside of it – a complete world, fully encapsulated – beneath a staircase in a cellar, as if to suggest the strangeness, perhaps even the ridiculousness, of attempts at universal representation. It is not wholly dissimilar from the player-God punctuating his assertions of the end with reminders of time: acknowledgement, or admission, that time and space, the very resources of representation,[4] undercut all attempts at full accounts.

But still such attempts are made, and not only in the Middle Ages or within the context of sacred history. In the twentieth century, space travel recontextualized our place in the universe, offering proof of a complete, spherical, finite earth, one that, with the aid of photography, could indeed be seen all at once (or perhaps one half at a time, in the manner that each crystal miraculously discloses half of the garden in *The Romance of the Rose*). In the 1970s, Carl Sagan tried to update the project of the global *arca* by loading a representative inventory of the earth into a spacecraft. That vessel, Voyager I, launched in 1979, finally departed the solar system in 2013, containing what have become known as the "golden records,"[5] holding sounds and images of our planet, including classical music, thunder, mathematical equations, artist-rendered silhouettes of a man and a woman, and lots of other things. The idea was to represent the earth to whatever new world existed to receive it, should its inhabitants be advanced enough to receive and access the records. "We are attempting," wrote then-President Carter, evoking the dream of Tomlinson's poetry in my epigram, "to survive our time so we may live into yours."[6]

Sagan chaired the NASA committee responsible for selecting the inventory for the Voyager project, realizing even as they sent the vessel outward, that it was not necessarily positioned toward encounter, but that it served as a call for its compilers to think about what the earth meant and how it might be understood, by themselves or by future others: how it might be represented in words, sounds, and images, its existence distilled into inventory. The compilers agonized over the selection, trying to figure out *which* music to include within the limited audio space and *how* to word a greeting. They acknowledged the ways in which contemporary mores shaped their compilational strategies and stumbled, at last, over the same problem encountered by the medieval Noah: how to include and represent a human, both a man and a woman. (A photograph of a naked man and a naked pregnant woman eventually was expunged from the record.) Fitting the whole world onto a golden record: there, too, the hopelessness of the writer or archivist begins.

This study has demonstrated how medieval thinkers and artists expressed a desire for that kind of comprehensive vision, even as it offers an additional method for partially recovering a now-vanished and perhaps always unrecordable experience of the fullness of time. It employs the resource of imagined adjacency,[7] by which I mean the possibility of thinking *with* medieval artists as they represent the impossibility of fully experiencing their own present and past and the even more difficult problem of bequeathing it, in all of its elusively capacious richness, to us. Because of our own extraordinary projects, we can begin to imagine (partially) what it might have been like to prepare the inheritance we now receive,[8] or to attempt to live on into some future time. I do not want to argue that such dreams of transmission are a universal desire, common across centuries to patriarchs, poets, and scientists alike, especially since part of the point of this study has been to put such claims of universality under pressure, to note, for instance, those things that elude official inventories and archival strategies. Methods for representing, accessing, and forgetting the past are always changing. What I want to suggest, however, is that perhaps what changes least of all is the impulse to think through those very changes, to contemplate what kind of world is ushered through time, and how that transmission occurs: to struggle over which music to load into a spacecraft; to imagine a universe in which time moves in multiple directions; or to add an additional perspective to a story of renewed origins, and give her space to speak.

Notes

Introduction

1. *The York Plays*, ed. Beadle, Doomsday, ll.69–70. All York quotations are from this edition, and hereafter are cited in the main text by line number.
2. In late medieval iconography, these reckonings or books of account sometimes took the form of codices superimposed upon the heart, suggesting that the heart itself contained or formed a textual record. See Jager, *The Book of the Heart*, 113–19.
3. Badir, reading this compression of time through Gil Harris, describes the Mercers' pageant wagon itself as "'untimely matter,' bringing together several or many historical periods at one time," in "'The whole past, the whole time': Untimely Matter and the Playing Spaces of York," in Bennett and Polito (eds.), *Performing Environments*, 18–22.
4. Clanchy describes how the *Anglo-Saxon Chronicle* exaggerates the reach and meticulousness of the Domesday records – "there was no single hide nor virgate of land, nor indeed – it is a shame to relate but it seemed no shame to him to do – one ox or one cow nor one pig which was there left out and not put down in his record" – in order "to emphasize the frightening – and shameful – thoroughness" of the project. Clanchy, *From Memory to Written Record, England: 1066–1307*, 18.
5. The phrase is from Blouin Jr. and Rosenberg, *Processing the Past: Contesting Authority in History and the Archives*, 5. See further, Craven (ed.), *What Are Archives? Cultural and Theoretical Perspectives: A Reader*, and Clanchy, who argues that the comparatively modern distinction between libraries and archives does not hold in the Middle Ages, in "'Tenacious Letters': Archives and Memory in the Middle Ages," 122–3.
6. *The Etymologies of Isidore of Seville*, ed. and trans. Barney et al., XX.ix.2. The Latin text is from *Etymologiarum sive originum*, 2 vols., ed. Lindsay: "Arca dicta quod arceat visum atque prohibeat. Hinc et arcivum, hinc et arcanum, id est secretum, unde ceteri arcentur." Hereafter, I cite from Barney et al. by book, chapter, and verse in the main text and provide the Latin from Lindsay's edition in the notes.
7. Hugutio of Pisa (Uguccione da Pisa), *Derivationes*, ed. Cecchini et al., A.308.5, 79.

8. *Summa Britonis Sive Guillelmi Britonis Expositiones Vocabularium Biblie*, ed. Daly and Daly, 49–50.
9. Clanchy, *From Memory to Written Record, England: 1066–1307*, 128, n. 49.
10. Blouin and Rosenberg, *Processing the Past*, 4.
11. Derrida, "Archive Fever: A Freudian Impression," trans. Prenowitz, 10.
12. Steedman, *Dust: The Archive and Cultural History*, 6, 4.
13. Foucault, *The Archaeology of Knowledge and the Discourse on Language*, trans. Smith, 129. Steedman, *Dust*, 2.
14. Steedman, *Dust*, 27.
15. Foucault, *The Archaeology of Knowledge*, trans. Smith, 129–130.
16. Ibid., 130, emphasis in original.
17. Steiner, *Documentary Culture and the Making of Medieval English Literature*, 93.
18. Steiner, *Documentary Culture and the Making of Medieval English Literature*, 94, quoting from Foucault, *The Archaeology of Knowledge*, 129. Steiner also is interested in Foucault's other discarded definition: "the sum of all those texts that a culture has kept on its person as documents attesting to its own past, or as evidence of a continuing identity," which she quotes at 94.
19. Farge, *The Allure of the Archives* (orig. *Le Goût de l'Archive*, 1989), trans. Scott-Railton, 12.
20. Ibid., 96, 9–12.
21. In several special issues, the journal *Archival Science* has invited archivists to consider the nexus among their profession, political power, and interpretive license after Foucault and Derrida. In their introduction to the second of a two-part special issue on archives, records, and power in 2002, Cook and Schwartz write, as part of their opening abstract, "Theory and practice are not opposites, not even polarities." Cook and Schwartz, in "Archives, Records, and Power: From (Postmodern) Theory to (Archival) Performance," 171. Another issue, also deliberately positioning itself after Foucault, Derrida, and "the theoretical appropriation of 'the archive' by postmodern theory," appeared in 2010, under the title "In and Out of the Archives," focusing on Europe 1400–1700 and introduced by Blair. The quotation is from a preface by Head, who notes the valuable work such an "appropriation" and the emergence of new questions have produced, especially for postcolonial studies. "Preface: Historical Research on Archives and Knowledge Cultures: An Interdisciplinary Wave," 191–2. See further Cook's introduction to a volume of essays he edited a year later as a festschrift for the archivist Helen Samuels, *Controlling the Past*, 1–28.
22. Greenblatt and Gallagher, *Practicing New Historicism*, Introduction, 1–19.
23. Gillespie's "History of the Book" surveys this trend and suggests how medieval manuscript study offers room for exciting new approaches in a field interested primarily in print culture. Some of this exciting work has taken the form of intersecting material and textual formalisms. See, for instance, Nichols' earlier call for a "material philology" in "Philology and its

Discontents," and "Philology in a Manuscript Culture," in Paden (ed.), *The Future of the Middle Ages*, as well as Lerer, "Medieval Literature and the Idea of the Anthology," and Bahr, *Fragments and Assemblages: Forming Compilations of Medieval London*. For more general studies on the history of the book, see Howsam, "The Study of Book History," in *The Cambridge Companion to the History of the Book*, ed. Howsam, and Chartier, *The Order of Books: Readers, Authors, and Libraries in Europe between the Fourteenth and Eighteenth Centuries*, trans. Cochrane.

24. In an early critique of new historicism, David Scott Kastan advocates for "more facts" and "definitive and usable historical knowledge," mined through methods of careful scrutiny; he argues that, without them, we fail to apprehend the past as fully as we might, or at all. Kastan, "Shakespeare After Theory," 365, 372. Ten years later, Peter D. McDonald revisits the subject of the relationship between theory and the (by then) more recognizable field of book history in "Ideas of the Book and Histories of Literature: After Theory?" See further, Howsam, *Old Books and New Histories: An Orientation to Studies in Book and Print Culture*, 4–5.

25. The need for such time-consuming, highly trained study is described by Taylor, who synthesizes and responds to criticism launched at book history and archival research in *Textual Situations: Three Medieval Manuscripts and their Readers*, 197–9.

26. LaCapra writes that such study risks "making a fetish of archival research," permitting one to mistake musty holdings for an actually irrecoverable past. LaCapra, *History and Criticism*, 20–1.

27. Reading through Derrida's "Archive Fever," Warner interestingly argues that the scarcity of inventory can, in fact, clarify the amount of interpretive authority afforded the *archon*. Warner, *The Myth of Piers Plowman: Constructing a Medieval Literary Archive*, 2–3.

28. Coletti and Gibson discuss early modern strategies of crafting a body of medieval drama in "The Tudor Origins of Medieval Drama," in *A Companion to Tudor Literature*, ed. Cartwright, 228–45. Summit interestingly writes: "If libraries reveal that the Middle Ages were a creation of the Renaissance, they also make it possible to see the Renaissance as a creation of the Middle Ages . . . later readers . . . touching these earlier books, could not fail to be touched by them in turn," in *Memory's Library: Medieval Books in Early Modern England*, 4. See further Echard, who describes how modern archives continue to remake the Middle Ages in "House Arrest: Medieval Manuscripts: Modern Archives," as well as Warner, *The Myth of Piers Plowman: Constructing a Medieval Literary Archive*, 3.

29. Kastan, "Shakespeare after Theory," 372.

30. Phelan, *Unmarked: The Politics of Performance*, 146.

31. Alexandra F. Johnston and Margaret (Dorrell) Rogerson (eds.), *Records of Early English Drama: York*, 2 vols, I: ix. (The first volume of REED, published in 1979, concerned York.)

32. Ibid.

33. Coletti, "Reading REED: History and the Records of Early English Drama," 270. Coletti makes it very clear that such a critique does not imply criticism of archival research in general, 251. Frantzen has made a similar point about certain projects in Anglo-Saxon studies in *Desire for Origins: New Language, Old English, and Teaching the Tradition*, esp. 85.

34. As Bennett and Polito write in the introduction to *Performing Environments: Site Specificity in Medieval and Early Modern English Drama*, 3: "The amassing of such a dense body of empirical evidence about these myriad events in places all over the mainland has allowed for speculative and theoretically engaged work." A similar argument about the productive intertwining of theory and the kind of research provided by REED can be found in Badir, "History, The Body, and Records of Early English Drama," which is in part a response to Coletti's essay.

35. LaCapra, *History and Criticism*, 92.

36. Geary, *Phantoms of Remembrance: Memory and Oblivion at the end of the First Millennium*, 8.

37. The idea that the Middle Ages had its own past(s) and methods for apprehending and organizing them may seem a basic one, but it is often one worth more actively remembering. Nicholas Watson describes how medieval strategies for reaching back toward the past might inform our own in a pair of related essays: "Desire for the Past" and "The Phantasmal Past: Time, History, and the Recombinative Imagination."

38. Clanchy refers specifically to the twelfth and thirteenth centuries in *From Memory to Written Record, England: 1066–1307*, 1–2.

39. A number of medievalist historians and scholars of literary history have charted the work of these bureaucratic offices, both ecclesiastical and royal. See Rouse and Rouse, "*Statim invenire:* Schools, Preachers, and New Attitudes to the Page," in Benson et al. (eds.), *Renaissance and Renewal in the Twelfth Century*, 201–25; Brown, *Governance of Late Medieval England, 1272–1461*; Britnell (ed.), *Pragmatic Literacy, East and West, 1200–1330*; and Declercq, "Originals and Cartularies: The Organization of Archival Memory (Ninth-Eleventh Centuries)," in Heidecker (ed.), *Charters and the Use of the Written Word*, 147–70. In addition, *The Cambridge History of Libraries in Britain and Ireland, Vol. 1: to 1640*, ed. Leedham-Green and Webber, offers chapters on all aspects of medieval libraries. Firth Green also considers the literary consequences of an increase in documentation and writing in general in *The Crisis of Truth: Literature and Law in Ricardian England*.

40. Richard fitzNigel, *Dialogus de Scaccario, The Dialogue of the Exchequer*, ed. and trans. Amt, 38–9. "In mundanorum enim tribulis mistici intellectus flores querere laudabile est. Nec in his tantum que commemoras set in tota scaccarii descriptione sacramentorum quedam latibula sunt. Officiorum namque diuersitas, iudiciarie potestatis auctoritas, regie imaginis impressio, citationum emissio, rotulorum conscriptio, uillicationum ratio, debitorum exactio, reorum condempnatio uel absolutio districti examinis figura sunt, quod reuelabitur cum omnium libri aperti erunt et ianua clausa."

41. Apocalypse, 20:12: "et libri aperti sunt." All Latin scriptural text is quoted from *Biblia Sacra: iuxta vulgatam versionem*, ed. Gryson, and all English translations are from *The Holy Bible: Douay–Rheims Version*, rev. Richard Challoner.

42. *Liber Albus: The White Book of the City of London*, trans. Riley, 3. "Quia labilitas humanae memoriae, brevitasque vitae, de singulis rebus memorandis, licet scriptis – praesertim irregulariter et confuse, – et multo magis de non scriptis, certam habere notitiam non permittunt; cumque, per frequentes pestilentias, subtractis velut insimul cunctis gubernatoribus longaevis magis expertis et discretioribus Civitatis Regalis Londoniarum ... necessarium videbatur a diu, tam superioribus quam subditis dictae civitatis, quoddam volume ... ex notabilibus memorandis tam in libris, rotulis, quam in chartis dictae civitatis inordinate diffuseque positis, compilari." *Munimenta Guildhallae Londoniensis: Liber Albus, Liber Custumarum, et Liber Horn*, ed. Riley, 3. For a discussion of this preface, see Knapp, *The Bureaucratic Muse*, 83–6.

43. Studies by Steiner (*Documentary Culture and the Making of Medieval English Literature*) and Knapp (*The Bureaucratic Muse: Thomas Hoccleve and the Literature of Late Medieval England*) have demonstrated not only how the intersection of bureaucracy and poetry helped to produce a documentary poetics in the later Middle Ages, but also how the categories of the "literary" and the "non-literary" were not so clearly demarcated.

44. Knapp, *The Bureaucratic Muse*, esp. 30–32.

45. Mead, "Chaucer and the Subject of Bureaucracy," 42.

46. Geoffrey Chaucer, *The Riverside Chaucer* 3rd edn., ed. Benson, "House of Fame," ll.653–4, 657. All Chaucer quotations are taken from this edition and hereafter are cited by line number (or, for the *Canterbury Tales*, by fragment and line number) in the main text.

47. "Continens in se tam laudibiles observantias non scriptas, in dicta civitate fieri solitas et approbatas, ne posterius deleat ipsas oblivio, quam notabilia memoranda, modo quo praedicitur sparsim et inordinate scripta" (4).

48. Dante Alighieri, *The Divine Comedy: Paradiso*, trans. Mandelbaum, 33.82–90. "Oh abbondante grazia ond' io presunsi / ficcar lo viso per la luce etterna, / tanto che la veduta vi consunsi! / Nel suo profondo vidi che s'interna, / legato con amore in un volume, / ciò che per l'universo si squaderna: / sustanze e accidenti e lor costume / quasi conflati insieme, per tal modo / che ciò ch'i' dico è un semplice lume." All Italian and English *Inferno* and *Paradiso* quotations are from Dante, *The Divine Comedy*, trans. Mandelbaum; hereafter, English translations are cited by canto and line number in the main text, with the Italian provided in the notes.

49. Helpful to this last pairing is Derrida's discussion of totality, lack, and supplement in "Structure, Sign, and Play in the Discourse of the Human Sciences," in Macksey and Donato (eds.), *The Structuralist Controversy: The Languages of Criticism and the Sciences of Man*, 260–1.

50. Ronquist discusses the innovative impatience of Dante's encyclopedic strategies in the *Comedy* in "Patient and Impatient Encyclopaedism," in Binkley (ed.), *Premodern Encyclopaedic Texts*, 39–40.

51. Emily Steiner, "Compendious Genres: Higden, Trevisa, and the Medieval Encyclopedia," 73–5.

52. For instance, Bernard Silvestris, in the dedication of his twelfth-century *Cosmographia*, immediately assents to the difficulty of representing the total universe. Silvestris, *Cosmographia*, trans. Wetherbee, 65.

53. Binkley, "Preachers' Responses to Thirteenth-Century Encyclopaedism," in Binkley (ed.), *Pre-Modern Encyclopaedic Texts*, 79.

54. Lerer suggests that the "book of wikked wives" from the *Wife of Bath's Prologue* also recalls Dante's volume in parodic form, in "Medieval English Literature and the Idea of the Anthology," 1254.

55. See Happé, *Cyclic Form and the English Mystery Plays: A Comparative Study of the English Biblical Cycles and Their Continental and Iconographic Counterparts*, 15–21, and Clopper, "From Ungodly *Ludi* to Sacred Play," in Wallace (ed.) *The Cambridge History of Medieval Literature*, 739–766.

56. Palmer suggests the importance of the town (or manor) of Wakefield to the Towneley cycle is exaggerated in "'Towneley Plays' or 'Wakefield Cycle' Revisited."

57. Coletti and Gibson, "The Tudor Origins of Medieval Drama," 235–6.

58. The codices that compile and preserve the plays, occasionally along with an accompanying banns – or the annotated, advertising table of contents, in some cases written considerably later – bring together a different kind of capacious record, documenting not only the events of sacred history, but also of regional dramatic efforts to dramatize that history across shifts in aesthetic and religious emphases. Mills thus describes the late texts associated with Chester, for instance, as a "record of change," making visible the adjustments and modifications that occur within a performance and scriptwriting tradition stretching across centuries. Mills, "The Editing of the Play-Manuscripts," in *The Chester Mystery Cycle: A Casebook*, ed. Harty, 11.

59. On staging the Eucharist, see Sofer, *The Stage Life of Props*, ch.1, 31–60, and Beckwith, "Ritual, Church, and Theatre: Medieval Dramas of the Sacramental Body," in Aers (ed.), *Culture and History, 1350–1500: Essays on English Communities, Identities, and Writing*.

60. Turner, *From Ritual to Theatre*, 13. Brantley discusses how Julian of Norwich's use of the word intersects with this sense in *Reading in the Wilderness: Private Devotion and Public Performance in Late Medieval England*, 18.

61. On the recursivity of verse, see Simpson, "Cognition Is Recognition: Literary Knowledge and Textual 'Face,'" 34.

62. Symes, *A Common Stage: Theater and Public Life in Medieval Arras*, 1–13, and "The Appearance of Early Vernacular Plays: Forms, Functions, and the Future of Medieval Theater," esp. 779. Such an approach is also the imperative of performance studies generally, as articulated in Schechner's "Performance Studies: The Broad Spectrum Approach."

63. Brantley, *Reading in the Wilderness: Private Devotion and Public Performance in Late Medieval England* and Enders, "Medieval Stages." Chaganti also provides a helpful overview of this discussion in "The *Platea* Pre- and Postmodern: A Landscape of Medieval Performance Studies."

64. Robert Mannyng of Brunne, *The Chronicle*, ed. Idelle Sullens, l.1–2.

65. Kolve, *The Play Called Corpus Christi*, 1.

1 Model Worlds

1. Genesis 2:8.

2. Delumeau provides an overview of these names in *History of Paradise: The Garden of Eden in Myth and Tradition*, trans. O'Connell, 4–5.

3. Minnis, *From Eden to Eternity: Creations of Paradise in the Later Middle Ages*, 1.

4. Geertz, *The Interpretation of Cultures*, 93.

5. Ibid.

6. Just to the side of this discussion, it would seem, is the question of "universals" and "particulars," which medieval thinkers inherited from Aristotle and Plato, via Boethius and Porphyry. The idea is that a "universal," something known through the intellect rather than through sensory experience – something abstract and yet participating in all subsequent particulars – at times seems to take its features through the initial sensation of particulars. See the discussion and excerpt of Boethius in Bosley and Tweedale (eds.), *Basic Issues in Medieval Philosophy*, 337–9. A helpful overview of the shifts that occurred in medieval apprehension of these ideas and their influence upon poetic possibilities is in Kay, *The Place of Thought: The Complexity of One in Late Medieval French Didactic Poetry*, 8–15.

7. *Le Jeu D'Adam (Ordo representacionis Ade)*, ed. Noomen, 17. Mittman, *Maps and Monsters in Medieval England*, 46–7.

8. See the British Library's Egerton 912, f.10.

9. See the British Library's Royal 14 E V f. 13v, a Dutch manuscript from the end of the fifteenth century, or the Hours of Catherine of Cleves, Morgan Library's MS M.917/945, p. 85.

10. *The Egerton Version of Mandeville's Travels*, ed. Seymour, 165.

11. Ibid.

12. "sed fons ascendebat e terra inrigans universam superficiem terrae / formavit igitur Dominus Deus hominem de limo terrae / et inspiravit in faciem eius spiraculum vitae / et factus est homo in animam viventem / plantaverat autem Dominus Deus paradisum voluptatis a principio / in quo posuit hominem quem formaverat." On the history of the translation of these opening chapters, see Scafi, *Mapping Paradise: A History of Heaven on Earth*, 32–6.

13. Augustine spends a considerable amount of time discussing the spring mentioned in Genesis, as well as growth rates and irrigation patterns, in *De*

Genesi ad litteram. For instance, he asks if it is plausible that the spring of paradise initially waters everything on earth, and then "later on, having planted Paradise, he [God] cut off the flow of that spring, and filled the earth with many springs, as we now see it, while he divided the flow from the one spring of Paradise into four huge rivers?" Augustine, *On Genesis*, trans. Hill, ed. Rotelle, 286 ". . . et postea plantato paradiso repressisse illum fontem, multisque fontibus, sicut jam nunc videmus, implevisse terram; de paradisi autem uno fonte quatuor ingentia flumina divisisse" (*PL* 34:0328–9). The Latin is from *De Genesi ad litteram Libri Duodecim.*

14. Scafi, *Mapping Paradise: A History of Heaven on Earth*, 40.
15. *Cursor Mundi*, ed. Morris, ll. 707–10. The Middle English quotation is from the Cotton manuscript in this edition.
16. Middle English text and modern translation are quoted from Rudd, *Greenery: Ecocritical Readings of Late Medieval English Literature*, 22. Rudd's whole reading depends on the flexibility of possible translations, but this is the one she offers.
17. Ibid., 23–4.
18. Ibid.
19. Derrida, "Archive Fever: A Freudian Impression," trans. Prenowitz, 57.
20. Ibid., 9, emphasis in the original.
21. On the difference between (human, active) beginnings and (passive, divine) origins, see Said, *Beginnings: Intention and Method*, xvii, 4–6.
22. Smith discusses the formative sense of beginnings in *The Book of the Incipit: Beginnings in the Fourteenth Century*, x.
23. *The N-Town Play: Cotton MS Vespasian D. 8* ed. Spector, Creation of the World; The Fall of Man, l.31. See also ll.16–17: "In erthelech paradys withowtyn wo / I graunt þe bydyng, lasse þu do blame" [In earthly paradise I allow you to stay, unless you do something blameworthy]. The N-Town plays hereafter will be cited by line number in the main text.
24. The *Jeu D'Adam* has actors' lines in Old French and stage directions in Latin. The quotation is from *Le Jeu D'Adam (Ordo representacionis Ade)*, ed. Noomen, 17. The English translation is from *Le Jeu D'Adam*, ed. and trans. van Emden.
25. This is how Schmitt stages her 1998 Toronto play of Eden, in accordance with contemporary imagery; Schmitt, "The Body in Motion in the York *Adam and Eve in Eden*," in Davidson (ed.), *Gesture in Medieval Drama and Art*, 161–2.
26. Bush, "The Resources of *Locus* and *Platea* Staging: The Digby *Mary Magdalene*," 139. See also Weimann, *Shakespeare and the Popular Tradition in the Theater: Studies in the Social Dimension of Dramatic Form and Function*, 73–85.
27. Marvin Carlson makes this point in his study of the semiotics of unbounded, urban theatrical space, a book he begins with an examination of the mystery plays. Carlson, *Places of Performance: The Semiotics of Theatre Architecture*, 17–19.

28. Beckwith, *Signifying God: Social Relation and Symbolic Act in the York Corpus Christi Plays*, xvi. Hugh of Saint Victor writes that the theater is not the only place where performance took place, in *Didascalicon*, 2:27. See further, William N. West, "The Idea of a Theater: Humanist Ideology and the Imaginary Stage in Early Modern Europe," James, "Ritual, Drama, and Social Body in the Late Medieval Town," and Ganim, "Landscape and Late Medieval Literature: A Critical Geography," in Howes (ed.) *Place, Space, and Landscape in Medieval Narrative*, xxiv.
29. Schmitt, "The Body in Motion in the York *Adam and Eve in Eden*," in Davidson (ed.), *Gesture in Medieval Drama and Art*, 162.
30. Beckwith, *Signifying God: Symbolic Relation and Symbolic Act in the York Corpus Christi Plays*, xvi.
31. The crowd, too, perhaps can play itself, or a version of itself. Agan turns to Turner's work on liminality to read the disparate energies animating the *platea* in the York and Towneley plays, the threshold space from which the audience members might watch the performances and serve as witnesses to sacred events. Agan, "The Platea in the York and Wakefield Cycles: Avenues for Liminality and Salvation," 353–67.
32. Justice discusses this dynamic as it pertains to the *Jeu d'Adam*, in "The Authority of Ritual in the Jeu D'Adam," 858.
33. Beckwith, *Signifying God: Social Relation and Symbolic Act in the York Corpus Christi Plays*, 31.
34. Ibid., 72. Beckwith's quotation is from Stanley Cavell's "The Avoidance of Love."
35. Ibid.
36. Douglas discusses the Latin "sacer" in *Purity and Danger: An Analysis of the Concepts of Pollution and Taboo*, 8.
37. Schechner, *Between Theater and Anthropology*, 102–5.
38. Frantzen, *Desire for Origins: New Language, Old English, and Teaching the Tradition*, 118–22. Frantzen indicates his debts to Derrida and Foucault in the sections from which I quote in this chapter. See further Warner, *The Myth of Piers Plowman: Constructing the Literary Archive*, 5.
39. Minnis, *From Eden to Eternity: Creations of Paradise in the Later Middle Ages*, 1.
40. Jager, *The Tempter's Voice: Language and the Fall in Medieval Literature*, 2.
41. Smith, *The Book of the Incipit*, 16.
42. Rather, argues Frantzen, scholars are invested in the "fragment" around which scholarship can be constructed, in *Desire for Origins*, 110.
43. Greenblatt, "Resonance and Wonder," 20–1.
44. However, as Augustine points out in *De Genesi ad litteram*, ed. Rotelle, trans Hill, 281–2, God perhaps newly plants green things in Paradise after he has already created them – that is, initially created the nature of their species – out in the larger world during the initial work of creation.
45. On England's particular relationship to Edenic imagery, see Staley, *The Island Garden*, 1, 17, and Sobecki, *The Sea and Medieval English Literature*, 75–82.

Lavezzo describes its association with a "holy wilderness" in *Angels on the Edge of the World*, 20.

46. See McLean, *Medieval English Gardens*, 16, and Miller, "Paradise Regained: Medieval Garden Fountains," in *Medieval Gardens*, ed. MacDougall, 137–153. Sometimes wealthy collectors (including Henry I) gathered flora and fauna from far-flung regions to stock paradise-like collections. One famous example, the park of Hesdin, offers, in French, a homonym for Eden. On this, see Colvin, "Royal Gardens in Medieval England," 18, and Van Buren, "Reality and Literary Romance in The Park of Hesdin," 130; both essays are in *Medieval Gardens*, ed. MacDougall.

47. Matter, *The Voice of My Beloved: The Song of Songs in Western Medieval Christianity*, 162, and Winston-Allen, "Gardens of Heavenly Delight: Medieval Gardens of the Imagination," 84, 90.

48. Bleeth, "Chaucerian Gardens and the Spirit of Play," in Howes (ed.), *Place, Space, and Landscape in Medieval Narrative*, 107.

49. Foucault, "Of Other Spaces," trans. Miskowiec, 25–6.

50. Findlen, "The Museum: Its Classical Etymology and Renaissance Genealogy," in *Museum Studies*, ed. Carbonell, 25–7.

51. Ibid., 28–32

52. Griffiths discusses the garden metaphor in *The Garden of Delights: Reform and Renaissance for Women in the Twelfth Century*, 134–7.

53. Quoted in Meyvaert, "The Medieval Monastic Garden," in *Medieval Gardens*, ed. MacDougall, 51. "Porro claustrum praesefert paradisum, monasterium vero Eden securiorem locum paradisi . . . Diversae arbores fructiferae sunt diversi libri sacrae Scripturae." Honorius Augustodunensis, *Gemma Animae, PL* 172:0590B.

54. Findlen, *Possessing Nature: Museums, Collecting, and Scientific Culture in Early Modern Italy*, 91.

55. We know Chaucer translated the *Romance of the Rose*, and we have Middle English translations of it, but we are not sure whether Chaucer wrote the fragments we have. The passage above is from Fragment A, which scholars suggest is the one most likely written by Chaucer (see Benson, *The Riverside Chaucer*, 686).

56. Pearsall and Salter, *Landscapes and Seasons of the Medieval World*, 58–9.

57. Toswell, *Borges the Unacknowledged Medievalist: Old English and Old Norse in His Life and Work*, 90–1.

58. Borges, "The Aleph," in *Collected Fictions*, trans. Hurley, 283–4.

59. Ibid., 284.

60. On the ontology of the image, see Gayk, *Image, Text, and Religious Reform in Fifteenth-century England*, esp. 5–6, 49–51.

61. Chaganti, *The Medieval Poetics of the Reliquary: Enshrinement, Inscription, Performance*, 15.

62. Julian of Norwich, *The Writings of Julian of Norwich: A Vision Showed to a Devout Woman and a Revelation of Love*, ed. Watson and Jenkins,

139. The "little thing" itself goes unnamed; maybe we can imagine an iridescent sphere, or a shining crystal stone. Borges, playing with the image of an immense universe in a tiny nut, chooses an early modern version; one of his epitaphs in "The Aleph" is from Hamlet: "O God! I could be bounded in a nutshell, and count myself a King of infinite space" (II.2).

63. Julian of Norwich, *The Writings*, ed. Watson and Jenkins, 201.

64. The classic study is: Walker Bynum, *Jesus as Mother: Studies in the Spirituality of the High Middle Ages*.

65. Jager, *The Tempter's Voice: Language and the Fall in Medieval Literature*, 60. Jager's book helpfully focuses research into Augustine's multiple writings on Eden and language.

66. Augustine, *On Genesis*, ed. Rotelle, trans. Hill, 176. "Deus nullo spatio syllabarum aeterna Verbi sui ratione dixerit" (*PL* 34:0253–0254).

67. See Bloch on the etymology linking "to divide" and "to describe" (*deviser*), as well as on the idea of narrative in pieces, in relation to the *Romance of the Rose* in *The Scandal of the Fabliaux*, 33.

68. This is from the York Adam and Eve in Eden.

69. Dante, *De vulgari eloquentia*, ed. and trans. Botterill, 9. All translations are hereafter cited by chapter divisions, followed by page numbers, in the main text, with the Latin (also from Botterill's edition) in the notes. ". . . quam dicimus locutionem" (8). On this passage, and how it relates to Dante's engagement with the figure of Adam at the end of *Paradiso*, see Arbery, "Adam's First Word and the Failure of Language in *Paradiso* XXXIII," in Wasserman and Roney (eds.), *Sign, Sentence, Discourse: Language in Medieval Thought and Literature*, 31–44.

70. "post confusionem illum" (20).

71. Eco, *The Search for the Perfect Language*, trans. Fentress, 8.

72. "omne enim quod vocavit Adam animae viventis ipsum est nomen eius."

73. Bloch, "Etymologies and Genealogies: History, Words, and the World," 50.

74. Ibid., 56.

75. Shoaf discusses the idea of "breaking up of the word" in the context of medieval poetry in "Medieval Studies after Derrida after Heidegger," in Wasserman and Roney (eds.), *Sign, Sentence, Discourse: Language in Medieval Thought and Literature*, esp. 10, 18.

76. Borges, *Collected Fictions*, Trans. Hurley, 282.

77. Ibid., emphasis in the original. Johnson discusses Chaucer's *Boece* and the idea of "successioun" as it relates to time, language, and literary form in *Practicing Literary Theory in the Middle Ages: Ethics in the Mixed Form in Chaucer, Gower, Usk, and Hoccleve*, 138.

78. Frantzen engages with Derrida to make this point in *Desire for Origins*, 110.

79. Ibid., 111.

80. On this kind of confusion, see Kuskin's discussion of M.C. Escher in the introduction of *Recursive Origins: Writing at the Transition to Modernity*.

2 Ark and Archive

1. Emily Steiner, "Compendious Genres: Higden, Trevisa, and the Medieval Encyclopedia," 79.
2. Ibid.
3. Ibid., 80.
4. Higden, Ranulph. *Polychronicon Ranulphi Higden monachi Cestrensis; together with the English translations of John Trevisa and of an unknown writer of the fifteenth century*, ed. Babington, 1:7. Higden's Latin: "Historia igitur, cum sit testis temporum ... Historia namque quadam famae immortalitate peritura renovat, fugitiva revocat, mortalia quodammodo perpetuat et conservat" (1:6). Quotations from Trevisa's Middle English translation hereafter will be cited by volume and page number in the main text; Higden's Latin, when included, is from the same edition, quoted in the notes or partly interpolated in the main text.
5. These are Noah's words, l.42.
6. See Mueller, *Translating Troy: Provincial Politics in Alliterative Romance*, 7–8.
7. Orderic Vitalis, *The Ecclesiastical History of Orderic Vitalis*, 6 vols., ed. M. Chibnall, III.285. The Latin: "ueterum monimenta ... quasi grando vel nix in undis cum rapido flumine irremeabiliter fluente defluunt" (284).
8. Nietzsche, *Unfashionable Observations*, trans. Gray, 100.
9. Elsner and Cardinal (eds.), *The Cultures of Collecting*, 1.
10. Ibid.
11. Stewart, *On Longing: Narratives of the Miniature, the Gigantic, the Souvenir, the Collection*, 152.
12. Ibid.
13. Ibid., 151–2.
14. John Tradescant's collection was called the "Ark" before it eventually became the Ashmolean; see Arnold, *Cabinets for the Curious: Looking Back at Early English Museums*, 19. Athanasius Kircher, whose *colegio* at Rome some consider the first museum of natural history, wrote, among many other things, a treatise on Noah's Ark. The collector Johann Kentmann presided over an *arca rerum fossilium*; and a famous curiosity shop in Paris was known colloquially as *Noah's Ark*. Findlen discusses Kentmann, Kircher, and other uses of the ark in *Possessing Nature*, 82–92; on the shop in Paris, see Arnold, 113.
15. Teeuwen, *The Vocabulary of Intellectual Life in the Middle Ages*, 31.
16. As does Capgrave in *John Capgrave's Abbreuiacion of Cronicles*, ed. Lucas, 18.
17. Carruthers, *The Book of Memory*, 7–8, 34. Lerud discusses the mystery play as a "storehouse" or "thesaurus" in relation to Carruthers' work on memory in *Memory, Images, and the English Corpus Christi Drama*, 34.
18. Carruthers, *The Book of Memory*, 231–40, and Zinn, "Hugh of Saint Victor and the Art of Memory."
19. Squire offers these dates in his introduction of Hugh of Saint Victor, *Selected Spiritual Writings*, ed. Squire and trans. a Religious of C. S. M. V., 25. I take

all English translations for *De Archa Noe*, which Squire calls *De Arca Noe Morali*, from this text. There is some debate about whether these texts are indeed separate works or components of a larger whole. See Squire as well as Weiss's introduction to her translation of *Libellus de formation Arche* – "A Little Book about Constructing Noah's Ark" – in Carruthers and Ziolkowski (eds.), *The Medieval Craft of Memory: An Anthology of Texts and Pictures*. I take all English translations of *Libellus de formatione Arche* from Weiss. All Latin quotations for both texts are from *De Archa Noe: Libellus de formatione arche*, ed. Sicard. I cite both English and Latin texts by page number.

20. A search through the *Patrologia Latina* locates the phrase in a number of places, and across centuries; for instance, in the homilies of Gregory the Great (5.3), *PL* 76:1094a-1094b and Rabanas Maurus (34), *PL* 110:0066a-0066b, in Aelred of Rielvaux's *Speculum Charitatis, PL* 195:0537b-0537c, and in Augustine's sermon 302, ch. 7, *PL* 38:1387–8.

21. See Woodward, "Medieval *Mappaemundi*," in *The History of Cartography, Vol. 1*, ed. Harley and Woodward, 312–13, and Barber, "The Evesham World Map: A Late Medieval English View of God and the World," 19.

22. See Allen, *The Legend of Noah: Renaissance Rationalism in Art, Science, and Letters*, 71–2.

23. Zinn discusses Hugh on the literal sense of the ark in "Hugh of Saint Victor and the Ark of Noah: A New Look."

24. *De arca Noe morali*, ed. Squire, 63; "tanta spatia longitudinis et latitudinis et altitudinis, que uere totius mundi reparanda germina" (20).

25. Ibid., 72. "cuius longitudo in fide Trinitatis trecentos cubitos habeat, in latitudine caritatis quinquaginta, in altitudine spei que in Christo est triginta" (32).

26. Ibid., "in bona operatione longus, in dilectione amplus" (32).

27. Hugh of Saint Victor, *Libellus*, trans. Weiss, 49; "incipio sursum a capite et primum nomen Ade taliter scribo" (128).

28. *De arca noe morali*, ed. Squire, 151. "Hec archa similis est apothece omnium deliciarum uarietate referte. Nichil in ea quesieris, quod non inuenias [. . .] Ibi historia rerum gestarum texitur, ibi mysteria sacramentorum inueniuntur [. . .] Ibi quoddam uniuersitatis corpus effingitur, et concordia singulorum explicatur. Ibi alter quidam mundus huic pretereunti et transitorio contrarius inuenitur" (115–16).

29. Hugh of Saint Victor, *De arca noe morali*, ed. Squire, 102. "peccati puluis superiectus cordi humano" (64).

30. Hugh of Saint Victor, *De arca noe morali*, ed. Squire, 103; Sicard, 65.

31. Hugh of Saint Victor, *Libellus*, trans. Weiss, 67–8. Sicard, 157, 160: "Hoc modo archa perfecta, circunducitur ei circulus oblongus qui ad singula cornua eam contingat; et spatium, quod circumferentia eius includit, est orbis terre. In hoc spatio mappa mundi depingitur, ita ut caput arche ad orientem conuertatur et finis eius occidentem contingat, ut mirabili dispositione ab eodem principio decurrat situs locorum cum ordine temporum, et idem sit

finis mundi qui est seculi. Conus autem ille circuli, qui in capite arche prominet ad orientem, paradisus est, quasi sinus Abrahe, ut post apparebit Maiestate depicta. Conus alter, qui prominet ad occidentem, habet uniuersalis resurrectionis iudicium: in dextera electos, in sinistra reprobos. In cuius coni angulo aquilonari est infernus, ubi dampnandi cum apostatibus spiritibus detrudentur. [...] Hoc modo constructa machina uniuersitatis, in parte eius superiori Maiestas a scapulis sursum, pedibusque deorsum eminens et quasi in solio sedens formatur; ita ut expansis hinc inde brachiis omnia continere uideatur; tribusque digitis, per medium protensis usque ad orbem terre et ceteris in palmum reflexis, celos concludit" (157, 160).

32. Hugutio writes: "et hic torax ... quam nos dicimus archam quia ibi archanum sit, idest secretum quo ceteri arcentur," in the *Derivationes*, ed. Cecchini, T.142.16, 1234.

33. Guy de Chauliac, *The Cyrurgie of Guy de Chauliac*, ed. Ogden, 53.

34. See, for instance, Carruthers' discussion of the *scrinium* in *The Book of Memory*, 39–40. On the relationship between history and memory in the Middle Ages, see Le Goff, *History and Memory*, trans. Rendell and Claman, xi–xii, 68–80, and Minnis "Medieval Memory and Imagination," in Kennedy, Minnis, et al. (eds.), *Cambridge History of Literary Criticism: Vol.2 The Middle Ages*, esp. 266.

35. *Summa Britonis*, ed. Daly and Daly, 49.

36. In Part 1, a Norwegian princess says her "luf is lokyn & leyd in ark" (l.2908), and in Part 2, it is a repository in which the order of Cluny might set aside funds (1.3341). Robert Mannyng of Brunne, *The Chronicle*, ed. Sullens.

37. *Henry Suso: The Exemplar, with Two German Sermons*, trans. Tobin, 70–71. See also Jager, *The Book of the Heart*, 97–8.

38. Jacobus de Voragine, *Golden Legend: Readings on the Saints*, trans. Ryan, 1:143.

39. Ibid.

40. "Life of Margaret of Città di Castello," *Analecta Bollandiana* 19, 27–8. Bynum discusses the case of Margaret in *Fragmentation and Redemption*, 197.

41. The phrase is frequently used; see, for instance, Declercq, in "Originals and Cartularies: The Organization of Archival Memory (Ninth-Eleventh Centuries)" in *Charters and the Use of the Written Word*, ed. Heidecker, 167.

42. Richards considers such Victorian projects in *Imperial Archive: Knowledge and the Fantasy of Empire*, esp. 11–13. Our own era, concerned like Noah's with apocalyptic weather, albeit a slower kind, has constructed at least one post-ark "seminaria" or seed vault buried deep in arctic ice. See Revkin, "Buried Seed Vault Opens in Arctic."

43. See "The Hypostasis of the Archons," trans. Layton, in *The Nag Hammadi Library in English*, ed. Robinson, 166. Epiphanius brings up the story of Noria who burns the ark *multiple* times – in order to dispute it – in *The Panarion*, trans. Williams, 1:90–1, which James comments on in *The Lost Apocrypha of the Old Testament*, 12–15.

44. For a description of works traditionally grouped within this category, see Kennedy, *Chronicles and other Historical Writing*, 2611–47; Albano, *Middle*

English Historiography, 3–5; Matheson, "The Chronicle Tradition," in *A Companion to Arthurian Literature*, ed. Fulton, 58–69; and Pagan (ed.) *Prose Brut to 1332*, 10–17.

45. Some histories also include the origin story of Diocletian and his thirty-three daughters, put to sea with six months' worth of rations; they give birth to giants after arriving in Albion, the island named after the eldest sister. The story of the thirty-three sisters can be found in *The Brut or The Chronicles of England*, ed. Brie, I.1–4, and *Castleford's Chronicle, or The boke of Brut*, ed. Eckhardt, I.1–226.

46. Jacques le Goff, *Medieval Civilization*, 171–2, Patterson, *Chaucer and the Subject of History*, esp. 90–9, 123–4, and Sobecki, *The Sea and Medieval English Literature*, 72–90. On different disruptions to the directional flow of *translatio imperii* and for other, less imperialistic engagements with Troy, see Robertson, "Geoffrey of Monmouth and the Translation of Insular Historiography," and Simpson, "The Other Book of Troy: Guido delle Colonne's *Historia destructionis Troiae* in Fourteenth- and Fifteenth-Century England."

47. Hanning discusses Augustine's influence on the writing of history in *The Vision of History in Early Britain*, 32–7, as does Patterson in *Chaucer and the Subject of History*, 86–90.

48. Staley, *The Island Garden*, 1–3, 42.

49. Geoffrey of Monmouth, *The History of the Kings if Britain*, ed. Reeve, 21.

50. For a discussion of the universal history genre, see Taylor, *English Historical Literature in the Fourteenth Century*, 90–109.

51. Matthew of Paris, *Flores historiarum per Matthaeum Westmonasteriensem collecti*, 4.

52. Ibid., 5.

53. Capgrave, *John Capgrave's Abberuiacion of Cronicles*, ed. Lucas, 31.

54. Caxton, *Caxton's Eneydos*, ed. Culley and Furnivall, 165.

55. Robert of Gloucester, *The Metrical Chronicle of Robert of Gloucester*, ed. Wright, l.204.

56. Ibid., ll.302–13.

57. Ibid., l.334

58. Curtius, *European Literature and the Latin Middle Ages*, trans. Trask, 128–30.

59. Spiegel, *The Past as Text*, 86–7.

60. Isidore of Seville, *Etymologies*, I.xlii.1.

61. Robert Mannyng, *The Chronicle*, ed. Sullens, ll.23–4, 31–2. All Mannyng quotations are from this edition, from Part 1, and are hereafter cited in the main text by line number.

62. Sullens inserts these lines, only appearing in the Lambeth MS 131 (her base text is Petyt MS 511 Vol. 7), at l. 1198. Wace has: "Mult fu hardiz, mult fu curteis / Cil ki fist nef premierement / E en mer se mist aval vent, / Terre querant qu'il ne veeit / E rivage qu'il ne saveit." Wace, *Roman de Brut*. ed. and trans. Weiss, II.11234–8. Sobecki suggests Wace's version of these lines are inspired by a passage from Seneca, in *The Sea and Medieval English Literature*, 25–6.

63. *Cursor Mundi*, ed. Morris, ll.1805–1806.

64. *The 'Gest Hystoriale' of the Destruction of Troy: An Alliterative Romance*, ed. Panton and Donaldson, ll.12903–4.

65. Summerfield, *The Matter of Kings' Lives: The Design of Past and Present in the Early Fourteenth-Century Verse Chronicles by Pierre de Langtoft and Robert Mannyng*, 170–1, 194–5.

66. Staley, *The Island Garden*, 16–17.

67. *Laȝamon's Brut*, ed. Brook and Leslie, ll.6–13, from MS. Cotton Caligula A. IX.

68. Woodward, "Medieval *Mappaemundi*," in *The History of Cartography, Vol. 1*, ed. Harley and Woodward, 334.

69. At this point, the Cotton manuscript (from which I quote) offers a diagram, spanning from Adam to Lameth. The Trinity and Göttingen manuscripts both read "Noe kinne" (or Noe kynne) instead of Adam, though it is, of course, different phases of the same family.

70. Capgrave, *John Capgrave's Abberuiacion of Cronicles*, ed. Lucas, 18.

71. Gilbert and Gubar, *The Madwoman in the Attic: The Woman Writer and the Nineteenth-Century Literary Imagination*, 4.

72. Shakespeare, "Sonnet XVIII," l.12.

73. Simpson, "The Other Book of Troy: Guido delle Colonne's *Historia destructionis Troiae* in Fourteenth- and Fifteenth-Century England," 406.

74. *Cursor Mundi*, ed. Morris, l.1690

75. LeGoff, *History and Memory*, 54; LeGoff discusses the medieval arts of memory, and the relationship among memory, religion, and record at 68–80.

76. Ibid., 73.

77. Turville-Petre, *England the Nation: Language, Literature and National Identity, 1290–1340*, 1.

78. See Knight, "Stealing Stonehenge: Translation, Appropriation, and Cultural Identity in Robert Mannyng of Brunne's *Chronicle*," 43–4, and, further, Lamont, "Becoming English: Ronwenne's Wassail, Language, and National Identity in the Middle English Prose *Brut*," esp. 285.

79. Genesis 4.24.

80. I am conceiving of the path of the arrow as a trajectory with a beginning, end, and carefully circumscribed movement in-between. This potentially flattens out the curve in the word *arc*, the arching of the *arc*. This is not to suggest that a streamlined plot cannot have a controlled curve (as in conversion narratives) or, of course, to suggest that an arrow in flight cannot gracefully curve from sky to earth. The shape of the bow (Latin *arcus*, also the word for rainbow) from which the arrow flies provides more of the curvature embedded in the primary meaning of the English word *arc*.

81. Nora, "Between Memory and History: Les Lieux de Mémoire," esp. 7–8.

82. Greenblatt discusses this "thickness" in the context of museum and cultural studies in "Resonance and Wonder."

83. Isidore of Seville, *Etymologies*, I.xl.1.

84. *De Arca Noe Morali*, ed. Squire, 51. "fac archam testamenti, fac archam diluuii, uel quocunque nomine appelles, una est domus Dei" (90).

85. See Alter, *The Five Books of Moses: A Translation with Commentary*, 312, n.3.
86. Shakespeare, *The Riverside Shakespeare*, ed., Evans, *Romeo and Juliet*, III.v.133–4
87. Ibid., V.iii.117–18.
88. See also Nelson, who uses Chaucer's *Man of Law's Tale* to theorize a more multivocal, "rhizomatic" process of transmission, one that relies on a variety of networks and bodies beyond the iconic figure of the Trojan remnant Aeneas, and in disruption of such singular narrative transmission. Nelson, "Premodern Media and Networks of Transmission in the *Man of Law's Tale*."
89. Helen Cooper, *The English Romance in Time: Transforming Motifs from Geoffrey of Monmouth to the Death of Shakespeare*, 119. Cooper's chapter "Providence and the Sea: 'No Tackle, Sea, nor Mast'" greatly informs my argument.
90. Ibid., 120.
91. Ingledew, "The Book of Troy and the Genealogical Construction of History," 668.
92. This excerpt is from Weiss's translation of the Anglo-Norman in *The Birth of Romance in England*, 2. The Anglo-Norman, from Pope's edition, reads: "'Sire,' fet il, 'purnez un de voz vielz chalanz, / Metez i cels valez, ki jo vei ici estanz; / K'il n'aient avirum dunt (a) seient aïdanz, / Sigle ne guvernail dunt il seient najanz; / Enz un altre metez xx bonisme serjanz, / Ke bien sacent nagier cume bon marinanz, / Ki[s] treient a la mer a dous leue[e]s granz./ Les cordes trenchent pus, dunt les erent trainanz, / E leissent les iluc al palagre walcranz. / N'en orrez pus parler, bien me sui (fic) purfichanz: / Ja nes garrat lur deus, en ki il sunt creanz, / Plus d'un tundu mutun ky est tut asotanz.'" Thomas, *The Romance of Horn*, ed. Pope, *ll.*58–69.
93. Cooper, *The English Romance in Time*, 110.
94. "Emaré." *Six Middle English Romances*, ed. Mills, l. 168.
95. Ibid., ll.427–8.
96. Carruthers writes that, "the favored means of cultural translation, especially in the early Middle Ages, was apt to be a living, breathing, thinking and speaking person," in "Mechanisms for the Transmission of Culture: The Role of 'Place' in the Arts of Memory," in *Translatio, or the Transmission of Culture in the Middle Ages and the Renaissance: Modes and Messages*, ed. Hollengreen, 1.
97. See Ladner, "*Homo Viator*: Mediaeval Ideas on Alienation and Order."
98. *The Pilgrimage of the Lyfe of the Manhode*, ed. Henry, 1:1.
99. "Havelock." *Middle English Romances*, ed. Shepherd, ll.587–606.
100. "Barm," which the *Middle English Dictionary* (MED) variously glosses as "lap," "breast," "bosom," "womb," and "bed," sometimes is used metaphorically to describe a boat. In *Beowulf*, ed. Klaeber, l. 35, the dead Scyld Scefing is placed in "bearm scipes," and the Old English "bearm" connects to the Middle English "barm."
101. Cooper, *The English Romance in Time*, 113.

102. Ibid., 114.

103. On the archive of the performing body, see Lepecki, "The Body as Archive: Will to Re-enact and the Afterlives of Dances."

104. *York Mystery Plays: A Selection in Modern Spelling*, ed. Beadle and King, 15, 21.

3   *Uxor Noe* and the Drowned

1. Roach, *Cities of the Dead: Circum-Atlantic Performance*, xiii; Beckwith applies Roach's formulation in *Signifying God: Social Relation and Symbolic Act in the York Corpus Christi Plays*, 72.

2. Schechner, *Between Theater and Anthropology*, 35–7.

3. Roach, *Cities of the Dead: Circum-Atlantic Performance*, 29.

4. Zumthor, *Essai de Poétique Médiévale*, 65–75.

5. Taylor, *The Archive and the Repertoire: Performing Cultural Memory in the Americas*, 16–33.

6. Nora, "Between Memory and History: Les Lieux de Mémoire," 7.

7. Ibid., 12.

8. Beckwith, *Signifying God: Social Relation and Symbolic Act in the York Corpus Christi Plays*, 10–12.

9. Ibid., 12.

10. *York Mystery Plays: A Selection in Modern Spelling*, ed. Beadle and King, 15, 21.

11. Yates, *The Art of Memory*, Chapter 6, 129–59, and Chapter 15, 320–41.

12. Yates suggests a connection between Fludd's design and the Globe Theater in *The Art of Memory*, Chapter 16, 342–67.

13. Clanchy, *From Memory to Written Record*, 127.

14. Carruthers, *The Book of Memory*, 34. Zinn also discusses Hugh of Saint Victor's use of the money purse in "Hugh of Saint Victor and the Art of Memory," 220.

15. These two are aligned with error in the Towneley Flood play when Noah's Wife suggests Noah send forth the raven first rather than the dove.

16. This phrase is from Tolmie, "Mrs. Noah and Didactic Abuses," 31.

17. See *de Mirabilibus Sacrae Scripturae Libri Tres*, Book 1, ch. 5. PL 35:2156.

18. Findlen, *Possessing Nature: Museums, Collecting, and Scientific Culture in Early Modern Italy*, 92.

19. Allen, *The Legend of Noah: Renaissance Rationalism in Art, Science, and Letters*, 71–2.

20. Utley, "The One Hundred and Three Names of Noah's Wife," 428, 430–31, 436–7. Bal theorizes the naming of nameless biblical women in the context of Jepthe's daughter in "Between Altar and Wondering Rock: Toward a Feminist Philology," in *Anti-Covenant: Counter Reading Women's Lives in the Hebrew Bible*, ed. Bal, 212.

21. Kolve, *Chaucer and the Imagery of Narrative: The First Five Canterbury Tales*, 203.

22. Mill, "Noah's Wife Again," 620, 623.

23. Kolve, *The Play Called Corpus Christi*, 150.

24. Kolve, *The Play Called Corpus Christi*, 147. Many critics agree with Kolve's general reading, including Woolf, *The English Mystery Plays*, 143, and Storm, "Uxor and Allison: Noah's Wife in the Flood Plays and Chaucer's Wife of Bath," 319. Beadle and King's edition of the York Mystery plays introduces "The Flood" with the suggestion that the stage direction that requires the family to sing at the play's end "signals the final restoration of harmony at all levels" (21). Sutherland, however, suggests that Uxor's "progress from doubt to belief" that allows a return to such stability is, at each point, "marked by an ambivalence never fully resolved," in "Not or I see more neede": The Wife of Noah in the Chester, York, and Towneley Cycles," in Elton and Long (ed.), *Shakespeare and Dramatic Tradition: Essays in Honor of S.F. Johnson*, 191.

25. Mannyng, *Handlyng Synne*, ed. Sullens, ll. 2933–6.

26. Davis, "Women on Top," in *Society and Culture in Early Modern France*, 131.

27. Tolmie, "Mrs. Noah and Didactic Abuses," 11.

28. Normington, *Gender and Medieval Drama*, 125–32.

29. Ibid., 121.

30. Ibid., 130.

31. Gibson, *The Theater of Devotion: East Anglian Drama and Society in the Late Middle Ages*, 164.

32. Coletti, "A Feminist Approach to the Corpus Christi Cycles," in Emmerson (ed.), *Approaches to Teaching Medieval English Drama*, 82.

33. McAvoy, *Authority and the Female Body in the Writings of Julian of Norwich and Margery Kempe*, 235, and Jager, "Did Eve invent writing? Script and Fall in the *Adam Books*." See in *The Canticum de Creatione* in *The Apocryphal Lives of Adam and Eve*, ed. Murdoch and Tasioulas, ll.899–912.

34. Tolmie, "Mrs. Noah and Didactic Abuses," 30–31.

35. *The Towneley Plays*, 2 vols, ed. Stevens and Cawley, Noah, ll.486–90. Towneley quotations from this edition are hereafter cited by line number in the main text.

36. Jacobus, "The Difference of View," in *Women Writing and Writing about Women*, 14.

37. Ibid., 12.

38. Dinshaw, "Medieval Feminist Criticism," in Plain and Sellers (eds.), *A History of Feminist Literary Criticism*, 24.

39. Kiser, "The Animals in Chester's *Noah's Flood*," 16.

40. Ibid., 26–30.

41. *The Chester Mystery Cycle*, 2 vols, ed. R. M. Lumiansky and David Mills, Noah's Flood, l.193. All Chester quotations are from this edition and are hereafter cited by line number in the main text.

42. There is no stage direction recorded, but the line occurs (at 244) immediately before Noah welcomes his wife into the boat at l.245.

43. Gilbert and Gubar, *The Madwoman in the Attic*, 13.

44. Derrida, "Archive Fever: A Freudian Impression," trans. Prenowitz, 10 (emphasis in original).
45. Ibid., 10, 58.
46. Ibid., 58.
47. Benjamin, *The Arcades Project*, trans. Eiland and McLaughlin, "The Collector," 205.
48. Jacobus, "The Difference of View," 12.
49. Woolf, *A Room of One's Own*, 24.
50. Moi, *Sexual/ Textual Politics: Feminist Literary Theory*, 65–8, quotation at 66.
51. I am especially influenced here by Moi's recent re-engagement with Simone de Beauvoir in "What Is a Woman?" in *What is a Woman and Other Essays*, 3–120.
52. Williams, *Inventing Womanhood: Gender and Language in Later Middle English Writing*, 4–5.
53. Ibid., 3.
54. Grosz, "Histories of the Present and Future: Feminism, Power, Bodies," in Cohen and Weiss (eds.), *Thinking the Limits of the Body*, 18, emphasis in original.
55. Gerald of Wales, *The History and Topography of Ireland*, trans. O'Meara, 92–3, my emphasis. The Latin is from *Giraldis Cambrensis Opera*, ed. Dimock, Vol. 5, 139–40: "Juxta antiquissimas igitur Hibernensium historias, Cæsara neptis Noe, audiens diluvium in proximo futurum, ad remotissimas occidentis insulas, quas necdum quisquam hominum habitaverat, cum suis complicibus fugam navigio destinaverat; sperans, ubi nunquam peccatum perpetratum fuerat, diluvii vindictam locum non habere. Amissis itaque quas in comitatu habebat naufragio navibus, una, qua cum viris tribus et quinquaginta mulieribus vehebatur, nave superstite, primo ante diluvium anno ad Hibernica litora forte devenit. Sed licet acute satis, et laudabili in femina ingenio, fatalitatem declinare statuerit, communem tamen interitum et fere generalem nullatenus potuit evitare. ... Verumtamen cunctis fere per diluvium jam deletis, qualiter rerum istarum, et tam eventus quam adventus memoria post diluvium retenta fuerit, non indignum videtur dubitatione. Sed qui historias istas primo scripserunt, ipsi viderint. Historiarum enimvero enucleator venio, non impugnator. Sed forte in aliqua materia inscripta, lapidea scilicet vel lateritia, sicut de arte musica legitur ante diluvium inventa, istorum memoria fuerat reservata."
56. Birkholz, "Mapping Medieval Utopia: Exercises in Restraint," 605, 606.
57. Ibid., 608–11.
58. On this word and acts of commemoration, see Bal, "Between Altar and Wondering Rock: Toward a Feminist Philology," in *Anti-Covenant: Counter Reading Women's Lives in the Hebrew Bible*, ed. Bal, 226–8.
59. Roach, *Cities of the Dead: Circum-Atlantic Performance*, 30.
60. *Canticum de Creatione*, in *The Apocryphal Lives of Adam and Eve*, ed. Murdoch and Tasioulas, ll.146, 130. Adam parts ways with his wife to stand in the Jordan, dutifully performing his forty days of penance there.
61. Shapcott, "Mrs. Noah: Taken after the Flood," in *My Life Asleep*, 10.

4 Infernal Archive

1. The classic overview is Le Goff, *The Birth of Purgatory*; on the "third place" designation, see 1–4.
2. Matsuda, *Death and Purgatory in Middle English Didactic Poetry*, 36–59.
3. Moore discusses the work in relation to drama and narrative as it exists in the three manuscripts (Auchinleck, Harley, and Digby) in "The Narrator within the Performance: Problems with Two Medieval 'Plays.'" On the potential for these versions of the *Harrowing of Hell* to be understood within the context of more secular entertainment, see Nelson, "The Performance of Power in Medieval English Households: The Case of the *Harrowing of Hell.*"
4. Several works explore the influence of classical and ancient underworlds upon medieval hells. See Patch's *The Otherworld, according to descriptions in medieval literature*; Himmelfarb, *Tours of Hell: An Apocalyptic Form in Jewish and Christian Literature;* Turner, *The History of Hell*; and Edmonds III, *Myths of the Underworld: Plato, Aristophanes, and the Orphic Golden Tablets.*
5. Marx, *The Devil's Rights and the Redemption in the Literature of Medieval England*, 4–5.
6. Dante, *Inferno*, trans. Mandelbaum, 4.37–9. All English translations of the *Inferno* are from this edition, and hereafter cited by canto and line number in the main text. The Italian text also is from this edition and hereafter provided in the notes.
7. "quando ci vidi venire un possente, / con segno di vittoria coronato. / Trasseci l'ombra del primo parente, / d'Abèl suo figlio e quella di Noè,/ di Moïsè legista e ubidente; / Abraàm patriarca e Davìd re, / Israèl con lo padre e co' suoi nati / e con Rachele, per cui tanto fé, / e altri molti, e feceli beati. / E vo' che sappi che, dinanzi ad essi, / spiriti umani non eran salvati."
8. In *The Harrowing of Hell in Medieval England*, 104, Tamburr suggests that a fifth-century manuscript, 'Latin A' was most influential for later medieval versions; see ch. 4, 102–47 for a general overview of the *Gospel of Nicodemus.*
9. *The Middle English Harrowing of Hell and Gospel of Nicodemus*, ed. Hulme, ll.1541–8. All quotations from the *Gospel* are from this edition, and hereafter cited in the main text by line number. Hulme draws on four manuscripts for the *Gospel*, all of them from the fifteenth century, though all of them, he believes, copied from earlier versions (xv–xvi). I quote from the Harley throughout.
10. This is a very general summary of the Harrowing; details, of course, vary. See, for instance, Butler, who discusses small but crucial differences between the Harrowing mystery plays in "The York/Towneley *Harrowing of Hell?*"
11. *The Gospel of Nicodemus: Gesta Salvatoris*, ed. Kim, 24.1, 44. Citation is by text division (chapter and verse) followed by page number.
12. These Christian narrative strategies for closing down a Jewish past are explored by Biddick in *The Typological Imaginary: Circumcision, Technology, History* and Kruger in the *Spectral Jew: Conversion and Embodiment in*

Medieval Europe. Cohen considers the "hermeneutical Jew," or "the Jew as constructed in the discourse of Christian theology," in *Living Letters of the Law: Ideas of the Jew in Medieval Christianity*, 2–3, and Tomasch examines depictions of Jews deployed in English narrative in "Postcolonial Chaucer and the Virtual Jew," in Cohen (ed.), *The Postcolonial Middle Ages.*

13. Biddick, *The Typological Imaginary: Circumcision, Technology, History*, 1–2.
14. Ibid., 22–3, 28–9.
15. The Auchinleck version is cut off at the beginning and the end. For a discussion of the relationship among the three versions, see Nelson, "The Performance of Power in Medieval English Households: The Case of the *Harrowing of Hell*," 51–5.
16. *The Middle English Harrowing of Hell and the Gospel of Nicodemus*, ed. Hulme, ll.85–90. All following lines from the Middle English poetic *Harrowing* also are from the Auchinleck version in Hulme, and hereafter cited by line numbers in the main text.
17. Bloom, *The Anxiety of Influence*, 141, emphasis in the original.
18. Gregory the Great, *Dialogues*, ed. and trans. Zimmerman, 236; On Gregory's description of volcanoes, see Easting, *Visions of the Other World in Middle English*, 11.
19. Virgil, *The Aeneid*, trans. Mandelbaum, 6.175–6; 179; the Latin: "facilis descensus Averno . . . sed revocare gradum superasque evadere ad auras, / hoc opus, hic labor est."
20. Friedman, *Orpheus in the Middle Ages*, esp. 57–8, 175–96.
21. *Sir Orfeo*, ed. Bliss, ll.387–90. All lines are from this edition, from the Auchinleck manuscript (1330s), and hereafter are cited by line number in the main text.
22. See Bliss on the first thirty-eight lines of the Auchinleck version, *Sir Orfeo*, xv.
23. On the relationship between the form of the lai and Orfeo's harping, see Lerer, "Artifice and Artistry in Sir Orfeo," esp. 106–7.
24. Liuzza "*Sir Orfeo*: Sources, Traditions, and the Poetics of Performance," 276, and Riddy, "The Uses of the Past in *Sir Orfeo*," 7.
25. Simpson, "Cognition is Recognition: Literary Knowledge and Textual 'Face,'" esp. at 26, 28, and 30.
26. Ibid., 40.
27. Ibid., 28.
28. Liuzza, "*Sir Orfeo*: Sources, Traditions, and the Poetics of Performance," 276–9.
29. On the relationship among poetry, song, and music – as well as between writing and performance – see Huot, *From Song to Book: The Poetics of Writing in Old French Lyric and Lyrical Narrative*, esp. 132, and Butterfield, *Poetry and Music in Medieval France*, esp. 8–9, 13–24.
30. Riddy, "The Uses of the Past in *Sir Orfeo*," esp. 13–15.
31. The EETS *St. Patrick's Purgatory*, ed. Easting, also includes the *Tractatus de Purgatorio Sancti Patricii* (c.1180–1184) and *The Vision of William of Stranton* (15th century), and discusses other versions of *Owayne Miles*.

32. "Owayne Miles, Auchinleck Version," in *St. Patrick's Purgatory*, ed. Easting, stanzas 23–25. I take all quotations, regardless of manuscript version, from Easting's edition.

33. "Owayne Miles, Cotton and Yale Version," in *St. Patrick's Purgatory*, ed. Easting, ll.89–100.

34. Ibid., l.156.

35. Ibid., l.70–1.

36. "The Vision of William of Stranton," in *Saint Patrick's Purgatory*, ed. Easting, p. 78. I quote from the Royal MS.

37. Cotton, ll.631–2.

38. Auchinleck, stanza 194.

39. Auchinleck, stanzas 3–4.

40. 2 Cor. 12:2. On this and the *Visio Sancti Pauli*, see Patch, *The Other World, According to Descriptions in Medieval Literature*, 91–3, and Matsuda, *Death and Purgatory in Middle English Didactic Poetry*, 34–6.

41. *Revelation of the Monk of Eynsham*, ed. Easting, 37.

42. On the range of possibility and its genres, see Newman, "What does it mean to say 'I saw'? The Clash between Theory and Practice in Medieval Visionary Culture."

43. "Quivi sospiri, pianti e alti guai / ... Diverse lingue, orribili favelle, / parole di dolore, accenti d'ira, / voci alte e fioche, e suon di man con elle."

44. "L'onrata nominanza / che di lor suona sù ne la tua vita ..."

45. "priegoti ch'a la mente altrui mi rechi."

46. "il nome tuo tra l'altra note."

47. Peter Comestor, *Historia Scholastica*, ed. Migne, *PL* 198:1101b-1101c. The Latin, from ch. 53, quoting from Genesis 19.26: "*Et respiciens uxor Lot retro, versa est in statuam salis*, quam Josephus dicit se vidisse, et hactenus manere."

48. Ginzburg, *Ecstasies: Deciphering the Witches' Sabbath*, trans. Rosenthal, 307.

5   The Harrowing of Hell: Closure and Rehearsal

1. Ginzburg, *Ecstasies: Deciphering the Witches' Sabbath*, trans. Rosenthal, 307. Ginzburg cites Benjamin's "The Storyteller," which argues that death authorizes narrative, and suggests that modernity has pushed death to the margins, an argument that Roach also will take up in literal form in his description of cemeteries in *Cities of the Dead: Circum-Atlantic Performance*, 50. Benjamin, *Illuminations*, ed. Arendt, 93–4.

2. Roach, "Performance: The Blunders of Orpheus," 1078.

3. Such a multivalent moment perhaps corresponds to the potential for a richer now that Dinshaw examines in *How Soon Is Now? Medieval Texts, Amateur Readers, and the Queerness of Time*; see especially, 1–7.

4. For the importance of understanding the conjunction of dramatic and icono-graphic traditions, see Lerud on "quick images," in *Memory, Images, and the English Corpus Christi Drama*.

5. The York Harrowing of Hell, ll.124, 190, 140.

6. This occurs after l.204 in the Chester Harrowing of Hell.

7. Dinshaw, *Getting Medieval: Sexualities and Communities, Pre- and Postmodern*, 1–54.

8. Schneider, *Performing Remains: Art and War in Times of Theatrical Reenactment*, 35.

9. Barthes, *Michelet*, trans. Howard, 81: "For Michelet the historical mass is not a puzzle to reconstitute, it is a body to embrace. The historian exists only to recognize a warmth ... The roots of historical truth are therefore the documents as voices, not as witnesses. Michelet considers in them, exclusively, that quality of having been an attribute of life, the privileged object to which clings a kind of residual memory of past bodies." See further, 17–25, and Dinshaw's discussion of this passage in *Getting Medieval*, 46–7.

10. *The Middle English Liber Aureus and Gospel of Nicodemus*, ed. William, 58–9.

11. See the British Library's Harley MS 1671, *The Weye of Paradys* (unfinished), last quarter of 14th century or 1st quarter of 15th century, England. f. 77r and 77v.

12. Stuart "The Stage Setting of Hell and the Iconography of the Middle Ages," 333–5, and Davidson, *The Primrose Way: A Study of Shakespeare's Macbeth*, 21–2. Woolf examines the potential staging of the *Jeu D'Adam* as well as the relationship between Harrowing of Hell iconography and the mystery plays in *The English Mystery Plays*, 50, 269–70.

13. Meredith, "The Iconography of Hell in the English Cycles: A Practical Perspective," in Davidson and Seiler (eds.), *The Iconography of Hell*, 159.

14. The line from Isaiah 9:2 is quoted in the Harrowing plays to refer to the shades that dwell there.

15. See Rastell, "The Sounds of Hell," in Davidson and Seiler (eds.), *The Iconography of Hell*.

16. Tamburr also suggests that similarities might be discerned in liturgical rituals associated with Easter, baptism, and with the consecration of new cathedrals (see for instance, the *Ordo Dedicationis Ecclesiae*, as used by the Bishop of Metz, in *Medieval Drama*, ed. Bevington, 12–13). Tamburr delineates several connections between the Latin liturgical play staged at the Abbey of Barking in the fourteenth century and the Harrowing of Hell plays: a knocking at the door, the call to open the gates, the release of the priest and his ministry figured as redeemed souls of the Old Testament, an entrance of bodies into the space of the church. Tamburr, *The Harrowing of Hell in Medieval England*, 10–13. See further Faulkner, "The Harrowing of Hell at Barking Abbey and in Modern Production," in Davidson and Seiler (eds.), *The Iconography of Hell*.

17. Sheingorn, "Who can open the doors of his face?" The Iconography of the Mouth of Hell," in Davidson and Seiler (eds.), *The Iconography of Hell*, 3.

18. Davidson, "Civic Drama for Corpus Christi at Coventry: Some Lost Plays," in Knight (ed.), *The Stage as Mirror: Civic Theatre in Late Medieval Europe*, 155–6. See further, Davidson, *Technology, Guilds and Early English Drama*, 83.

19. Ingram (ed.), *Coventry: Records of Early English Drama*, 237, 475, and 230.

20. Schmidt, *The Iconography of the Mouth of Hell: Eighth-Century Britain to the Fifteenth Century*, 165, 167.

21. Sheingorn, "Who can open the doors of his face?" in Davidson and Seiler (eds.) *The Iconography of Hell*, 2.

22. Isidore, *Etymologies*, XI.i.49.

23. Sheingorn, "Who can open the doors of his face?" in Davidson and Seiler (eds.), *The Iconography of Hell*, 7.

24. Examples range from the scriptures (Proverbs 23:8) to the sagas (*Egil's Saga*, ed. and trans. Fell, 133–4.)

25. The *de Lisle Psalter* is Arundel 83 II at the British Library. This image of Satan and the hell mouth appears on fol. 132 v. See Sandler, *The Psalter of Robert de Lisle in the British Library*, 71. See also Tamburr, *The Harrowing of Hell in Medieval England*, 152.

26. Translated in Jager, "Speech and Chest in Old English Poetry: Orality or Pectorality?" 855.

27. Augustine, *Saint Augustine's Confessions*, trans. Chadwick, 192. *Confessionum*, ed. Lucas Verheijen, 166: "Forte ergo sicut de uentre cibus ruminando, sic ista de memoria recordando proferuntur." All Latin quotations are from this edition. All translations, hereafter cited in the main text by chapter divisions, are Chadwick's.

28. Carruthers, *The Book of Memory: A Study of Memory in Medieval Culture*, 53–4.

29. On eating and "glosing," see Minnis, *From Eden to Eternity*, 6.

30. Bardsley, *Venomous Tongues: Speech and Gender in Late Medieval England*, 51.

31. Biddick, *The Typological Imaginary: Circumcision, Technology, History*, 6.

32. Carlson, *The Haunted Stage: The Theatre as Memory Machine*, 15.

33. Ibid., 2, 4.

34. Kruger, *The Spectral Jew: Conversion and Embodiment in Medieval Europe*, xvi–xvii.

35. Ibid., 2–3, 5.

36. Derrida, *Specters of Marx: The State of the Debt, The Work of Mourning and the New International*, trans. Kamuf, 13, emphasis in the original.

37. Ibid., 12, emphasis in the original.

38. Diamond, *Performance and Cultural Politics*, 2.

39. Derrida, *Specters of Marx*, trans. Kamuf, 10. Gil Harris, *Untimely Matter in the Time of Shakespeare*, 11–12.

40. Schneider, *Performing Remains*, 109.

41. Derrida, *Specters of Marx*, trans. Kamuf, 5.

42. Freccero, "Infernal Irony: The Gates of Hell."

43. Kruger, *The Spectral Jew*, xx. Kruger considers iconography of the Harrowing in the opening pages of his book, xiv–xv.

44. See Ingham's recent engagement with Deleuze on how the dynamic of repetition and the new might be understood within a medieval context, in *The Medieval New: Ambivalence in an Age of Innovation*, 16.

45. Gervase of Tillbury, *Otia Imperialia: Recreation for an Emperor*, ed. and trans. Banks and Binns, 777. On this see Matsuda, *Death and Purgatory in Middle English Didactic Poetry*, 18.
46. Matsuda, *Death and Purgatory in Middle English Didactic Poetry*, 26.
47. This is the stage direction for God's positioning at the beginning of the Chester flood play. See further, Meredith, "Some High Place: Actualizing Heaven in the Middle Ages," in Muessig and Putter (eds.), *Envisaging Heaven*, 139–54.
48. Lumiansky reads the scene as thematically integrated into the rest of the play because it offers a point of comparison to "those who live righteously on earth," in "Comedy and Theme in the Chester *Harrowing of Hell*," 12.
49. Boethius, *Consolation of Philosophy*, trans. Stewart et al., V.vi. 58–9.
50. Dante, *Inferno*, 24.100–105.
51. Augustine, *Confessions*, trans. Chadwick, 229. "Respondeo non illud, quod quidam respondisse perhibetur iocunlariter eludens quaestionis uiolentiam: "Alta," inquit, "scrutantibus gehennas parabat" (201).
52. Ibid., 230. "Si autem ante caelum et terram nullum erat tempus, cur quaeritur, quid tunc faciebas? Non enim erat tunc, ubi non erat tempus" (202).
53. Novacich, "Repetition and Redemption: *On Saint Pierre et le Jongleur*," 330–2.
54. Smith, *Book of the Incipit*, 22.
55. See "harrow, v.2," "harrow, v.1," and "rehearse, v." in the *Oxford English Dictionary*.
56. Cohen suggests that this is also the familiar refrain of the monstrous, who (in some ways) similarly "haunt" and who also solicit a resurrection or re-membering: "The monster commands, "Remember me": restore my frag-mented body, piece me back together, allow the past its eternal return," in *Monster Theory: Reading Culture*, ed. Cohen, ix.

Epilogue

1. The N-Town Joachim and Anne's Presentation of Mary at the Temple, l. 304.
2. This involved the now lost "Fergus," which Evans discusses in "When a Body Meets a Body: Fergus and Mary in the York Cycle," 199.
3. Accounts of the Mercers' props and the bishop's amazement both are discussed in Meredith's "Actualizing Heaven in Medieval Drama," in Muessing and Putter (eds.), *Envisaging Heaven*, 139–41. The translation of bishop Abraham's description is Meredith's.
4. "God gyve you tyme and space!" cries Knowledge in "Everyman," admittedly a very different kind of medieval drama. "Everyman," in *Early English Drama*, ed. Coldewey, l.608.
5. Barnes, "In Breathtaking First, NASA's Voyager I Exits the Solar System."
6. Sagan et al. (eds.), *Murmurs of Earth: The Voyager Interstellar Record*, 28.

7. Here, I find particularly useful Waller's discussion of "sidling up" to thinkers – he borrows the term from Irigaray through the religious studies scholar Tina Beattie – in his study of the Virgin Mary in medieval thought. Though Waller discusses sidling up specifically to postmodern theorists, he first uses the phrase after suggesting the past can never speak "on its 'own' terms, but only through and for the ever-changing present." But, as Waller suggests, we can sidle up "to different struggles toward the truth" simultaneously, without firmly committing to any one, and thus we might attempt to think both *with* and about that past. See Waller, *The Virgin Mary in Late Medieval and Early Modern Literature and Popular Culture*, 5.

8. On recalling the anticipated future of the medieval past, see Schmitt, "Appropriating the Future," trans. Rand, and Boitani, "*Those who will call this time ancient:* The Futures of Prophecy and Poetry," both in Burrow and Wei (eds.), *Medieval Futures: Attitudes to the Future in the Middle Ages.*

Bibliography

Primary Texts

Alain, de Lille. *De Planctu Naturae*. Trans. Douglas M. Moffat. New Haven: Yale Studies in English, 1908.

The Apocryphal Lives of Adam and Eve. Eds. Brian Murdoch and J.A. Tasioulas. Exeter: University of Exeter Press, 2002.

Augustine. *Confessionum libri XIII*. Ed. Lucas Verheijen CCSL 27. Turnhout: Brepols, 1981.

    Saint Augustine's Confessions. Trans. Henry Chadwick. Oxford: Oxford University Press, 1991.

    De Genesi ad Litteram Libri Duodecim. PL 34:0245–0486.

    On Genesis. Trans. Edmund Hill. Ed. John E. Rotelle. Hyde Park, NY: New City Press, 2013.

Beowulf and the Fight at Finnsburg, 3rd edn. Ed. Fr. Klaeber. Lexington, MA: D.C. Heath and Company, 1950.

Bevington, David, ed. *Medieval Drama*. Boston: Houghton Mifflin, 1975.

Biblia Sacra: iuxta vulgatam versionem, 5th edn. Ed. Roger Gryson. Stuttgart: Deutsche Bibelgesellschaft. 2007.

Boethius. *The Consolation of Philosophy*. Trans. H.F. Stewart, E.K. Rand, and S.J. Tester. Loeb Classical Library, Vol. 74. Cambridge: Harvard University, 1973.

The Brut, or The Chronicles of England. Ed. Friedrich W.D. Brie. EETS o.s. 131 London: Oxford University Press, 1906, repr. 1960.

Capgrave, John. *Abbreuiacion of Cronicles*. Ed. Peter J. Lucas. EETS 285. Oxford: Oxford University Press, 1983.

Castleford's Chronicle, or The Boke of Brut. Ed. Caroline Eckhardt. EETS 305. Oxford: Oxford University Press, 1996.

Caxton, William. *Eneydos*. Ed. W.T. Culley and F.J. Furnivall. EETS e.s. 57. London: Oxford University Press, 1890, repr. 1962.

Chaucer, Geoffrey. *The Riverside Chaucer*, 3rd edn. Ed. Larry Benson. Boston: Houghton Mifflin, 1987.

The Chester Mystery Cycle, 2 vols. Eds. R. M. Lumiansky and David Mills. EETS s. s. 3. London: Oxford University Press, 1974.

Comestor, Peter. *Scolastica Historia: Liber Genesis*. Ed. Agneta Sylwan. Turnhout: Brepols, 2004.

Cursor Mundi. Ed. Richard Morris. London: K. Paul, Trench, Trübner et al., 1874–1893.

Dante Alighieri. *Inferno.* Trans. Allen Mandelbaum. Berkeley: University of California Press, 1980.

   Paradiso. Trans. Allen Mandelbaum. Berkeley: University of California Press, 1982.

   De Vulgari Eloquentia. Ed. and Trans. Steven Botterill. Cambridge: Cambridge University Press, 1996.

Epiphanius of Salamis. *The Panarion of Epiphanius of Salamis,* 2 vols. Trans. Frank Williams. Leiden: Brill, 2009.

Fitzgerald, Christina M. and John T. Sebastian, eds. *The Broadview Anthology of Medieval Drama.* Ontario: Broadview, 2013.

fitzNigel, Richard. *Dialogus de Scaccario: The Dialogue of the Exchequer.* Ed. and Trans. Emilie Amt, with *Consititutio Domus Regis: Disposition of the King's Household.* Ed. and Trans. S.D. Church. Oxford: Oxford University Press, 2007.

Geoffrey of Monmouth. *The History of the Kings of Britain,* an edition and translation of *De gestis Britonum (Historia Regum Britanniae).* Ed. Michael D. Reeve. Trans. Neil Wright. Woodbridge: Boydell, 2007.

Gerald of Wales. *Giraldi Cambrensis Opera: Vol. 5: Topographia Hibernica, et Expugnatio Hibernica.* Ed. James F. Dimock. London: Longman et al., 1867. Kraus Reprint, 1964.

   The History and Topography of Ireland. Ed. and Trans. John O'Meara. Mountrath, Portlaoise, Ireland: Dolmen Press, 1982.

Gervase, of Tilbury. *Otia Imperialia: Recreation for an Emperor.* Ed. and Trans. Banks, S.E. and J. W. Binns. Oxford: Oxford University Press, 2002.

The Gest Hystoriale of the Destruction of Troy: An Alliterative Romance. Ed. G.A. Panton and D. Donaldson. EETS. o.s. 39 and 56. London: Oxford University Press, 1968.

The Gospel of Nicodemus: Gesta Salvatoris. Ed. H.C. Kim. Toronto: Pontifical Institute of Medieval Studies, 1973.

Saint Gregory the Great: Dialogues. Ed. and Trans. Odo John Zimmerman. Washington D.C.: Catholic University Press of America Press, 1959.

Guy de Chauliac. *Cyrurgie of Guy de Chauliac.* Ed. Margaret S. Ogden. EETS o.s. 265. Oxford: Oxford University Press, 1971.

Henry Suso. *The Exemplar, with Two German Sermons.* Ed. and Trans. Frank Tobin. New York: Paulist Press, 1989.

Herzman, Ronald B., Graham Drake, and Eve Salisbury, ed. *Four Romances of England.* Kalamazoo, MI: Medieval Institute Publications, 1999.

Higden, Ranulph. *Polychronicon Ranulphi Higden monachi Cestrensis; together with the English translations of John Trevisa and of an unknown writer of the fifteenth century.* Ed. Churchill Babington. London: Longman, et al., 1865.

The Holy Bible: Douay–Rheims Version. Rev. Richard Challoner. Rockford, IL: Tan Books and Publishers, 1989.

Honorius Augustodunensis. *Gemma Animae. PL* Vol. 172:0541–0738B.

Hugh of Saint-Victor. *The Didascalicon of Hugh of St. Victor: A medieval guide to the arts*. Trans. Jerome Taylor. New York: Columbia University Press, 1961.

    De Archa Noe: Libellus de formatione arche, 2 vols. CCCM. 176–176a. Ed. Patrice Sicard. Turnhout: Brepols, 2001.

    Selected Spiritual Writings. Ed. Aelred Squire. Trans. A Religious of C. S. M. V. Eugene, OR: Wipf and Stock, 2009.

Hugutio of Pisa (Uguccione da Pisa). *Derivationes*, 2 vols. Ed. Enzo Cecchini et al. Florence: Edizioni del Galluzzo, 2004.

Isidore of Seville. *Etymologiarum sive originum*, 2 vols. Ed. W.M Lindsay. Oxford: Oxford University Press, 1911.

    The Etymologies of Isidore of Seville. Ed. and Trans. Stephen A. Barney et al. Cambridge: Cambridge University Press, 2006.

Jeu D'Adam. Ed. Willem Noomen. Paris: Champion, 1971.

Le Jeu d'Adam. Ed. and Trans. Wolfgang van Emden. Edinburgh: Société Rencesvals, British Branch, 1999.

Julian of Norwich. *The Writings of Julian of Norwich: A Vision Showed to a Devout Woman and A Revelation of Love*. Ed. Nicholas Watson and Jacqueline Jenkins. University Park, PA: Penn State Press, 2006.

Laʒamon's Brut. Ed. G. L. Brook and R.F. Leslie. EETS o.s. 250. London: Oxford University Press, 1963–1978.

Liber Albus: The White Book of the City of London, compiled A.D. 1419 by John Carpenter, common clerk. Richard Whitington, Mayor. Trans. from the Original Latin and Anglo-Norman by Henry Thomas Riley. London: Richard Griffin and Co., 1861.

Liber Albus, Liber Custumarum, et Liber Horn. Ed. Henry Thomas Riley. London: Longman, Brown, Green, Longmans, and Roberts, 1859.

Life of Margaret of Città di Castello. *Analecta Bollandiana* 19 (1900).

Mandeville, John. *The Egerton Version of Mandeville's Travels*. Ed. M.C. Seymour. Oxford: Oxford University Press 2010.

Mannyng, Robert of Brunne, *Handlyng Synne*. Ed. Idelle Sullens. Binghamton, NY: Center for Medieval and Early Modern Studies, 1983.

    The Chronicle. Ed. Idelle Sullens. Binghamton, NY: Center for Medieval and Early Renaissance Studies, 1996.

Matthew of Paris, *Flores historiarum per Matthaeum Westmonasteriensem collecti*. London: Ex officina Thomæ Marshij, 1570. EEBO.

The Middle English Harrowing of Hell and Gospel of Nicodemus. Ed. William Henry Hulme. EETS e.s. 100. London: Oxford University Press, 1907, repr. 1961.

The Middle English Liber Aureus and Gospel of Nicodemus. Ed. William Marx. Heidelberg: Universitätsverlag, 2013.

Mills, Maldwyn, ed. *Six Middle English Romances*. London: J.M. Dent, 1973.

The N-Town Play: Cotton MS Vespasian D.8. Ed. Stephen Spector. EETS s.s. 11. Oxford: Oxford University Press, 1991.

The Nag Hammadi Library in English. ed. James M. Robinson. Leiden: Brill, 1988.

Origen. *Homilies on Genesis and Exodus*. Trans. Ronald E. Heine. Washington, DC: The Catholic University of America Press, 1982.

Pilgrimage of the Lyfe of the Manhode, 2 vols. Ed. Avril Henry. EETS o.s. 288, 292 Oxford: Oxford University Press, 1985.

Prose Brut to 1332. Ed. Heather Pagan. Manchester: Anglo-Norman Text Society, 2011.

Revelation of the Monk of Eynsham. Ed. Robert Easting. EETS o.s. 318. Oxford: Oxford University Press, 2002.

Robert of Gloucester. *The Metrical Chronicle of Robert of Gloucester*. Ed. William Aldis Wright. London: Printed for H.M. Stationery off., by Eyre and Spottiswoode, 1887. Kraus Reprint, 1965.

Shakespeare, William. *The Riverside Shakespeare*, 2nd edn. Eds. G. Blakemore Evans, J.J.M. Tobin et al. Boston: Houghton Mifflin, 1997.

Shapcott, Jo. *My Life Asleep*. Oxford: Oxford University Press, 1998.

Silvestris, Bernardus. *Cosmographia*. Trans. Winthrop Wetherbee. New York: Columbia University Press, 1990.

Sir Orfeo, 2nd edn. Ed. A.J. Bliss. Oxford: Clarendon Press, 1966.

Shepherd, Stephen, ed. *Middle English Romances*. New York: Norton, 1994.

St. Patrick's Purgatory. Ed. Robert Easting. EETS o.s. 298. Oxford: Oxford University Press, 1991.

Summa Britonis, sive Guillelmi Britonis Expositiones Vocabulorum Biblie. Ed. Lloyd W. Daly and Bernadine A. Daly. Padua: Editrice Antenore, 1975.

Thomas, *Romance of Horn*, 2 vols. Ed. Mildred K. Pope. Oxford: Blackwell, 1955–1964.

The Towneley Plays, 2 vols. Ed. Stevens, Martin, and A.C. Cawley. EETS s. s. 13. Oxford: Oxford University Press, 1994.

Virgil. *The Aeneid*. Trans. Allen Mandelbaum. Berkeley: University of California Press, 1971.

Vitalis, Orderic. *The Ecclesiastical History of Orderic Vitalis*, 6 vols. Ed. Marjorie Chibnall. Oxford: Oxford University Press, 1972.

de Voragine, Jacobus. *The Golden Legend: Readings on the Saints*. Trans. William Granger Ryan. Princeton: Princeton University Press, 1993.

Wace, *Wace's Roman de Brut: A History of the British, Text and Translation*, rev. edn. Ed. and Trans. Judith Weiss. Exeter: University of Exeter Press, 2002.

Weiss, Judith, trans. *The Birth of Romance in England: The Romance of Horn, The Folie Tristan, the Lai of Haveloc and Amis and Amilun*. Tempe, AZ: Arizona Center for Medieval and Renaissance Studies, 2009.

Woolf, Virginia. *A Room of One's Own*. New York: Harcourt Brace Jovanovich, 1957.

The York Plays: A Critical Edition of the York Corpus Christi Play as recorded in British Library Additional MS 35290, 2 vols. Ed. Richard Beadle. EETS s.s. 23. Oxford: Oxford University Press, 2009.

York Mystery Plays: A Selection in Modern Spelling. eds. Richard Beadle and Pamela M. King. Oxford: Oxford University, 1999.

Criticism

Aers, David, ed., *Culture and History, 1350–1500: Essays on English Communities, Identities, and Writing*. Detroit: Wayne State University Press, 1992.

Agan, Cami D. "The Platea in the York and Wakefield Cycles: Avenues for Liminality and Salvation." *Studies in Philology* 94.3 (1997): 344–67.

Alač, Morana, and Patrizia Violi, eds. *In the Beginning: Origins of Semiosis*. Turnhout, Belgium: Brepols, 2004.

Albano, Robert A. *Middle English Historiography*. New York: Peter Lang, 1993.

Allen, Don Cameron. *The Legend of Noah: Renaissance Rationalism in Art, Science, and Letters*. Urbana, IL: University of Illinois Press, 1963.

Alter, Robert. *The Five Books of Moses: A Translation with Commentary*. New York: W.W. Norton and Company, 2004.

Arnold, Ken. *Cabinets for the Curious: Looking Back at Early English Museums*. Aldershot: Ashgate, 2006.

Badir, Patricia. "History, The Body, and Records of Early English Drama." *Exemplaria* 9.2 (1997): 255–79.

Bahr, Arthur. *Fragments and Assemblages: Forming Compilations of Medieval London*. Chicago: University of Chicago Press, 2013.

Bal, Mieke. *Anti-Covenant: Counter Reading Women's Lives in the Hebrew Bible*. Sheffield: Almond Press, 1989.

Barber, Peter. "The Evesham World Map: A Late Medieval English View of God and the World." *Imago Mundi* 47 (1995): 13–33.

Bardsley, Sandy. *Venomous Tongues: Speech and Gender in Late Medieval England*. Philadelphia: University of Pennsylvania Press, 2006.

Barnes, Brooke. "In Breathtaking First, NASA's Voyager I Exits the Solar System." *The New York Times*. September 12, 2013.

Barthes, Roland. *Michelet*. Trans. Richard Howard. New York: Farrar, Strauss, and Giroux, 1987.

Beckwith, Sarah. *Signifying God: Social Relation and Symbolic Act in the York Corpus Christi Plays*. Chicago: University of Chicago Press, 2003.

Benjamin, Walter. *The Arcades Project*. Trans. Howard Eiland and Kevin McLaughlin. Cambridge: Harvard University Press, 1999.

  Illuminations: Essays and Reflections. Ed. Hannah Arendt. Trans. Harry Zohn. New York: Schocken Books, 2007.

Bennett, Susan, and Mary Polito, eds. *Performing Environments: Site-Specificity in Medieval and Early Modern English Drama*. New York: Palgrave Macmillan, 2014.

Benson, Robert L., and Giles Constable with Carol D. Lanham, eds. *Renaissance and Renewal in the Twelfth Century*. Cambridge: Harvard University Press, 1982.

Biddick, Kathleen. *The Typological Imaginary: Circumcision, Technology, History*. Philadelphia: University of Pennsylvania Press, 2003.

Binkley, Peter, ed. *Pre-modern Encyclopaedic Texts: Proceedings of the second COMERS Congress, Groningen, 1–4 July 1996*. Leiden: Brill, 1997.

Birkholz, Daniel. "Mapping Medieval Utopia: Exercises in Restraint." *Journal of Medieval and Early Modern Studies* 36:3 (2006): 585–618.

Blair, Ann. "Introduction." *Archival Science* 10 (2010): 195–200.

Bloch, R. Howard. *The Scandal of the Fabliaux*. Chicago: University of Chicago Press, 1986.

Bloom, Harold. *The Anxiety of Influence: A Theory of Poetry*, 2nd edn. (orig. 1973). New York: Oxford University Press, 1997.

Blouin Jr, Francis X. and William G. Rosenberg. *Processing the Past: Contesting Authority in History and the Archives*. Oxford: Oxford University Press, 2011.

Bosley, Richard N., and Martin M. Tweedale, eds. *Basic Issues in Medieval Philosophy*, 2nd ed. Ontario: Broadview Press, 2006.

Brantley, Jessica. *Reading in the Wilderness: Private Devotion and Public Performance in Late Medieval England*. Chicago: University of Chicago Press, 2007.

Britnell, Richard, ed. *Pragmatic Literacy, East and West, 1200–1330*. Woodbridge: Boydell Press, 1997.

Brown, A.L. *Governance of Late Medieval England, 1272–1461*. Stanford: Stanford University Press, 1989.

Burrow, J.A. and Ian P. Wei, eds. *Medieval Futures: Attitudes to the Future in the Middle Ages*. Woodbridge: Boydell Press, 2000.

Bush, Jerome. "The Resources of Locus and Platea Staging: The Digby Mary Magdalene." *Studies in Philology* 86 (1989): 139–65.

Butler, Michelle. "The York/Towneley *Harrowing of Hell*." *Fifteenth-Century Studies* 25 (1999): 115–26.

Butterfield, Ardis. *Poetry and Music in Medieval France: From Jean Renart to Guillaume de Machaut*. Cambridge: Cambridge University Press, 2002.

Bynum, Caroline Walker. *Jesus as Mother: Studies in the Spirituality of the High Middle Ages*. Berkeley: University of California Press, 1982.

    Fragmentation and Redemption: Essays on Gender and the Human Body in Medieval Religion. New York: Zone Books, 1991.

Carbonell, Bettina Messias, ed. *Museum Studies: An Anthology of Texts and Contexts*. Malden, MA: Blackwell Publishing, 2004.

Carlson, Marvin. *Places of Performance: The Semiotics of Theatre Architecture*. Ithaca, NY: Cornell University Press, 1989.

    The Haunted Stage: The Theatre as Memory Machine. Ann Arbor: University of Michigan Press, 2003.

Carruthers, Mary. *The Book of Memory: A Study of Memory in Medieval Culture*. Cambridge: Cambridge University Press, 2006.

Carruthers, Mary, and Jan M. Ziolkowski, eds. *The Medieval Craft of Memory: An Anthology of Texts and Pictures*. Philadelphia: University of Pennsylvania Press, 2002.

Cartwright, Kent, ed. *A Companion to Tudor Literature*. Chichester: John Wiley and Sons, 2010.

Chaganti, Seeta. *The Medieval Poetics of the Reliquary: Enshrinement, Inscription, Performance*. New York: Palgrave MacMillan, 2008.

"The Platea Pre- and Postmodern: A Landscape of Medieval Performance Studies." *Exemplaria* 25.3 (2013): 252–64.

Chartier, Roger. *The Order of Books: Readers, Authors, and Libraries in Europe between the Fourteenth and Eighteenth Centuries*. Trans. Lydia G. Cochrane. Stanford: Stanford University Press, 1994.

Clanchy, M.T. *From Memory to Written Record, England 1066–1307*. Cambridge: Harvard University Press, 1979.

""Tenacious Letters": Archives and Memory in the Middle Ages." *Archivaria* 11 (1980): 115–25.

Cohen, Jeffrey Jerome, ed. *Monster Theory: Reading Culture*. Minneapolis: University of Minnesota Press, 1996.

The Postcolonial Middle Ages. New York: St. Martin's Press, 2000.

Cohen, Jeffrey Jerome, and Gail Weiss, eds. *Thinking the Limits of the Body*. Albany: State University of New York, 2003.

Cohen, Jeremy. *Living Letters of the Law: Ideas of the Jew in Medieval Christianity*. Berkeley: University of California Press, 1999.

Cook, Terry. *Controlling the Past*. Chicago: Society of American Archivists, 2011.

Cook, Terry, and Joan M. Schwartz, "Archives, Records, and Power: From (Postmodern) Theory to (Archival) Performance." *Archival Science* 2.3–4 (September 2002): 171–85.

Cooper, Helen. *The English Romance in Time: Transforming Motifs from Geoffrey of Monmouth to the Death of Shakespeare*. Oxford: Oxford University Press, 2004.

Craven, Louise, ed., *What Are Archives? Cultural and Theoretical Perspectives: A Reader*. Hampshire: Ashgate, 2008.

Curtius, Ernst Robert. *European Literature and the Latin Middle Ages* (1948). Trans. Willard R. Trask. Princeton: Princeton University Press, 1967.

Davidson, Clifford. *The Primrose Way: A Study of Shakespeare's Macbeth*. Iowa: John Westburg, 1969.

Technology, Guilds, and Early English Drama. Kalamazoo: Medieval Institute Publications, 1996.

ed., *Gesture in Medieval Drama and Art*. Western Michigan University: Medieval Institute Publications, 2001.

Davidson, Clifford, and Thomas H. Seiler, eds. *The Iconography of Hell*. Kalamazoo: Medieval Institute Publications, 1992.

Davis, Natalie Zemon. *Society and Culture in Early Modern France*. Stanford: Stanford University Press, 1975.

Delumeau, Jean. *History of Paradise: The Garden of Eden in Myth and Tradition*. Trans. Matthew O'Connell. Champaign, IL: University of Illinois Press, 2000.

Derrida, Jacques. *Specters of Marx: The State of the Debt, The Work of Mourning and the New International*. Trans. Peggy Kamuf. New York: Routledge, 1994.

"Archive Fever: A Freudian Impression." Trans. Eric Prenowitz. *Diacritics* 25.2 (1995): 9–63.

Diamond, Elin, ed. *Performance and Cultural Politics*. New York: Routledge, 1996.

Dinshaw, Carolyn. *Getting Medieval: Sexualities and Communities, Pre- and Postmodern.* Durham, NC: Duke University Press, 1999.
  How Soon is Now? Medieval Texts, Amateur Readers, and the Queerness of Time. Durham, NC: Duke University Press, 2012.
Douglas, Mary. *Purity and Danger: An Analysis of the Concepts of Pollution and Taboo* (orig. 1966) London: Routledge and Kegan Paul, 1979.
Easting, Robert. *Visions of the Other World in Middle English.* Cambridge: D.S. Brewer, 1997.
Echard, Sian. "House Arrest: Medieval Manuscripts: Modern Archives." *Journal of Medieval and Early Modern Studies* 30:2 (Spring 2000): 185–210.
Eco, Umberto. *The Search for the Perfect Language.* Trans. James Fentress. Oxford: Blackwell, 1995.
Edmonds, Radcliffe G. III. *Myths of the Underworld: Plato, Aristophanes, and the Orphic Golden Tablets.* Cambridge: Cambridge University Press, 2004.
Elsner, John, and Roger Cardinal, eds. *The Cultures of Collecting.* London: Reaktion Books, 1994.
Elton, W.R. and William B. Long, eds. *Shakespeare and Dramatic Tradition: Essays in Honor of S.F. Johnson.* Newark: New Jersey: University of Delaware Press, 1989.
Emmerson, Richard K, ed. *Approaches to Teaching Medieval English Drama.* New York: Modern Language Association, 1990.
Enders, Jody. "Medieval Stages." *Theatre Survey* 50 (2009): 317–25.
Evans, Ruth. "When a Body Meets a Body: Fergus and Mary in the York Cycle." *New Medieval Literatures* 1 (1997): 193–212.
Farge, Arlette. *The Allure of the Archives* (orig. *Le Goût de l'Archive*, 1989). Trans. Thomas Scott-Railton. New Haven: Yale University Press, 2013.
Findlen, Paula. *Possessing Nature: Museums, Collecting, and Scientific Culture in Early Modern Italy.* Berkeley: University of California Press, 1996.
Foucault, Michel. "Of Other Spaces." Trans. Jay Miskowiec. *Diacritics* 16.1 (1986), 22–7.
  The Archaeology of Knowledge and the Discourse on Language. Trans. A.M. Sheridan Smith. New York: Vintage, 2010.
Frantzen, Allen J. *Desire for Origins: New Language, Old English, and Teaching the Tradition.* New Brunswick: Rutgers University Press, 1990.
Freccero, John. "Infernal Irony: The Gates of Hell." *MLN* 99.4 (1984): 769–86.
Friedman, John Block. *Orpheus in the Middle Ages.* Cambridge: Harvard University Press, 1970.
Fulton, Helen, ed. *A Companion to Arthurian Literature.* Oxford: Blackwell, 2009.
Gallagher, Catherine, and Stephen Greenblatt. *Practicing New Historicism.* Chicago: University of Chicago Press, 2001.
Gayk, Shannon. *Image, Text, and Religious Reform in Fifteenth-Century England.* Cambridge: Cambridge University Press, 2010.
Geary, Patrick J. *Phantoms of Remembrance: Memory and Oblivion at the end of the First Millennium.* Princeton, NJ: Princeton University Press, 1994.
Geertz, Clifford. *The Interpretation of Cultures.* New York: Basic Books, 2000.

Gibson, Gail McMurray. *The Theater of Devotion: East Anglian Drama and Society in the Late Middle Ages*. Chicago: University of Chicago Press, 1994.

Gilbert, Sandra M., and Susan Gubar. *The Madwoman in the Attic: The Woman Writer and the Nineteenth-Century Literary Imagination*. New Haven: Yale University Press, 1979.

Gillespie, Alexandra. "Analytical Survey: The History of the Book." *New Medieval Literatures* 9 (2007): 245–77.

Ginzburg, Carlo. *Ecstasies: Deciphering the Witches' Sabbath*. trans. Raymond Rosenthal. London: Penguin, 1991.

Green, Richard Firth. *The Crisis of Truth: Literature and Law in Ricardian England*. Philadelphia: University of Pennsylvania Press, 1999.

Greenblatt, Stephen. "Resonance and Wonder." *Bulletin of the American Academy of Arts and Sciences* 43.4 (1990): 11–34.

Griffiths, Fiona J. *The Garden of Delights: Reform and Renaissance for Women in the Twelfth Century*. Philadelphia: University of Pennsylvania Press, 2007.

Hanning, Robert W. *The Vision of History in Early Britain: From Gildas to Geoffrey of Monmouth*. New York: Columbia University Press, 1966.

Happé, Peter. *Cyclic Form and the English Mystery Plays: A Comparative Study of the English Biblical Cycles and Their Continental and Iconographic Counterparts*. Amsterdam: Rodopi, 2004.

  The Towneley Cycle: Unity and Diversity. Cardiff: University of Wales Press, 2007.

Harley, J.B. and David Woodward, eds. *The History of Cartography, Vol. 1: Cartography in Prehistoric, Ancient, and Medieval Europe and the Mediterranean*. Chicago: University of Chicago Press, 1987.

Harris, Jonathan Gil. *Untimely Matter in the Time of Shakespeare*. Philadelphia: University of Pennsylvania Press, 2009.

Harty, Kevin J., ed. *The Chester Mystery Cycle: A Casebook*. New York: Garland Publishing, 1993.

Head, Randolph. "Preface: Historical Research on Archives and Knowledge Cultures: An Interdisciplinary Wave." *Archival Science* 10 (November 2010): 191–4.

Heidecker, Karl ed. *Charters and the Use of the Written Word*. Turnhout, Belgium: Brepols, 2000.

Himmelfarb, Martha. *Tours of Hell: An Apocalyptic Form in Jewish and Christian Literature*. Philadelphia: University of Pennsylvania Press, 1983.

Hollengreen, Laura H., ed. *Translatio, or the Transmission of Culture in the Middle Ages and the Renaissance: Modes and Messages*. Turnhout: Brepols, 2008.

Howes, Laura, ed. *Place, Space, and Landscape in Medieval Narrative*. Knoxville, TN: The University of Tennessee Press, 2007.

Howsam, Leslie. *Old Books and New Histories: An Orientation to Studies in Book and Print Culture*. Toronto: University of Toronto Press, 2006.

  ed., *The Cambridge Companion to the History of the Book*. Cambridge: Cambridge University Press, 2015.

Huot, Sylvia. *From Song to Book: The Poetics of Writing in Old French Lyric and Lyrical Narrative Poetry*. Ithaca: Cornell University Press, 1987.

Ingham, Patricia Clare. *The Medieval New: Ambivalence in an Age of Innovation*. Philadelphia: University of Pennsylvania Press, 2015.

Ingledew, Francis. "The Book of Troy and the Genealogical Construction of History: The Case of Geoffrey of Monmouth's *Historia regum Britanniae*." *Speculum* 69.3 (1994): 665–704.

Ingram, Reginald W., ed. *Coventry: Records of Early English Drama*. Toronto: University of Toronto Press, 1981.

Jacobus, Mary, ed. *Women Writing and Writing about Women*. London: Croom Helm in Association with the Oxford University Women's Committee, 1979.

Jager, Eric. "Did Eve Invent Writing? Script and Fall in the Adam Books." *Studies in Philology* 93.3.

"Speech and Chest in Old English Poetry: Orality or Pectorality?" *Speculum* 65.4 (1990): 845–59.

The Tempter's Voice: Language and the Fall in Medieval Literature. Ithaca, NY: Cornell University Press, 1993.

The Book of the Heart. Chicago: University of Chicago Press, 2000.

James, Mervyn. "Ritual, Drama, and Social Body in the Late Medieval Town." *Past and Present* 98 (1983): 3–29.

James, Montague Rhodes. *The Lost Apocrypha of the Old Testament*. London: Society for Promoting Christian Knowledge, 1920.

Johnston, Alexandra, and Margaret (Dorrell) Rogerson. "The York Mercers and Their Pageant of Doomsday, 1433–1526." *Leeds Studies in English* 6 (1972): 10–35.

Records of Early English Drama: York, 2 vols. Toronto: Toronto University Press, 1979.

Johnson, Eleanor. *Practicing Literary Theory in the Middle Ages: Ethics and the Mixed Form in Chaucer, Gower, Usk, and Hoccleve*. Chicago: University of Chicago Press, 2013.

Justice, Steven. "The Authority of Ritual in the *Jeu d'Adam*." *Speculum* 62.4 (1987): 851–64.

Kastan, David Scott. "Shakespeare after Theory." *Textus* 9.2 (1996): 357–74.

Kay, Sarah. *The Place of Thought: The Complexity of One in Late Medieval French Didactic Poetry*. Philadelphia: University of Pennsylvania Press, 2007.

Kennedy, Edward. *Chronicles and other Historical Writing*, Hartung et al., eds. *A Manual of the Writings in Middle English, 1050–1500*., vol. 8. New Haven: Connecticut Academy of Arts and Sciences, 1989.

Kiser, Lisa J. "The Animals in Chester's Noah's Flood." *Early Theatre* 14.1 (2011): 15–44.

Knapp, Ethan. *The Bureaucratic Muse: Thomas Hoccleve and the Literature of Late Medieval England*. University Park, PA: The Pennsylvania State University Press, 2001.

Knight, Alan E., ed. *The Stage as Mirror: Civic Theatre in Late Medieval Europe*. Cambridge: D.S. Brewer, 1997.

Knight, Rhonda. "Stealing Stonehenge: Translation, Appropriation, and Cultural Identity in Robert Mannyng of Brunne's Chronicle." *Journal of Medieval and Early Modern Studies* 32.1 (2002): 41–58.

Kolve, V.A. *The Play Called Corpus Christi*. Stanford: Stanford University Press, 1966.

  Chaucer and the Imagery of Narrative: The First Five Canterbury Tales. Stanford: Stanford University Press, 1984.

Kruger, Steven F. *The Spectral Jew: Conversion and Embodiment in Medieval Europe*. Minneapolis: University of Minnesota Press, 2006.

Kuskin, William. *Recursive Origins: Writing at the Transition to Modernity*. Notre Dame: University of Notre Dame Press, 2013.

LaCapra, Dominick. *History and Criticism*. Ithaca: Cornell University Press, 1985.

Ladner, Gerhart B. "Homo Viator: Mediaeval Ideas on Alienation and Order." *Speculum* 42.2: 233–59.

Lamont, Margaret. "Becoming English: Ronwenne's Wassail, Language, and National Identity in the Middle English Prose Brut." *Studies in Philology* 107.3 (2010): 283–309.

Lavezzo, Kathy, *Angels on the Edge of the World: Geography, Literature, and English Community, 1000–1534*. Ithaca: Cornell University Press, 2006.

Leedham-Green, Elisabeth, and Teresa Webber. *The Cambridge History of Libraries in Britain and Ireland, Vol. 1: to 1640*. Cambridge: Cambridge University Press, 2006.

Le Goff, Jacques. *The Birth of Purgatory*. Trans. Arthur Goldhammer. Chicago: University of Chicago Press, 1981.

  History and Memory. Trans. Steven Rendall and Elizabeth Claman New York: Columbia University Press, 1992.

  Medieval Civilization, 400–1500. Trans. Julia Barrow. Oxford: Blackwell, 1992.

Lepecki, André. "The Body as Archive: Will to Re-enact and the Afterlives of Dances." *Dance Research Journal* 42.2 (2010): 28–48.

Lerer, Seth. "Artifice and Artistry in Sir Orfeo." *Speculum* 60.1 (1985): 92–109.

  "Medieval English Literature and the Idea of the Anthology." *PMLA* 118.5 (2003): 1251–67.

Lerud, Theodore K. *Memory, Images, and the English Corpus Christi Drama*. New York: Palgrave MacMillan, 2008.

Le Saux, Françoise, ed. *The Text and Tradition of Laȝamon's Brut*. Cambridge: D.S. Brewer, 1994.

Lindblom, Andreas. *La Peinture Gothique en Suède et en Norvège*. London: Bernard Quaritch, 1916.

Liuzza, Roy. "Sir Orfeo: Sources, Traditions, and the Poetics of Performance." *Journal of Medieval and Renaissance Studies* 21:2 (1991): 269–84.

Lumiansky, R.M. "Comedy and Theme in the Chester Harrowing of Hell." *Tulane Studies in English* 10 (1960): 5–12.

MacDougall, Elisabeth, ed. *Medieval Gardens*. Washington D.C.: Dumbarton Oaks, 1986.

Macksey, Richard, and Eugenio Donato, eds. *The Structuralist Controversy: The Languages of Criticism and the Sciences of Man.* Baltimore: Johns Hopkins Press, 1970.

Marx, C.W. *The Devil's Rights and the Redemption in the Literature of Medieval England.* Cambridge: D.S. Brewer, 1995.

Matsuda, Takami. *Death and Purgatory in Middle English Didactic Poetry.* Cambridge: D.S. Brewer, 1997.

Matter, E. Ann. *The Voice of My Beloved: The Song of Songs in Western Medieval Christianity.* Philadelphia: University of Pennsylvania Press, 1990.

McAvoy, Liz Herbert. *Authority and the Female Body in the Writings of Julian of Norwich and Margery Kempe.* Cambridge: D.S. Brewer, 2004.

McDonald, Peter D. "Ideas of the Book and Histories of Literature: After Theory?" *PMLA* 121.1 (2006): 214–28.

McLean, Teresa. *Medieval English Gardens.* New York: The Viking Press, 1980.

Mead, Jenna. "Chaucer and the Subject of Bureaucracy." *Exemplaria* 19.1 (2007): 39–66.

Mill, Anna Jean. "Noah's Wife Again." *PMLA* 56.3 (1941): 613–26.

Minnis, Alastair, George Alexander Kennedy, et al. Eds. *Cambridge History of Literary Criticism: Vol.2 The Middle Ages.* Cambridge: Cambridge University Press, 1989.

Minnis, Alastair, *From Eden to Eternity: Creations of Paradise in the Later Middles Ages.* Philadelphia: University of Pennsylvania Press, 2015.

Mittman, Asa. *Maps and Monsters in Medieval England.* New York: Routledge, 2006.

Moi, Toril. *Sexual/ Textual Politics: Feminist Literary Theory,* 2nd ed. New York: Routledge, 2002.

What is a Woman? and Other Essays. Oxford: Oxford University Press, 2006.

Moore, Bruce, "The Narrator within the Performance: Problems with Two Medieval 'Plays.'" *Comparative Drama* 22.1 (1988): 21–36.

Mueller, Alex. *Translating Troy: Provincial Politics in Alliterative Romance.* Columbus: The Ohio State University Press, 2013.

Muessig, Carolyn, and Ad Putter, eds. *Envisaging Heaven in the Middle Ages.* New York: Routledge, 2007.

Nelson, Ingrid. "The Performance of Power in Medieval English Households: The Case of the Harrowing of Hell." *JEGP* 112.1 (2013): 48–69.

"Premodern Media and Networks of Transmission in the Man of Law's Tale." *Exemplaria* 25.3 (2013): 211–30.

Newman, Barbara. "What does it mean to say 'I Saw'? The Clash between Theory and Practice in Medieval Visionary Culture." *Speculum* 80.1 (2005): 1–43.

Nichols, Stephen. "Philology in a Manuscript Culture." *Speculum* 65.1 (1990): 1–10.

Nietzsche, Friedrich. *Unfashionable Observations.* Trans. Richard T. Gray. Ed. Ernst Behler. Stanford: Stanford University Press, 1995.

Nissé, Ruth. *Defining Acts: Drama and the Politics of Interpretation in Late Medieval England.* Notre Dame, IN: University of Notre Dame Press, 2005.

Nora, Pierre. "Between Memory and History: Les Lieux de Mémoire." *Representations* 26 (1989): 7–24.

Normington, Katie. *Gender and Medieval Drama.* New York: DS Brewer, 2004.

Novacich, Sarah Elliott. "Repetition and Redemption: On St. Pierre et le Jongleur." *Viator* 47.1 (2016): 313–32.

Paden, William D., ed. *The Future of the Middle Ages: Medieval Literature in the 1990s.* Toronto: University of Toronto Press, 1994.

Palmer, Barbara D. "'Towneley Plays' or 'Wakefield Cycle' Revisited." *Comparative Drama* 21 (1987): 318–48.

Patch, Henry Rollins. *The Otherworld, according to Descriptions in Medieval Literature.* Cambridge: Harvard University Press, 1950.

Patterson, Lee. ed. *Literary Practice and Social Change in Britain, 1380–1530.* Berkeley: University of California Press, 1990.

  Chaucer and the Subject of History. Madison: University of Wisconsin Press, 1991.

Pearsall, Derek, and Elizabeth Salter. *Landscapes and Seasons of the Medieval World.* Toronto: University of Toronto Press, 1973.

Phelan, Peggy. *Unmarked: The Politics of Performance.* New York: Routledge, 2001.

Plain, Gill, and Susan Sellers, eds. *A History of Feminist Literary Criticism.* Cambridge: Cambridge University Press, 2007.

Revkin, Andrew C. "Buried Seed Vault Opens in Arctic." *The New York Times.* February 26, 2008.

Richards, Thomas. *The Imperial Archive: Knowledge and the Fantasy of Empire.* New York: Verso, 1993.

Riddy, Felicity. "The Uses of the Past in *Sir Orfeo.*" *The Yearbook of English Studies* (1976): 5–15.

Robertson, Kellie. "Geoffrey of Monmouth and the Translation of Insular Historiography." *Arthuriana* 8.4 (1998): 42–57.

Roach, Joseph. *Cities of the Dead: Circum-Atlantic Performance.* New York: Columbia University Press, 1996.

  "Performance: The Blunders of Orpheus." *PMLA* 125.4 (2010): 1078–86.

Rudd, Gillian. *Greenery: Ecocritical Readings of Late Medieval English Literature.* Manchester: Manchester University Press. 2007.

Sagan, Carl, et al., eds. *Murmurs of Earth: The Voyager Interstellar Record.* New York: Random House, 1978.

Said, Edward. *Beginnings: Intention and Method.* New York: Basic Books, 1985.

Sandler, Lucy Freedman. *The Robert de Lisle Psalter in the British Library.* London: Harvey Miller, 1983.

Scafi, Alessandro. *Mapping Paradise: A History of Heaven on Earth.* Chicago: Chicago University Press, 2006.

Schechner, Richard. "Performance Studies: The Broad Spectrum Approach," *TDR* 32.3 (1988): 4–6.

Schechner, Richard, and Victor Turner, *Between Theater and Anthropology*. Philadelphia: University of Pennsylvania Press, 1985.

Schmidt, Gary D. *The Iconography of the Mouth of Hell: Eighth-Century Britain to the Fifteenth Century*. Selinsgrove: Susquehanna University Press, 1995.

Schneider, Rebecca. *Performing Remains: Art and War in Times of Theatrical Reenactment*. New York: Routledge, 2011.

Simpson, James. "The Other Book of Troy: Guido delle Colonne's *Historia destructionis Troiae* in Fourteenth- and Fifteenth-Century England." *Speculum* 73.2 (1998): 397–423.

"Cognition is Recognition: Literary Knowledge and Textual "Face." *New Literary History* 44.1 (2013): 25–44

Smith, D. Vance. *The Book of the Incipit: Beginnings in the Fourteenth Century*. Minneapolis: University of Minnesota Press, 2001.

Sobecki, Sebastian I. *The Sea and Medieval English Literature*. Woodbridge: D.S. Brewer, 2008.

Sofer, Andrew. *The Stage Life of Props*. Michigan: University of Michigan Press, 2003.

Spiegel, Gabrielle M. *The Past as Text: The Theory and Practice of Historiography*. Baltimore: Johns Hopkins University Press, 1997.

Spearing, A.C. "The Journey to Jerusalem: Mandeville and Hilton." *Essays in Medieval Studies* 25 (2008): 1–17.

Staley, Lynn. *The Island Garden: England's Language of Nation from Gildas to Marvell*. Indiana: University of Notre Dame Press, 2012.

Stallybrass, Peter. "The Library and Material Texts." *PMLA* 119.5 (2004): 1347–52.

Steedman, Carolyn. *Dust: The Archive and Cultural History*. New Brunswick, NJ: Rutgers University Press, 2001.

Steiner, Emily. *Documentary Culture and the Making of Medieval English Literature*. Cambridge: Cambridge University Press, 2003.

"Compendious Genres: Higden, Trevisa, and the Medieval Encyclopedia." *Exemplaria* 27.1–2 (2015): 73–92.

Stewart, Susan. *On Longing: Narratives of the Miniature, the Gigantic, the Souvenir, the Collection*. Baltimore: Johns Hopkins University Press, 1984.

Stolzenberg, Daniel, ed. *The Great Art of Knowing: The Baroque Encyclopedia of Athanasius Kircher*. Stanford: Stanford University Libraries, 2001.

Storm, Melvin. "Uxor and Alison: Noah's Wife in the Flood Plays and Chaucer's Wife of Bath." *Modern Language Quarterly: A Journal of Literary History* 48 (1987): 303–19.

Stuart, Donald Clive. "The Stage Setting of Hell and the Iconography of the Middle Ages." *Romanic Review* 4 (1913): 330–42.

Summerfield, Thea. *The Matter of Kings' Lives: The Design of Past and Present in the Early Fourteenth-Century Verse Chronicles by Pierre de Langtoft and Robert Mannyng*. Amsterdam: Rodopi, 1998.

Summit, Jennifer. *Memory's Library: Medieval Books in Early Modern England*. Chicago: University of Chicago Press, 2008.

Symes, Carol. "The Appearance of Early Vernacular Plays: Forms, Functions, and the Future of Medieval Theater." *Speculum* 77.3 (2002): 778–831.

  A Common Stage: Theater and Public Life in Medieval Arras. Ithaca: Cornell University Press, 2007.

Tamburr, Karl. *The Harrowing of Hell in Medieval England*. Cambridge: D.S. Brewer, 2007.

Taylor, Andrew. *Textual Situations: Three Medieval Manuscripts and their Readers*. Philadelphia: University of Pennsylvania Press, 2002.

Taylor, Diana. *The Archive and the Repertoire: Performing Cultural Memory in the Americas*. Durham, NC: Duke University Press, 2003.

Taylor, Jerome, and Alan H. Nelson, eds. *Medieval English Drama: Essays Critical and Contextual*. Chicago: University of Chicago Press, 1972.

Taylor, John. *English Historical Literature in the Fourteenth Century*. Oxford: Oxford University Press, 1987.

Teeuwen, Mariken. *The Vocabulary of Intellectual Life in the Middle Ages*. Turnhout: Brepols, 2003.

Tolmie, Jane. "Mrs. Noah and Didactic Abuses." *Early Theatre* 5.1 (2002): 11–35.

Toswell, M.J. *Borges the Unacknowledged Medievalist: Old English and Old Norse in His Life and Work*. New York: Palgrave MacMillan, 2014.

Turner, Alice K. *The History of Hell*. New York: Harcourt, Brace, and Co., 1993.

Turner, Victor. *From Ritual to Theatre: The Human Seriousness of Play*. New York: PAJ, 1982.

Turville-Petre, Thorlac. *England the Nation: Language, Literature and National Identity, 1290–1340*. Oxford: Clarendon Press, 1996.

Utley, Frances Lee. "The One Hundred and Three Names of Noah's Wife." *Speculum* 16.4 (1941): 426–52.

Wallace David, ed. *The Cambridge History of Medieval English Literature*. Cambridge: Cambridge University Press, 2005.

Waller, Gary. *The Virgin Mary in Late Medieval and Early Modern Literature and Popular Culture*. Cambridge: Cambridge University Press, 2011.

Watson, Nicholas. "Desire for the Past." *Studies in the Age of Chaucer* 21 (1999): 59–97.

  "The Phantasmal Past: Time, History, and the Recombinative Imagination." *Studies in the Age of Chaucer* 32 (2010): 1–37.

Warner, Lawrence. *The Myth of Piers Plowman: Constructing a Medieval Literary Archive*. Cambridge: Cambridge University Press, 2014.

Wasserman, Julian N., and Lois Roney, eds. *Sign, Sentence, Discourse: Language in Medieval Thought and Literature*. Syracuse: Syracuse University Press, 1989.

Weimann, Robert. *Shakespeare and the Popular Tradition in the Theater: Studies in the Social Dimension of Dramatic Form and Function*. Baltimore: Johns Hopkins University Press, 1978.

West, William N. "The Idea of a Theater: Humanist Ideology and the Imaginary Stage in Early Modern Europe." *Renaissance Drama* 28 (1997): 245–87.

Williams, Tara. *Inventing Womanhood: Gender and Language in Later Middle English Writing*. Columbus: The Ohio State University Press, 2011.

Winston-Allen, Ann. "Gardens of Heavenly Delight: Medieval Gardens of the Imagination." *Neuphilologische Mitteilungen* 99.1 (1998): 83–92.

Woolf, Rosemary. *The English Mystery Plays*. Berkeley: University of California Press, 1972.

Yates, Frances A. *The Art of Memory*. Chicago: University of Chicago Press, 1974.

Zinn, Grover. "Hugh of Saint Victor and the Ark of Noah: A New Look." *Church History* 40.3 (1971): 261–72.

"Hugh of Saint Victor and the Art of Memory." *Viator* 5 (1974): 211–34.

Zumthor, Paul. *Essai de Poétique Médiévale*. Paris: Éditions du Seuil, 1972.

Index

CAMBRIDGE STUDIES IN MEDIEVAL LITERATURE